"Too Good a Town"

"Too Good a Town"

William Allen White, Community,
and the Emerging Rhetoric of Middle America

Edward Gale Agran

THE UNIVERSITY OF ARKANSAS PRESS
FAYETTEVILLE ■ 1998

02   01   00   99   98   5   4   3   2   1

Designed by Ellen Beeler

⊚ The paper used in this publication meets the minimum requirements of the American National Standard for Permanence of Paper for Printed Library Materials Z39.48-1984.

Library of Congress Cataloging-in-Publication Data

Agran, Edward Gale, 1949–
    Too good a town : William Allen White, community, and the emerging rhetoric of middle America / Edward Gale Agran.
       p. cm.
    Includes bibliographical references and index.
    ISBN 1-55728-520-9 (cloth : alk. paper). —ISBN 1-55728-521-7 (paper : alk. paper)
    1. White, William Allen, 1868–1944. 2. Journalists—United States—Biography. 3. Emporia gazette (Emporia, Kan. : 1899) 4. Emporia (Kan.)—Social life and customs. 5. Middle class—United States.   I. Title.
PN4874.W52A63   1998
070'.92—dc21   98-19839
  [B]   CIP

For Charlotte Fairlie

Acknowledgments

THANKS naturally are in order. I may leave out an individual or institution here or there; if so, it is most unintentional, as I feel indebted to all who have helped to shape this work. William Vance Trollinger Jr., Barbara Melosh, Paul Boyer, John Sharpless, and Stanley Schultz have been attentive readers and sources of strong support. Conference participants in the United Kingdom and in Seattle, New York, and Topeka offered valuable comments on portions of this work. Numerous individuals read, edited, and helped to publish the journal articles. Editors and their readers at assorted presses provided helpful advice. The University of Wisconsin, Centre College, and Wilmington College gave me institutional and financial aid. Librarians in Madison, Wisconsin; Danville and Lexington, Kentucky; Wilmington, Ohio; and Emporia, Kansas assisted in my research. I particularly appreciate the close interest Mary Bogan and Dick Garvey of Emporia State University took in my work. And I want to thank David Walker and Barbara White Walker for their unqualified encouragement to publish this study. Fellow graduate students and countless undergraduates with whom I have sat in provocative seminars have given me a lot to think about. Certain teachers meant a lot to me at just the right moment—Daniel Francois and Thomas Kincaid at U.C.L.A., Robert Athearn and Robert Pois at the University of Colorado, and Stanley Kutler and Walter Rideout at the University of Wisconsin. Finally, I am indebted to the hard-working staff at the University of Arkansas Press in Fayetteville.

I owe most to Charlotte Fairlie and Hannah and Thomas. Thanks, and naturally, all shortcomings in this work are my own.

Contents

INTRODUCTION
Simple Points   1

CHAPTER ONE
"Too Good a Town": White, Community, and Rhetoric   31

CHAPTER TWO
The Progressive Promise I: Portraying the Idyllic Community   47

CHAPTER THREE
The Progressive Promise II: Politicking for the Ideal   65

CHAPTER FOUR
Fashioning the Model American Community   89

CHAPTER FIVE
Raising Middle American Barricades: Smith, Depression,
        and War   129

CHAPTER SIX
Forging a Middle American Ethos   159

Notes   179

Bibliography   219

Index   235

Introduction

Simple Points

THIS STUDY has been in the works for a long time. Fortunately, it has kept my interest, not simply for academic reasons but for personal ones, too. Graduate school, family, employment, unemployment, publication complications—I've run the typical gamut. In their own fashion I have found that my story and this book's story are parts of a cloth more whole than I had ever expected. Slowly, over the years, I have perceived a tie, but it is only in the last year that the tightness of the weave has materialized for me. Hence, this introduction attempts to place not only this study but myself as well, in relationship to it.

Over the past two years as I have prepared my final revisions, I have come to recognize, too, that the passage of time has been more an aid than a hindrance. This study began as my dissertation, and for the most part its findings and structure have remained intact. Early on I worried that the story was good, but the scholarship could be better; I knew there were holes. All along I received encouraging support and salient criticism from careful readers; in the final stage I have had the good fortune to be able to access more recent scholarship. I have questioned my own values and worked to hone my writing skills. The end product has a good deal to do with me as well as William Allen White and small-town rhetoric. I believe this study makes a strong complementary contribution to current scholarship. Equally important to me, and I hope of value to others, I believe this study reads well; I believe it tells a tale which William Allen White lived. White sensed that a good many others held to his value system as a north star of sorts, as a provocative story line for their own lives. Ultimately, in his ability to sense "what mattered" to folks, in his strategic positioning of himself within America's changing mainstream, and owing to his journalistic skills, William Allen White was able to weave together a rhetoric that made sense to people as they weighed their own lives against their perceptions of the worlds around them. If this story indeed does read well, it is because White, in today's idiom, genuinely connected. I have depended a good deal upon his writing, because it is his voice, in its appeal and in its message, which rang true for so many. There was a resonance in what this Kansas journalist had to say that struck a number of right chords in his own day and, I have found, in this day as well.

The most intriguing criticism of my work has rested upon the issue of White's soundness: "I was surprised at what a light-weight he was." "The study reads well, but it's a lot more like journalism than history." "I'm curious: White seemed so ordinary . . . I want to know what you make of this?" "He was no intellectual." "Funny, I was really disappointed in him; I thought I would like him." "There seems to be no core." I now better grasp Gertrude Stein's apocryphal deathbed retort to the query "Gertrude, Gertrude, what is the answer?": "I don't know . . .what is the question?" I've had to plead, What is the core?

■ ■ ■

I'd like to try to supply some preliminary answers to these questions I have wrestled with over the years. First, having read a good number of biographies, autobiographies, and memoirs of twentieth-century activist journalists—Ida Tarbell, H. L. Mencken, Lincoln Steffens, Dorothy Thompson, Henry Luce, Walter Lippmann, and Gore Vidal, amongst others—I find it difficult, as so many do, to sight where that line between journalism and history is to be drawn. More to the point, I don't understand why it has to be drawn—more questions. Is it a matter of substance? Of style? Ideology? What constitutes an intellect? An audience? Who does one want to reach? What is lightweight? How do I get out of this tangle? Where do I find the straight and narrow? Should it matter?[1]

Yes, it should matter. William Allen White, one might say, made his career by repeatedly, literally, asking the question, "What is the matter?" First with Kansas Populism, later with Bull Moose progressivism, then within twenties America, the Depression, and finally the world at large, he attempted to provide answers. Years ago in graduate school a professor with whom I taught set up the U.S. history survey course, on the first day of class, with the final question, "How would you define the core American experience?" It was a great question for a host of reasons. Most of the answers gravitated, fractured and fissured as they might be, toward the "middle." I hadn't really thought about the issue before. Once the question was posed, the response was not surprising: the middle is a seductive, comforting resting spot for individuals, where most can find the company they seek. And so this is where William Allen White sat, quite firmly, but not quite so comfortably as many critics might think; and this, for me, is the starting point for answering my readers' challenging questions as to what ought to matter.

White positioned himself in the middle, in the mainstream where most Americans stand, and where I tend to think many who find it disconcerting that William Allen White was not more an intellect or lacked a core have personally and politically positioned themselves, in his day and in our own. The vast majority of us, by almost every conceivable measure, attempt to comport ourselves on a cushioned middle ground. The core is pretty solid, it is pretty broad, and it generously accommodates most; but we all know it is not always so comfortable, not a particularly easy chair. Place oneself within the security of the academy's walls; within the voting booth opting Democrat or Republican; within the school district agonizing over public or private education; within the work force, pro-union or anti-union; within mind, body, and heart, pro-choice or pro-life; at the breakfast table or in a booth reading the *New York Times, USA Today,* or the *National Enquirer;* in front of the television weighing the simplistic pros and cons of a networked debate on the trials and tribulations of celebritydom. It's not a difficult spot, but it's not an easy spot either. For a few who never sit in the middle, naturally, it seldom is easy. But for most it's a sensible, acceptable, accepted, and—God forbid—a respectable position. So where does this lead? Well, hardly to the straight and narrow.

This middle ground, this core of tangled experiences, is in fact an old and fractious tract of land. Americans have long been at work attempting to define who we are as a people, a culture, and a society, searching for old and new norms, pressing, progressing, defining, moving westward if you like, and looking backward, too. Noah Webster, James Fenimore Cooper, Jane Addams, Henry Luce, Eleanor Roosevelt, Martin Luther King Jr.— one can name a thousand individuals, hundreds of groups and movements. William Allen White stood, and moved, smack in the middle of it all for a good fifty years. His writing made for interesting reading in his own day, roughly the first half of the twentieth century, and makes for intriguing study today, at the end of the century. He was, indeed, an ordinary guy—one of us, really, just trying to figure it all out.

William Allen White, on the other hand, was not simply a bit actor in some sort of attenuated, local, all-American historical pageant of the earlier part of the century. In today's lexicon he was a major player. It would be difficult to find a live or dead player with few critics. White played the game well; he not only lodged himself within the national mainstream, he helped to channel it. Ah, and so perhaps here is the rub. How can one be a popular journalist, a player, and an intellect, an erudite, midstream analyst of the world around? Few if any have qualified. Walter Lippmann might fit the bill, but who else? And how popular was he? To whom did he speak? How many really listened? And how many charged him with arrogance, naivete, blindness, hypocrisy? Certainly today, across our society, none is beyond criticism, especially the successful, and all the more especially those we have pronounced successful. We are dealing with a pack of imponderables. But we must attempt to sort it out. Who speaks for whom? Who shapes the debate? What exactly is the debate? Where do we place people? Why are those who seem to represent us somehow lightweight? Why is the middle disparaged?

■ ■ ■

Most important for the significance of this study, I must place William Allen White. Not really—White placed himself; I simply need to locate him and that place in their proper, and I hope decipherable, context. William Allen White, again, strategically, repeatedly landed himself right in the middle, the deified and disparaged middle: the early-twentieth century Progressives ("Why can't we figure those folks out?"); Harding's popular backward glance (Or was it forward?) toward Normalcy; FDR's New Deal, the Four Freedoms, and their homogenization by Norman Rockwell; the *Saturday Evening Post*, the *Saturday Review, Life, Look, Collier's*, the *Atlantic Monthly*, and *Time*; 1950s consensus theorists and Arthur Schlessinger Jr.'s vital center—Eisenhower preached dynamic conservatism, Lyndon Johnson beseeched us to reason together, and Richard Nixon laid claim to the silent majority. Everyone knows there is indeed a silent majority, but Nixon was mocked by a vociferous minority for claiming it as his own. As Tom Wicker attests in his biography of Richard Nixon, *One of Us*, Nixon was simply one of our own. So, too, later on would be Ronald Reagan—after all, wasn't it most fitting toward the end of Hollywood's century to elect as first couple not an A team, a Tracy and Hepburn, but a more facile duo more in touch with the folks, B actors like Ronald Reagan and Nancy Davis? One scholar provocatively asks of American history, are we dealing with American myths or American realities? Again, core experiences? Can one possibly exist? Is it tangible? Ephemeral? Can one address it? Explain it? Them?[2]

Richard Slotkin astutely assesses "what is the matter" in *The Fatal Environment: The Myth of the Frontier in the Age of Industrialism, 1800–1890*. In the chapter "Myth Is the Language of Historical Memory," historian Slotkin explains how one myth across time orchestrates itself toward a new myth: "An environment, a landscape, a historical sequence is infused with meaning in the form of a story, which converts landscape to symbol and temporal sequence into 'doom'—a fable of necessary and fated actions." The myths are regenerative, current, and ideologically laden; they are "central to the cultural functioning of the society that produces them." The frontier myth lives on and thrives. In fact, in the rhetoric of the recent presidential campaign, it fast approaches a "bridge into the twenty-first century": "It is this industrial and imperial version of the Frontier Myth whose categories still inform our political rhetoric of pioneering progress, world mission, and eternal strife with the forces of darkness and barbarism." Darkness and barbarism, rights and wrongs, these are the simple threads with which tales and an American Experience are woven together. Slotkin posits the question, "Why has this constellation of stories, fables, and images been for so long one of the primary organizing principles of our historical memory?"

> Historical experience is preserved in the form of narrative; and through periodic retellings those narratives become traditionalized. These formal qualities and structures are increasingly conventionalized and abstracted, until they are reduced to a set of powerfully evocative and resonant "icons"—like the landing of the Pilgrims, the rally of the Minutemen at Lexington, the Alamo, the Last Stand, Pearl Harbor, in which history becomes a cliché. At the same time that their form is being simplified and abstracted, the range of reference of these stories is being expanded. Each new context in which the story is told adds meaning to it, because the telling implies a metaphoric connection between the storied past and the present. . . .

Ultimately myths merge with the language, and they emerge as "deeply encoded . . . metaphors that may contain all of the 'lessons' we have learned from our history, and all of the essential elements of our world view." Simply, myths have the ability to key word our traditions.[3]

And so one lands, by means of Slotkin's treatment of the frontier, Custer, cowboys, and Indians, within the expansive bounds of any other myth as one finds "history successfully disguised as archetype." Slotkin points out that myth performs a cultural mission by "generalizing particular and contingent experiences into the bases of universal rules of understanding and conduct; and it does this by transforming secular history into a body of sacred and sanctifying legends."

> If appreciated historically, the rules . . . cease to function as rules and appear as a set of forms generated by a particular set of cultural producers in a peculiar historical moment—and as continually modified from period to period by changing ideological pressures. The present

forms in which our myths appear embody not only the solutions to past problems and conflicts; they contain the questions as well, and they reflect the conflicts of thought and feeling and action that were the mythmakers' original concern.

Slotkin concludes:

> If we can understand where and how in history the rules of the game originated, what real human concerns and social relationships the rules conceal or distort, and what the historical consequences of playing the game have been, we may be able to respond more intelligently the next time an infantry captain or a senator or a president invokes it.[4]

Here is the making of powerful history and mighty tales. William Allen White definitively spun yarns out of whole cloth. He was a player; history and storytelling was the game; language, rhetoric, and metaphor translated into narrative power; conversely, power made, and when necessary remade, language, rhetoric, and metaphor. Power writes the narrative; by some individuals' reckoning, power is the narrative. How, then, is the tale told, the game played?

According to Slotkin, as we study complex ceremonies, journalistic responses to seminal events, or "the literary fiction of a writer who works in the language of his society's preferred mythology, we engage ourselves with a complex reflecting mechanism, whose complications echo—in a special way—all of the complexities of social life and cultural history." But alas, such studies run perplexing ahistorical paths: "What is lost when history is translated into myth is the essential premise of history—the distinction of past and present itself. The past is made metaphorically equivalent to the present; and the present appears simply as a repetition of persistently recurring structures identified with the past." Values, beliefs, social conditioning, maxims, ancient and modern forces at work—"knowledge, intention, politics, and contingency"—all come to the fore, and "those who use mythic speech appear to be vehicles rather than inventors." Slotkin elicits the support of cultural scholar Roland Barthes:

> They have transformed "history into nature." . . . Their assertions are taken for definitions, their intentions as reflections of natural conditions; their declarations are read "not . . . as a motive, but as a reason." So the complex politics of cultural and social life is concealed beneath a "harmonious display of essences" or embedded in "bundles of meaning" too densely knotted for simple skepticism to unravel.[5]

But the skeptics are there, and those sensitized to hegemonic power see red. And the establishment is reflexive, and it is resilient. A culture is not a "harmonious display of essences." A culture is not "static, immune to the infection of innovation and progress, free of history." "Myth-ideological systems are affected by crises in material conditions; they are prone to internal contradictions of form and content; and the human intentions that shape cultural politics change, meet with opposition, stumble over difficulties." And especially, in modern societies, "the continual agitation and disruption of social forms and systems of value appears to be the characteristic fate . . . in these circumstances, the formal distinction between myth and ideology may become the basis of crucial distinctions." Different groups compete for power, attempts are made to articulate party or class ideology: "As the carrier of 'received wisdom,' myth is challenged. . . . When myths prove inadequate as keys to interpreting and controlling the changing world, systematic ideologies are developed to reestablish the lost coherence between facts and values." Truths are malleable, and they serve the purposes both of inclusion and exclusion. Slotkin makes the critical connection between myth, reality, perceived truth, and power:

> Since even a shattered mythology preserves elements of the cultural past, the new mythology will inevitably find connection with the old; indeed, the readiest way to renew the force of a weakened mythology is to link new ideology to the traditional imagery of existing myth. Thus discontent born of experience creates a cognitive dissonance that disrupts the [idyllic perception of a] "harmonious display of essences," degrading sacred myth to secular ideology; and ideology in the hands of a class seeking to establish and justify its hegemony reaches out to coopt myth. This process of mythogenesis, breakdown, cooptation, and mythic renewal informs the history of culture.

Myths are the prey, the hunted rationales. The "ideology of a class striving for ascendancy will seek to appropriate the moral authority of the myth."[6]

So, where does one start to locate the keepers of the myth? Slotkin explains that in a post-primitive stage of cultural development "it becomes possible to identify authorial activity in the production of myth, to specify who the producers are, what their concerns or interests may be, and how they relate to their discipline or art, their materials, their sponsors, their audiences, their fellow producers." Myth makers are elusive; Slotkin positions himself amongst the contentious scholarly sleuths:

> It is essential to my approach to myth to insist that the substance of mythic materials and genres is provided by human "authors"; men and women who fabricate or compose the stories, and promulgate them; who bring to the work their needs, intentions, and concerns. However, this premise of human authorship is the very thing that myth is organized to deny.

Still, social and historical factors are at work. And authors can be identified. It is a problematic process, made less easy by elusive audiences. But the chase has value. Slotkin makes his case:

> If we choose to study national popular culture, we should see it not as a national folklore but as the myth medium of the victorious party in an extended historical struggle. It has come to represent the mythology and ideology of those groups or classes whose political and economic concerns and cultural predilections have by and large dominated and directed the course of American social, economic, and political development—entrepreneurs and corporate directors, salesmen and promoters, entertainers and purveyors of grand ideas.[7]

Slotkin's goal is "to trace the historical development of a single major American myth, and to offer a critical interpretation of its meanings." He relates its waxing and waning to the marketplace: producers of myth, creative and marketing processes, historical crises, artistic genius, "and the special necessities and possibilities that arise from working within specific forms and genres." I have no such far-reaching goal. But through White's work, and with Slotkin's aid, I can better place White, decipher portions of a myth, grasp for the core, and come to terms with elusivity. In a more restrictive, complementary case study, I can demonstrate the power of a wordsmith. And in the process I can answer those gnawing questions about White's importance; simply, I can place him.[8]

■ ■ ■

White by some measures was a promoter of small matters, a purveyor of grandiose ideas, a creator, a marketer, a producer, and a consumer; he was in ways a small man and a big man. In his own words he was an average bloke, a common man, but he occupied center stage in the long-running national narrative. White was, most definitively, in the thick of things. If "myth is the language of historical memory," here was an individual who grew up on the frontier, understood its industrial and imperial dimensions, finessed the subtleties of myth making across time and place, drew lessons from myths and applied them to a world view through simplification, abstraction, and expansion, created and amplified key words, and preached universal rules of understanding and conduct. He was an active journalist and novelist, keenly perceptive of essences and bundles of meaning, a great blender of history and myth, the living personification of both. White was a grand orchestrater of matters many might tag small but which were in fact labeled quite important within their own purportedly broader perspectives and grounded ideologies; he was in essence an articulate spokesperson for an attractive middle ground.

White, one might say, came to live by "deeply encoded metaphors." He was the great townsman. There were few more adept carriers of the "received wisdom"; but such wisdom is always in flux. White played the hegemonic game the best; insider, outsider, angler, potshotter, he covered all fronts. The prey, the hunted, the author, the narrator, the reporter, the entrepreneur, and the politician—he criss-crossed a multitude of landscapes. He exclaimed at the end of his life, "What a show I have seen, what a grand show!" He really loved it; he really lived it, right on center stage in one fixed pageant after another, in one locale after another, deciphering, encoding, across time coming to represent the blended, received wisdom of the day. He was the "Sage of Emporia," grandstanding in the vital center of the national arena.[9]

Consider once more Slotkin's statement: "An environment, a landscape, a historical sequence is infused with meaning in the form of a story, which converts landscape to symbol and temporal sequence into 'doom'— a fable of necessary and fated actions." Slotkin is preoccupied with the frontier myth. He argues that the nation has long held to the myth and long will. For the past century students of American culture have wrestled, almost in their own mythic fashion, with the frontier first unleashed by the eminent historian Frederick Jackson Turner. At the end of the nineteenth century Turner observed, with so many others, that the physical frontier was closing; amidst the upheavals of the day he pondered the frontier's place in America's progressive saga; and so the conceptual frontier became freshly contested terrain. Western historian Patricia Nelson Limerick observes in her striking confessional, "Turnerians All: The Dream of a Helpful History in an Intelligible World," that despite Turner's acknowledged shortcomings there is no doubting the resilient power of the frontier and the fundamental ideals it conveys across time. Presentist critics, she declares, beware. But this is an old saw; many have been caught up short on this intellectual terrain.[10]

Shortly after World War II, Henry Nash Smith helped launch American Studies with his seminal work, *Virgin Land: The American West as Symbol and Myth*. Reconsidering his work two decades later, he recalled that "history cannot happen—that is, men cannot engage in purposive group behavior—without images which simultaneously express collective desires and impose coherence on the infinitely numerous and infinitely varied data of experience." Smith would be criticized for homogenizing too much of that experience into a singular, consensual national experience. But he sensed the power of an ideal and the power of words to convey it. They read well across time. Smith cites that a "thousand rivers flow into the mighty Mississippi," and he quotes Philip Frenau's 1782 tribute to the imperial glory of a western vision, speaking of the Mississippi,

> who from a source unknown collecting his remotest waters, rolls forward through the frozen regions of the north, and stretching his extended arms to the east and west, embraces those savage groves, as yet uninvestigated by the traveller, unsung by the poet, or unmeasured by the chain of the geometrician; till uniting with the Ohio, and turning due south, receiving afterwards the Missori [sic] and a hundred others, this prince of rivers, in comparison of whom the Nile is but a Rivulet and the Danube a mere ditch, hurries with his immense flood of waters to the Mexican sea, laving the shores of many fertile countries in his passage, inhabited by savage nations as yet almost unknown, and without a name.

But Anglicized, of course, they shall be. Later Smith records geopolitician William Gilpin's sweeping assessment of Manifest Destiny, written in 1846 as the nation approached the Mexican Borderlands:

> The "untransacted" destiny of the American people is to subdue the continent—to rush over this vast field to the Pacific Ocean—to animate the many hundred millions of its people, and to cheer them upward . . . —to teach old nations a new civilization—to confirm the destiny of the human race—. . . to emblazon history with the conquest of peace—to shed a new and resplendent glory upon mankind—to unite the world in one social family—. . . and to shed blessings round the world!

The words ring; they moved many; at times such words moved a nation. America treks westward, it progresses into the twentieth century as an urban-industrial behemoth, and at points it stumbles. Smith's work is filled with visions, apocalyptic prophesies, danger, and change. Again, he surveys the claim of a singular, consensual American experience; it is 1950 and an American century is ascendent. His study was deep; today he stands accused of being shallow. Smith was a young academic, a product of his time, and naturally his work was representative of his heritage.[11]

Just a few years earlier, as William Allen White neared the end of his life, he delivered a series of Harvard lectures later published as *The Changing West: An Economic Theory about Our Golden Age.* It was 1939; war clouds darkened a long-depressed domestic horizon. America was under seige; but the West always had offered an escape. The West, so sweeping in its destiny, the progenitor of progress itself, "here it is, the story of America's golden age . . . the vast magic carpet of prairie and plain and mountain, of lakes and rivers, deserts and forests, all yielding their wealth . . . in a widening, deepening stream of social and economic justice." White espied barbarism, warned of apocalypse, and cited destiny. He sounded a lot like Smith would in a few years, and he sounded a lot like his eighteenth- and nineteenth-century forebears Frenau and Gilpin. White wanted to; he was proud of the connection; he was assiduously striving to make the tie. He always had. He had made a career out of connecting.[12]

Environment, landscape, history, story, symbol, and necessary and fated actions—what a tale we have woven, and how well it has served us. Changing venues, all of the same pattern, the same cloth, make a whole. And this is the point. White knew the terrain well, he knew his history, and he knew his audience. And what a story he helped to tell: a comforting fable laden with messages for the many. He seemed so comfortable within his environment; he was the embodiment of necessary, fated actions and a born salesman to boot.

William Allen White, in the best sense of the measure, proofed out as "100 percent American." He was a cultural icon, a moveable feast, not always serving up the most popular fare of his day, but clearly in touch with popular preferences. He relished life, and he hit its and his own highs and lows. He certainly fit well the model sketched in Henry May's trail-blazing account *The End of American Innocence: A Study of the First Years of Our Own Time, 1912–1917*. White over this five-year span was in high stride. What a crossing it was: tradition was in the saddle, and modernist hounds were nipping at its exposed heels. May grapples with "the thought of the day." He cites William James's 1907 view of pragmatism: "For the philosophy which is so important in each of us is not a technical matter: it is more or less dumb sense of what life honestly and deeply means. It is only partly got from books. It is our individual way of just seeing and feel-ing the total push and pressure of the cosmos." May expands: "It is in philosophy in this sense that I have tried to center this book. The sense of what life means was what was stable in prewar America, and it was this that was beginning to change. . . . The change started in America to effect small groups of people directly. Soon . . . its indirect effects spread through the whole society."[13]

May goes on to explain the fit of such personages as the aging, urbane William Dean Howells, the young and exuberant Theodore Roosevelt, the "Great Commoner" William Jennings Bryan, "Fighting Bob" La Follette, and a host of other players of the day. They spoke a simple and confident language: forces for good, real truths, moral goodness, faith in both poli-tics and literature, and unembarrassed patriotism. Of Howells May writes, "He had always believed that American civilization was treading a sure path, whatever the momentary failures, toward moral and material improvement." The "whole people," led by the educated and able inheritors of tradition, "had some special responsibility for maintaining standards."[14]

This was a world of "smiling realism," of "practical idealism." The social gospel made sense, radicalism had been mainstreamed, and optimism reigned. In 1912 Theodore Roosevelt told a San Francisco gathering that it was all simple "because the great facts of life are simple." He continued, "A cultivated and intellectual paper once complained that my speeches lacked subtlety. So they do! I think that the command or entreaty to clean living and decent politics should no more be subtle than a command in battle should be subtle." Roosevelt rarely, if ever, marched alone. One of his excited compatriots was the Harvard-educated, rising young lion Walter Lippmann. No one doubted Lippmann's intellectual credentials. How subtle was he? A week after the United States embarked on its First World War crusade he predicted there would be a "transvaluation of values as radical as anything in the history of intellect." "We are living," he declared, "and shall live all our lives now in a revolutionary world."[15]

On one level it sounds silly today, as silly as it sounded by 1919, and tragic on too many levels. It would all collapse—morality, progress, culture, all that was good and right as defined by the dominant, aged WASP credo. But what resonance it carried in its day. Perhaps it is not a matter of composed or disjunctive soundings that matters but the leveling effect of language which cuts to the core. Theodore Roosevelt wrote to sociologist Edward D. Ross about the impact of the sociologist's 1901 study, *Social Control:* "Your plea is for courage, for uprightness, for far-seeing sanity, for active constructive work... You insist, as all healthy-minded patriots should insist, that public opinion, if only sufficiently enlightened and aroused, is equal to the necessary regenerative tasks and can yet dominate the future." These shapers of public opinion put their faith in the practical, in a call not to class but to "the general sense of right." It was a middle-class message, one which could regenerate a nation. It rang well because it harked back to old verities; all would be well. No wonder it still sounds good today—and yes, for some silly, too.[16]

It has sounded good to all sorts of folks for a long time. White had no tin ear. It is telling how many memoirs, autobiographies, and biographies of the first half of this century make laudatory references to that "most American of Americans," William Allen White. He seemed to intersect with so many lives, with so many streams of thought. Particularly amongst those active within or heavily influenced by Progressive Era reform, White's name crops up again and again. When I first became aware of Jean B. Quandt's study, *From the Small Town to the Great Community: The Social Thought of Progressive Intellectuals,* I thought surely she was off the mark.

Quandt's progressive intellectuals constituted an impressive lot: Josiah Royce, John Dewey, Mary Parker Follett, Jane Addams, Frederick Howe, Franklin Giddings, Charles Horton Cooley, Robert Park, and William Allen White. William Allen White? I had come to recognize his stature, but he clearly was no intellectual. I assumed that Quandt's dissertation committee, or her editors, made the point that she needed to include a popular lightweight in this study. But she knew exactly what she was doing; I only got the point years later. White was in particularly good form in the Progressive Era, and he was in most comfortable company with the likes of a John Dewey, a Jane Addams, or a Charles Horton Cooley. None would presume to call White an intellectual, but he was in step with a good number of intellectuals, walking diverse paths, merging with the mainstream public, skirting by at times, but clearly in touch—all of them—with issues of general concern. They certainly did not always agree. They did love to talk of an ephemeral sense of community. Quandt notes, "The benchmark of community was not coordination of function but consciousness of common ends. . . . Only when cooperation was accompanied by identification with a common cause could they speak of community." Ah yes, they loved to talk shop, and they were out to manufacture, in a most abstract sense of togetherness, a great society.[17]

What remains fascinating about this progressive lot is their intimacy, their casual intermingling, their widespread participation in public affairs, the similarity of backgrounds they possessed; they shared a faith in an egalitarian community, in a politicized, classless democracy. Their commitment to progressivism was profound; and so, too, was their commitment to the frontier, now epitomized by "building community," as towns were built throughout the "West." Quandt writes that for White "the greatest achievement of the West was always the collective creation of the country town." White's perspective was shaped by many factors; it was not provincial, nor was philosopher Josiah Royce's:

> For Royce, as for the others, early experience of the small town guided the later search for new and wider forms of community. The easy sense of belonging, the similarity of experience, and the ethic of participation might be more easily maintained in the small locality than anywhere else, but this did not preclude their cultivation in different soil.

The philosopher and the townsman tilled common ground.[18]

Yes, the soil, a place—America moves forward; a fertile land and a fervent dream beckon. The power and the persuasiveness of progressivism was contagious. A fever gripped the reformers; a fervor gripped the "nation." The "people" were admired. Millions enlisted in the "cause," however one might define it; all could lay claim to the people as once they laid claim to land. They shared common ground. But the exact locale of the movement never was clear. It was not structured; it in fact canvassed a fluid, highly publicized landscape. And progressivism flowed on beyond the Progressive Era. Scholars argue its direction, its strength, its integrity, its very life as well as its death, but those who subscribed to progressivism never forgot its power or its arching message. And it shaped the twentieth century. One study after another, calculating one element after another of twentieth-century history, refers to the movement, its participants, its energy, its direction. Twentieth-century community was in the making. Still, few have been able to grasp what exactly this means, what has been the end product.

The progressives, as Quandt sees it, staked their lot in communication: "Communication... would strengthen the psychic sources of unity: mutual sympathy, consensus, or common values, and the sense of one's special function in the whole which a complex social organism required." Drawing upon the new psychology, they believed "that the nature of the self is social; then they used this idea to show how communication might expand mutual identification beyond the bounds of family, town, class, or section." They had great faith in the communications revolution. Quandt cites White's view that the new inventions contained the fresh promise of making "the nation a neighborhood." She asserts it made a lot of sense: "Mutual sympathy would flourish on a larger scale than ever before. What firsthand acquaintance provided on Main Street, the communications media could create for the whole society." They did believe it.[19]

And so White was part of a formidable group. Jean Quandt had it right; he did fit. She erred in distinguishing the journalist as an intellectual, but she was on target in marking him comfortable within overlapping intellectual circles. White was part of this huge progressive reform movement. But it and he were part of a much greater tradition. White's links to the frontier were self-evident: he grew up on the frontier, and he addressed the nation's frontier heritage. Progressivism burst forth as the old frontier was fading off into the sunset. The movement incorporated multiple nineteenth-century legacies. Generations now have diagnosed, dissected, and prescribed the meaning of progressivism. The bibliographical guides are plentiful, and they are rich. And community is a constant refrain.[20]

White embraced it all. Progressive Republican, Bull Mooser, confidante to Theodore Roosevelt, publisher, editor, journalist, founder and contributor to progressive journals, Protestant, Midwesterner, prohibitionist, civil rights advocate, Jeffersonian and Hamiltonian, townsman and cosmopolite, isolationist and internationalist, traditional novelist and modernist—White was all of these. In trying to structure some sort of progressive profile, historian John Chambers writes,

> In diverse ways and with divergent goals, the progressives sought to modernize American institutions while attempting to recapture the ideals and sense of community that they believed had existed in the past. They battled conservatives, radicals, other reformers, and often each other. But despite their disagreements and difficulties, progressives played a major role in helping Americans to adjust to new conditions and create new institutions for coping with the challenges of the time. They took the lead in establishing a social agenda for modern America.

Both a communicator and a communitarian, White was a key author of that agenda.[21]

■ ■ ■

William Allen White was part of a rich progressive tradition. But progressivism spun out of and toward other traditions. It is not difficult to trace its roots. But where did it lead? The modern order? Whatever that might mean. Cultural historian Lawrence Levine helps direct the way. Levine in his retrospective compendium *The Unpredictable Past: Explorations in American Cultural History* attempts to place himself and his work within America's historical mainstream. He looks into a variety of cultural currents at work: theater, rhetoric, photography, jazz, literature, soaps, and film. He recognizes the subtleties of semiotics and the brute force of hegemony. He brilliantly jumps about from William Shakespeare and William Jennings Bryan to Marcus Garvey and Al Smith, and from Frank Capra to Jefferson Smith and John Doe. He attempts to come to terms with popular culture. He warns historians to take it seriously, to see it in its proper context, to understand the process of interaction: texts are complex; so, too, are audiences who "embody more than monolithic assemblies of compliant people but who are in fact complex amalgams of cultures, tastes, and ideologies." The people are not simple:

> It is a mistake, then, to divide the world up too easily into reality and representations of reality. The latter—the representations—when they become embodied in theater, tales, radio, movies, become forms of reality themselves. I don't mean by this that audiences necessarily "confuse" them with reality. Indeed, I think the opposite is more often true. Rather, the entire setting constitutes an important form of reality in which many essential things are realized: lessons are learned, values enunciated and repeated, modes of behavior scrutinized, social institutions and their effects explored, fantasies indulged.

Here, indeed, Levine finds the real multifarious stuff of America's urban-industrial society. Levine quotes folklorist Bruce Jackson's view that all of our stories are co-authored, "No story exists out there by itself. The story takes life from two of us: the teller and the listener, writer and reader, actor and watcher, each a necessary participant in the creation of space in which the utterance takes life, in which all our utterances take life." Levine continues,

> heterogeneity and variety do not necessarily connote chaos and loss of meaning. One has to look not for an unvarying central message but for "patterns" of meaning and consciousness across the genres and among different segments of the population. This is crucial but it does not negate the fact that whatever patterns we find will have to live along side the inconsistencies, tensions, and cacophony of voices. . . . Indeed, it is the very asymmetry and diversity in Popular Culture that should convince us it can be used as an indispensible guide to the thought and attitudes of an asymmetrical and diverse people.[22]

Levine talks a lot about "revitalization." The culture works at revitalization. Elements within the culture work at it. The historian gains support from anthropologist Anthony F. C. Wallace. Levine writes,

> When a perceptible gap arises between the images and expectations a culture has created . . . and the realities of the culture, the resulting anxiety can often be relieved only through the agency of what he has called a "revitalization movement": "a deliberate, organized conscious effort by members of a society to construct a more satisfying culture," one that comes closer to their longstanding dreams and expectations.

Levine concludes that in the United States such revitalization movements "have tended to stress the revival of central cultural beliefs and values and the elimination of alien influences." So, here is Middle America? Here is hegemony? As Levine explains, no, the people are not singular:

> Those who have seen in Popular Culture an overriding instrument of hegemony have misunderstood its nature. Popular Culture does not present us with a single face or an orderly ideology. Certainly it is true that even in as heterogeneous a society as the United States, there can be deeply internalized points of view and these will inevitably be reflected in the Popular Culture, but there will be myriad fundamental disagreements and contradictions as well. . . .

Within this heterogeneous mix, Levine recognizes the power of nostalgia and the presence of ambivalence, but he argues this

> is not to deny the realities of change. The desire to have things both ways—to accept the fruits of progress without relinquishing the funda-

mentals of the old order—explains many of the tensions in American life, but it has never led to complete paralysis. In spite of the persistent lag between actuality and perception, there has been a gradual acceptance of changes and a reordering of desires, expectations and action throughout American history. Americans ... turn to the past in their ideology and rhetoric more than in their actions.[23]

Yes, the actions—another formidable cultural historian, in another compendium of professional progress, assesses American actions in the twentieth century. Warren Sussman in *Culture as History: The Transformation of American Society in the Twentieth Century* writes of origins, arguing that progressivism in a fashion was also an aesthetic movement: "it proposed as a social 'and' political end the opportunity for each man and woman to know some experience that was creative and satisfying, an aesthetic experience that was the consequence of communal and political life. This kind of vision is strikingly new as a political goal in America." A culture of abundance was in the works amidst communication and organization revolutions; a new middle class, an end product in itself, would be the recipient of the goods. This new class would have a common ideology if not a clear political perspective or social strategy: "their position in the social order affected their perceptions, their consciousness, and the way they performed in everyday life." Public opinion would be shaped, and personality, too. It may have gone bust by aesthetic standards, but the goal was no less laudable.[24]

But bust it did. Sussman surveys a commercial rush of twentieth-century groups, figures, venues, and frameworks: progressives, latter-age puritans, eugenicists, filmmakers, consensus theorists, Frederick Jackson Turner, Willa Cather, Henry Ford, Babe Ruth, Bruce Barton, Herbert Croly, Archibald MacLeish, Rheinhold Niebuhr, Dale Carnegie, the American Dream, the American Way of Life, the Depression, and the Second World War. He concludes that the common man came of age in the 1930s, not quite what a host of progressives had anticipated:

> The concept of the average was born, a kind of statistical accounting of the people seen as a unit. For a culture that originally had enshrined individualism as its key virtue, interest in the average was now overwhelming. The Average American and the Average American Family became central to the new vision of a future culture. ... Increasingly, this statistical creature ... was invested as well with the sentimental aura that went with the more mystical notion of the people. If the people seemed pleasingly poetic and the average American suitably scientific, both versions of the idea nevertheless regarded society as a single entity.

No, this was not what most progressives had had in mind. The end product was in fact as fissured as progressives themselves, but it was commercially sealed and ultimately vacuum-packed as a body politic.[25]

A host of cultural studies confirm Sussman's view of the packaged transformation of American society, although the chosen "date of use" may vary. Amongst many complementary perspectives—represented here by David Glassberg's observation of American historical pageantry, T. J. Jackson Lears's work on antimodernism, Joan Shelley Rubin's view of middlebrow culture, Robert L. Dorman's study of the regionalist movement, and Roland Marchand's look at advertising—there repeatedly arises the issue not simply of the creation of a middling society, but one in its own way eager to establish a strong sense of community. Rubin cites a persistently changing middle ground; one element of her study focuses upon the establishment of the Book of the Month Club in the 1920s. She notes the congruence of a quest for knowledge, the rise of advertising, and new forms of marketing within a culture in extreme flux. An expanding sense of anxiety was relieved by joining a club. The club targeted the "average intelligent reader." In particular the club aimed to heal a modern ailment. With membership, an upper-middle-class American could assuage "anxiety about the self." The club made a great pitch: "The backward glances involved in the 'guarantee of satisfaction,' the rhetoric of service, and the construct of a 'club' suggest that [Robert Scherman, the BOMC's progenitor] sensed within his audience longings for a world inhabited by models of character, even as it strove to cultivate personality for the sake of impressing others."[26]

The Book of the Month Club was definitively something new for a "New Era." No wonder, as David Glassberg demonstrates, historical pageantry was biting the dust. The promoters of pageantry were looking ahead, but the medium was decidedly old-fashioned: "American historical pageantry, especially when in the hands of pageant-masters distinctly sympathetic with the forward-looking progressive movements around them, presented history in a setting that emphasized the continuities between past, present, and an ideal future." This relic of the nineteenth century could not find a meaningful spot in the modern age. The aim was to calm, to assuage, to clarify in simple pictorial form stability, cohesiveness, and hierarchy. More important, it increasingly looked backward: "the sequence of historical episodes reenacted in pageants of the 1920s offered little in the way of a rhythm of social evolution between past and present that local residents could imaginatively project into their future." It was no match for the greater communal allure of films, radio, and advertising. Advertising, as Roland Marchand makes abundantly clear, refined the sale:

Advertising leaders recognized the necessity of associating their selling messages with the values and attitudes already held by their audiences. They sought to strike only those notes that would evoke a positive
resonance. . . . Whatever the results in ad content and audience reaction,
advertising people clearly invested more time, energy, and money than
any other mass communicators in the effort to discover such fundamental beliefs.

They discovered them, they shaped them, and they hit pay dirt:

Advertisers, then as now, recognized a much larger stake in reflecting
people's needs and anxieties than in depicting their actual circumstances
and behavior. It was in their efforts to promote the mystique of modernity in styles and technology, while simultaneously assuaging the anxieties of consumers about losses of community and individual control,
that they most closely mirrored historical reality—the reality of a cultural dilemma.[27]

Marchand brilliantly displays the growth of an industry that mar-
velously negotiated the commercial crisis of the thirties. That fundamental need for community and identity would be expressed, pressed, and
impressed by Madison Avenue. It was a real need. People looked back, and
they looked ahead. Far from Madison Avenue, as Robert L. Dorman
unearths, from 1920 through 1945, provincialism was in revolt. A vast
array of intellectuals did not always catch the public imagination, but they
tapped into fundamentals. Lewis Mumford, Howard Odum, B. A. Botkin,
Mary Austin, and a troop of others offered pluralistic, region-specific alter-
natives. They wanted to forge a new ethos: "Regionalists would, in sum,
join this interwar modernist generation in the search for a new 'integrated'
culture and society." Unlike "New York–centered" groups, the regionalists
were older stock, and they were principally concerned with "rural America,
its traditions, folk, farms, towns, and wildernesses; even the prominent
urban-planning wing under Mumford was to take as a chief project the
'ruralizing' of the metropolis." They were not provincial; they possessed a
modernist agenda.[28]

T. J. Jackson Lears in his seminal work *No Place of Grace: Antimodernism and the Transformation of American Culture, 1880–1920,* sums
up well the dilemma facing the even older old-stock, late-nineteenth-
century Americans who had for so long set the cultural agenda.
"Antimodernists were far more than escapists: their quests for authentic-
ity eased their own and others' adjustments to a streamlined culture of
consumption." A grave transition was in the making. Lears wants to place
the antimodernists, those WASP elites who supposedly could not adjust to
the new twentieth-century order, in their proper role: "They helped both

to revitalize familiar bourgeois values and ease the transition to new ones at a critical historical moment." Lears argues that the "revolution in manners and morals" began long before the 1920s amongst the bohemian literati and the respectable bourgeoisie; "it was part of a broader shift from a Protestant to a therapeutic orientation within the dominant culture."[29]

■ ■ ■

We've come a long way from simple progressive platitudes about truth and honesty, coming to terms with a prescriptive therapeutic—as opposed to a restrictive, Protestant—cultural orientation. No wonder the progressives are tough to pin down. Maybe that is why White is so difficult to frame and nail to the wall. He's not Jello, as they say. But what was he? White was not only closely associated with a good number of the men and women, thoughts and movements, ideas and goods noted above; in numerous ways he summed them up. He was a progressive innocent, and he was a twentieth-century modernist; he appreciated popular culture and high culture, but he expressly styled himself an average man; he was capable of appreciating historical pageantry, and he was an original selection panelist for the Book of the Month Club; he was representative of WASP elites (with whom he so well identified that he, too, suffered periodic mental breakdowns), and he easily grasped the over-the-counter prescriptives of a consumer culture. The advertisers were selling goods; therapy was in demand, and so was White—right on the cover of one magazine, journal, or newspaper after another, for decades. Maybe there is a likeness to Jello; White would have made a great barker for this twentieth-century soul food, for this comfort food long hawked by the likes of a Jack Benny or a Bill Cosby—one of us, really.[30]

White stood for Levine's story elements: the teller and the listener, the writer and the reader, the actor and the watcher. He took it all in. Lears, again, refers to revitalization. William Allen White was the great revitalizer. In a culture hooked on the horns of a cultural dilemma, he was the great middle man who could deliver the goods—fundamental beliefs cut to fashionable demand. Dorman's regionalists, too, desperately sought to deliver the goods:

> Or was there another alternate solution to the crisis, another route to the "accomodating middle ground" between the modern and the traditional? Poets, folklorists, editors, historians, painters, and novelists were codiscoverers of the "region" with sociologists, conservationists, urban planners, and architects, who saw in the organicism embodied by the region—and its ethical and aesthetic implications as well—a sophisticated new tool for mitigating the effects of "Progress."

The regionalists sought an arena from which they could negotiate progress. White was in that arena. And he had the audience to prove it.[31]

White would argue they should look to Emporia, his town, the epitome of Middle America. But he never meant Emporia as such; he meant it as that community, that identity that could work better. The work of four scholars places White well: D. W. Meinig's "Symbolic Landscapes," James R. Shortridge's *The Middle West: Its Meaning in American Culture*, Carl Becker's "Kansas," and David E. Shi's *The Simple Life* focus on place as an idea. Meinig discusses the classic New England townscape as evocative of "a particular kind of place rather than a precise building or locality." He knows it is difficult to extract exact meaning from such imagery, but one can easily ponder,

> it seems clear that such scenes carry connotations of continuity (of not just something important in our past, but a visible bond between past and present), of stability, quiet prosperity, cohesion and intimacy. Taken as a whole, the image of the New England village is widely assumed to symbolize for many people the best we have known of an intimate, family-centered, Godfearing, morally conscious, industrious, thrifty, democratic "community."

It has been abundantly clear to those familiar with American high, low, middle, and popular culture that the Middle West in the twentieth century similarly has connoted such an emotive wholeness. It has stood as a pastoral ideal, a crossroads between uncivilized wilderness and urban-industrial evil. Shortridge makes the point:

> This identification is the unwavering fact of Middle-western existence— a root identity equivalent to New England's puritanism. It has failed to produce a simple unified regional image, however, because values associated with pastoralism have changed, the rural character of the Middle West itself has lessened, and the physical area said to be Middle Western has been modified. The basic pattern is thus something of a paradox— continuity yet change; and this melange is a key to the cultural confusion that has characterized the region throughout much of its history.

Still, despite the confusion, the "Middle West came to symbolize the nation, and to be seen as the most American part of America."[32]

For millions, from deep thinkers to moviegoers, from radio audiences to academics, Kansas came to represent the high spots and the low spots of this middle ground. Historian Carl Becker, contemplating his thirteen-year sojourn in Kansas, caught the symbol at its richest: "The Kansas spirit is the American spirit double distilled. It is a new grafted product of American individualism, American idealism, American intolerance.

Kansas is America in microcosm. . . . Within its borders, Americanism, pure and undefiled, has a new lease on life." In the midst of progressive enlightenment, Becker proclaimed, "The light on the altar, however neglected elsewhere, must ever be replenished in Kansas. If this is provincialism, it is the provincialism of faith rather than of the province."[33]

Provincialism, faith—all a bit too simplistic? Few would charge Carl Becker as being provincial or simplistic. He had faith; a leading progressive historian, he wrote "Kansas" in 1910 in honor of Frederick Jackson Turner. And he reprinted, with no qualifications, the Turnerian piece in 1935 as Kansas suffered the ravages of the Dust Bowl. Something else is at work here. David Shi refers to some sort of "Middle Kingdom" in the making. In fact, as Shi lucidly argues, for America a quest for a simple life has long reigned over the cultural landscape. Americans, burdened by jeremiads and prophecies of regeneration, have driven westward, carrying with them a powerful idea of retaining a simple life, which harks not backward but forward; and they have acted upon it:

> But ideas in the abstract are inert; they tell us little about the mystery of daily living. To bring texture—indeed, to bring life to the study of cultural beliefs—requires going beyond symbolic analysis; it entails examining how people have struggled to translate myths into practice. For this reason, I have treated the simple life both as a sentimental ideal and as an actual way of living, revealing in the process the personal implications for many of those who have tried to live according to its dictates. At the same time, I have also studied the way in which the larger public has viewed the simple life over the years. Doing so will tell us more about ourselves—perhaps more than some may want to know.

Perhaps, but what a captivating panorama Shi offers. Carl Becker, one might guess, would approve, and Frederick Jackson Turner, too.[34]

Legions of post-Columbian Americans across five centuries have sought a blend of old and new ways and guidelines for sorting out hopes, aspirations, and moral and social concerns; these Americans included Jeffersonian Republicans, Transcendentalists, Gilded Age patricians, early-twentieth-century progressives, twenties Agrarians, Ralph Borsodi, Lewis Mumford, Scott and Helen Knothe Nearing, E. F. Schumacher, and Ronald Reagan—what an array. Reagan could be both Hamiltonian and Jeffersonian. He told businessmen he looked toward "an end to giantism, for a return to the human scale—the scale that human beings can understand and cope with; the scale of the local fraternal lodge, the church congregation, the block club, the farm bureau." Who was Reagan fooling? No one, of course. We all know; we all have been raised on the language. Reagan's revivified community, he told us, would serve as "a framework for the creation of abundance and liberty." How far was the "Great Communicator" from Thoreau's simplified life in Concord, the "temperate zone" balancing the wild and the urbane? Shi writes, "Periodic excursions into the wilderness would provide necessary raw materials for the soul, and civilization would provide necessary finished products." Reagan, too, made it simple: "If he was Jeffersonian in his sentimental political vision . . . he was Hamiltonian in his refusal to emphasize any moral limits on the individual pursuit or consumption of wealth or on the size and influence of corporations." It was all very American, making sense across time, and across balance sheets.[35]

Certainly plenty of individuals looked further back than ahead. Some allowed nostalgia to get the edge. Charles Eliot Norton in the Gilded Age lamented that Greek culture presented a "lesson of moderation, of self-control, of sweet, simple, temperate living." The Harvard president would find refuge in Ashfield, a New England rural village. For Norton the town was homogeneous, ordered, and beautiful, a pleasant spot to reside where "everyone has self-respect, where there are no differences of condition." Ashfield, of course, was no such idyllic spot, nor was Norton as he claimed, "a farmer up here." But in Ashfield he found the rural, domestic simplicity he increasingly sought as he soured on the world around him; he looked back to a time when the "habits of life were simpler; the interests of men less mixed and varied; there were more common sympathies, more common and controlling traditions and associations."[36]

Most, however, looked ahead for simplicity, with the past a guiding line. In the 1920s Lewis Mumford and a host of architects, social theorists, and urban planners sought a means to rejuvenate simpler habits within the new order. America's peculiar blend of individualism and cooperation would be put to its severest test in the Great Depression; within the calamity, Mumford and others looked toward building "a new living environment that would combine the best features of town and country, farm and factory, and thereby establish a habitat in equilibrium with nature and civilization." Garden cities, bordering the metropolis, would overlook economic differences and eliminate economic waste, they would be "fresh communities planned on a human scale," capable of restoring "a little happiness and freedom in those places where things have been pretty well wrung out."[37]

Mumford possessed an intense, humane vision. He spoke of life "in no vague sense": "One means the birth and nurture of children, the preservation of human health and well-being, the culture of the human personality, and the perfection of the natural and civic environment. . . ." Shi summarizes, "Life in his planned communities would be a richly integrated and cooperative social experience in which people, regardless of their economic circumstances, would enjoy a sense of belonging with each other, with nature, and with their work." Once more there would be an enlightened middle ground, the American Dream, a middle-class haven. The vision was fresh; it looked ahead blending old and new; it revived, it revivified, and it revitalized.[38]

■ ■ ■

What a stretch from Charles Eliot Norton's Ashfield to Lewis Mumford's Greenbelt, from Athens to Concord. Simplicity never worked out well as a societal ethic, but it has "exercised a powerful influence on the complex patterns of American culture."

> As a myth of national purpose and as a program for individual conduct, the simple life has been a perennial dream and a rhetorical challenge, displaying an indestructible vitality even in the face of repeated defeats. It has, in a sense, served as the nation's conscience, reminding Americans of what the founders had hoped they would be and thereby providing a vivifying counterpoint to the excesses of materialist individualism.

Complex cultural patterns; national myths and rules for individual conduct; dreams, challenges, vitality and defeats; the nation's conscience; here is a vivifying counterpoint: progressivism looking back, and progressivism charging ahead. It is intriguing that within this lucid study of the simple life Shi never glimpses the prominence of the small-town protagonist. It is a constant, across generations and centuries; it threads its way through all elements of his study. But Shi missed its continuing twentieth-century stature in the same manner that so many accounts skirt its edges. Yet the small-town ideal has persisted throughout the century. So, too, has the progressive ideal; and so, too, have the cultural permutations which we conjure together as the twentieth-century American Way of life. Lawrence Levine plumbed the alchemy in Alfred North Whitehead's observation, "The health of a people depends largely on their ability to question their inherited symbols in light of contemporary actualities, to keep them fluid, vibrant, and responsive." America's small-town idyll has served as a responsive symbol. It has been mocked, it has been praised, it has been understood and misunderstood, and it has been taken for granted. It epitomizes the search for the simple life, the search which runs through so much of our lives.[39]

The town has had quite a run. And so, too, did William Allen White. Neither the small-town ideal nor White had a weighty influence upon events. Both seemed to be in the middle of it all. One historical study, one Progressive Era autobiography, the biography of this intellect, that journalism study, a few more histories, biographies, a politician's life, a film study, this view of community and that of urbanization, more studies on advertising and class, more memoirs, Middle Western backgrounds, small-town ties, pastoral hopes, the nation's conscious and unconscious longings backward and forward—certainly White related to all of this. He crops up again and again, and practically all agree he conveyed particular concerns of and to others. In Lears's therapeutic culture, White appears to have been some sort of mediator, perhaps facilitator, or, best of all, enabler. If White served as some sort of cultural enabler for half a century, surely then his codependent was his appreciative public. No wonder, then, that so many have trouble giving him due weight. In a therapeutic world, in a consumer-driven rush for simplicity, how many observers are prepared to comment that they, too, need the goods, especially the more common variety? This is a society in desperate need of community—whatever that might mean to whoever is beating the drum. William Allen White was a champion at delivering the goods. What's the matter? William Allen White, hardly alone but nevertheless prominent, offered appealing fixes.

David Shi summarizes that the simple life is a personal ethic. If he is correct, surely then one can be allowed a malleable model. "If the decision to live a simple life is fundamentally a personal matter, then so, too, is the nature and degree of simplification." White connected with Frederick Jackson Turner, with Lewis Mumford, with homogeneity and heterogeneity, with nostalgia, ambivalence, and change, with fundamentals and progress. White was the ultimate middle man. Yes, Jean B. Quandt had it right when she placed William Allen White in the middle of her intellectual communitarians. He touched all the bases; he translated important beliefs into the common-sense dialect. He would be the first to discount his own intellect. But he grasped the deeper issues, and he possessed a huge public which listened to him. Quandt wrote, "If the new media were to contribute to an enlarged social conscience, [the communitarians] reasoned, the means of communication must draw strength from intimate community life." Dewey could design schools, Addams could live in Hull House, and Josiah Royce could philosophize at Columbia. But White could relate to and through twentieth-century mass culture in a way few intellectuals could. Walter Lippmann, from his tower at the New York *World,* wrote Felix Frankfurter of his respect for his boss, "I have a great deal of affection and admiration for Frank Cobb. He's a sort of humorous Yankee titan, 100% American as William Allen White is and as none of the 100% professionals are." White cut a malleable American figure.[40]

Quandt argues that the communitarians lost their bearings after the First World War. She argues that the small-town perspective lost its intellectual grip. But she's wrong. The idea that the core face-to-face community must be the foundation for the greater society continued to carry weight. White, along with Quandt's other subjects, had embraced the view of Charles Horton Cooley: Cooley hoped that modern technology might foster a "sense of community, or of sharing in a common social or spiritual whole, membership in which gives to all a kind of inner equality, no matter what their special parts may be." From such common ground "would flow the concrete social and economic measures necessary for a just society." Cooley trusted in the small-town ideal; as a student of the communications revolution, he assumed social harmony, fair play, and kindness could be successfully communicated across an urban-industrial landscape. White shared with all too many the postwar disillusionment with a good number of abstract and concrete ideals seemingly gone bust; yet he continued to adhere, in a positive fashion, to the small-town ideal. Somehow, Quandt missed this important, vital element of the story. Progressivism and community lived on. Perhaps it all had a lot more to do with therapy than with bedrock Protestant values, but it did live on. The culture changed, and William Allen White changed, too; he kept communicating and communing in twentieth-century fashion.[41]

White fit well with the progressives, and for close to a hundred years the progressives have fit well with America. Progressivism is a knotty concept. As Chambers noted, again, these diverse reformers were good at adapting and "helping Americans to adjust to new conditions and create new institutions for coping with the challenges of the time." They were particularly good at using words. Daniel T. Rodgers catches the drift, across centuries:

> For it is largely through a string of words—be they "freedom," or "equality," or the "sanctity of property," or the claims of race—that individuals separated from normal sight of each other are shaken into consciousness that their grievances, ambitions, angers, and desires are not peculiarly theirs, but, at some slightly altered level of generalization, the material of politics. Abstract generalizing talk makes private matters public.

Rodgers goes on to conclude that the larger and more sonorous the words, "the more private desires they can bind together, the more new desires they can create." It sounds like a lesson right out of the Madison Avenue offices of Batten, Barton, Durstine and Osborn. Possibly over the past century the key words have destructively crashed on the rocky shores of commercialism. Rodgers demonstrates their longevity; they certainly carried clout during the Progressive Era. He believes we "get closest to the language of politics not by looking for paradigms nor by stringing our best writers together in traditions but by noticing what the talkers and scribblers are doing with the big words at their disposal." They were assiduously working the language during the Progressive Era; "no one looking back on the years before the First World War has failed to be struck by the vigor, the massive confidence of the era's appeal to ideals. The big, highbrow words which had fueled political argument so long went out not with a whimper, but unexpectedly, in full career."[42]

White was of another era. He came of age, a bit late one might say, with the twentieth century, with the Progressive Era. For Rodgers it clearly signaled an end. The nation moved on, politics were swallowed up by the interests, and key words were regurgitated as nonsense: "It is the story of how, in a world transformed by admen, propagandists, and public opinion shapers, among men shaken by these hucksters into a deeply skeptical attitude toward words of every sort, a mud-stained term of opprobrium swallowed up the whole of politics." Progressivism evolved into, or devolved within, a commercial culture. Community, peddled wholesale, descended to the bargain basement. But individuals like White carried on. You had to keep carrying on, of course. Those men and women like White, unlike a Borsodi or the Nearings, made vast connections that mattered, and, they carried a responsibility. Again, White always asked, What's the matter? He provided answers which made a good deal of common sense. They were simple truths really, perhaps not credible on one level, but highly accomodating on most.[43]

■ ■ ■

I noted at the beginning that this was my tale, too. It, naturally, belongs to us all. My own understanding of place, my own values, and where I have placed myself over the years clearly inform and influence this story. Here I write in Madeira, Ohio. Madeira is an old Cincinnati suburb which consciously retains a powerful small-town identity. I've landed here by way of Aspen and Boulder, Colorado; Madison, Wisconsin; Danville, Kentucky; and Wilmington, Ohio—an odd lot of small-town habitats. A decade and a half ago, when historian John Sharpless in Madison suggested the topic for my dissertation, it was perfect, and I immediately embraced it. Of course it was changed this way and that, and, I guess, so was I. I learned a lot. Small-town America—it meant a lot to me, a kid who grew up in Studio City, California, in the fifties and sixties. It seemed funny at first: my origins always were good for some laughs, but ultimately it proved to be a refreshingly provocative insight. William Allen White persistently searched for a conceptual sense of community that worked for him and others. When I was a child, I daydreamed, strangely enough in retrospect, about an idyllic life in an Ohio small town. My life was good, but my idea of the good life rested in a Middle Western idyll: large elms, front porch, very green, comfortably old, pleasantly shaded, with neighboring homes not too close, and certainly not too distant. Over the past five decades I've learned a lot about place. As it happens, I've ended up living in a quiet, small town smack in the middle of a bustling city. It's not the "place" as such that counts, but how it is situated within one's purview of what matters. For me, this small town, in the most relative of terms, assuages my interest in the simple life. And oddly enough—no, not odd at all—it strongly resembles the small town I in fact inhabited in Studio City, California, smack in the middle of Los Angeles's suburban expanse.

In the early part of the swiftly changing twentieth century, White tangled with the idea of place and concluded we may all live here or there, but in our hearts we long for some small town, some Emporia: "In America most of us are Emporians in one way or another. Some of us live in towns ranging from five thousand to a quarter of a million, others were born in or around these towns, and still others of us cherish golden dreams of going back to some Emporia." Perhaps I found this focus so appealing, so perplexing, and finally so fulfilling because I, as so many in the middle of America's broad mainstream, invest great stock in the idea of place, of some sort of intangible, meaningful, and in part physical community. It's all a muddle: Main Streets and shopping malls; old towns and newly manufactured "small-town" subdivisions; neighborhood druggists dispensing pharmaceutical homilies in million-dollar network ads; William McKinley's Canton, Warren Harding's Marion, Harry Truman's Independence, Ike's Abilene, Nixon's Whittier, Reagan's Dixon, and William Jefferson Clinton and a town called Hope. They are not substantial places in any sense of the word; they are mythical, metaphoric, political, nostalgic, and hyperbolic, but not substantive.[44]

It is not so surprising that a kid who grew up in Southern California —Studio City, of all places—valued a sense of Middle Western place. Studio City was very much a small town in what it offered to me and so many others in the fifties and early sixties; it offered security, family, and place. Emporia rested someplace inside of me, too. This was an American Dream long in the making. It held center stage in the consciousness of many. It was a key chapter in the national narrative. This narrative was ridiculed as millions struggled through the late sixties and seventies. Towns and suburbs, security and family, Ozzie and Harriet, all took heavy hits. Security and family again take center stage in a values-panicked society. But the show seems skewed. In the same manner that staged pageantry bit the dust in the mid-1930s, old values, the standards, have become sepia-toned. Jimmy Stewart has just been buried; the obituaries underscored the message: it was the end of an era. Jefferson Smith played well in the middle of the twentieth century, but we're now at the end of that run.

Well, Jimmy Stewart, for all his genuine apple-pie traits, did, after all, live in Beverly Hills, California, a long way off from his Indiana, Pennsylvania, roots. Cowboy humorist Will Rogers, everyone's Middle American, didn't linger in Oklahoma; he traveled east to Broadway and settled west in Hollywood. Ronald Reagan hardly ever returned to Dixon, Illinois, except for a campaign shoot. At Thanksgiving the cameras rolled as he and Nancy sat down to homespun fixings on the Santa Barbara ranch; at New Year's the shutters were closed as the first couple partied in star-studded Palm Springs. It's all really been a mix of fact and fancy. It's all been a good show, but it's old, and today we all know too much about what's going on back stage—some say too much for our own good. It was more comforting, perhaps, not to be so perceptive of our own fantasies, others' hegemonic powers, and our shared hard-core vulnerabilities. Perhaps David Shi was correct; investigating the means by which myths are put into practice can be risky: "Doing so will tell us more about ourselves —perhaps more than some may want to know."[45]

■ ■ ■

Middle class became the norm, and Middle America, the place. But now we are increasingly skeptical. We urbanize, we advertise, we dissemble, we homogenize, and we balkanize. And we really do seem today to be moving far away from a small-town idyll that most Americans could genuinely in some fashion relate to not so long ago. When I began this study in the early eighties, small-town imagery still resonated. Now, it seemingly drifts off, lost in the cacophony of cultural angst, fading back into the folklore of the yeoman, the independent farmer, the cowboy. Goods and comfort, the American Dream, the meaning of a middle-class way of life, all take on new connotations, new directions. Wealthy, preppie George Bush appealed to "front porch democracy," and baby-boomer Bill Clinton claimed to hail from a poor boy's past and a town called Hope. None of the coinage carried much weight in the public domain. Advertising, consumption, boxed politicians, untethered journalism, and a confession-mad tabloid society—many argue we are a jaded and worn out people, a tarnished and a tinny commodity. Jimmy Stewart's eulogists got it right: it was an end of an era, a faraway world that doesn't make so much sense any more. Ronald Reagan sang the swan song; a B actor could play one last sentimental, small-town scenario in Washington. Bob Dole, a real American hero, was pilloried in the recent presidential campaign for harking back to his small-town roots. It didn't sell; he was mispackaged for the day. Bill Clinton turned it all around with empty allusions to a bridge into the next century. Few seem to care about the message or the messenger—not much substance to the hope.

A hundred years have passed since corporate-aligned William McKinley similarly cut down to fashionable size Nebraska's William Jennings Bryan. McKinley, of course, did it sitting on his front porch in Canton, Ohio, while industrial tycoon Mark Hanna railroaded millions to view him as representing real America as opposed to Bryan's rural throwback. It's all a long time ago. We live in another world. Rural America had its day, and the small town has had its century. Patricia Limerick is right: never write off the frontier. Still, its small-town conception may be dying fast. A town called Hope is pretty forgettable.

We all are, in some fashion, middle class at our core; and we all are, as we have been for the past century, in search of community. Progressivism still makes a lot of sense. Slotkin and Shi had it right, and Lears caught the prescriptive edge to it all: the millenium beckons us to new frontiers, simple and comforting. I have tried to answer the call of others, and I urge those interested to explore this matter further. Academics and non-academics can share in this journey. It is, as David Shi pointed out, a personal ethic, and we all have a hefty stake in it.

CHAPTER ONE

"Too Good a Town"

White, Community, and Rhetoric

RONALD REAGAN, in his late-twentieth-century quest to revitalize the American nation, spent his eight years in the White House stressing the need to reassert "old community values," emphasizing such qualities as thrift, charity, neighborliness, and trust. The president implied that these values were rooted in the nation's past, in the more close-knit communities of yesterday, as in his own hometown of Dixon, Illinois. Reagan used the idea of the small town as an effective rhetorical device. Dixon and all the small towns of America importantly have reminded Americans of the supposedly tried and true values of a great people. The connection for Reagan was natural, and for many it was highly evocative.

Ronald Reagan was not the first American social commentator to couch his philosophy in terms of the small town. He was the latest in a long line of spokespersons to use this powerful rhetorical device both to praise and to abuse American values and norms. As the people moved from the farms and small towns to the medium-sized cities and metropolises of twentieth-century America, and as they blended into the rapidly expanding American middle class, a small-town rhetoric came to encapsule a homogenized, idealized set of values. It can be argued that the idea of the small town, epitomized by a Middle Western sense of community, came to be the yeoman myth of the twentieth century. While declining in relative demographic stature, the small-town community, as an idea, came to loom large over the nation as it adopted modern ways.[1]

One of the earliest and most important twentieth-century purveyors of the small town as an idea was the journalist, newspaper editor and publisher, political activist and reformer, and novelist William Allen White. White strongly associated himself with the ethos of small-town America. He purposefully based himself in Emporia, Kansas, a slowly growing county seat of ten to twenty thousand denizens, and preached the "gospel of Emporia" to a national audience for close to half a century. White spoke out upon a variety of social, political, and moral issues, fashioning himself as a progressive and constructing a fairly consistent world view. Yet while he expressed this view in terms of small-town values, a closer examination reveals that he tailored his rhetoric to the needs and values of the growing middle class living in developing urban centers throughout the nation. White's conception of small-town America more closely fit the sociology of Middletown America, so adroitly uncovered in the 1920s by Robert S. and Helen Merrell Lynd in Muncie, Indiana. White selectively used and idealized a set of small-town norms to highlight his own vision of the vast, emerging middle-class society. It was a utopian view of a rapidly changing, highly urbanized nation, and a sizable portion of the anxious citizenry of newly arrived Middle America apparently listened with interest to the Sage of Emporia.

This study analyzes the relationship between William Allen White's small-town rhetoric and his philosophy that was attuned to the emergence of a twentieth-century Middle American culture. Understanding White's use of the rhetoric of the small town provides an important step toward better grasping the social concerns and cultural values of Americans in the twentieth century. Much of the small-town rhetoric cropping up in political and social commentaries too often, in academic analyses, has been taken at face value. Many social and cultural conflicts have been interpreted within a framework of rural-urban, small town–metropolis dichotomies which miss the vast middle ground of people caught in the tides of change. This work studies the successful contribution of a leading spokesperson who helped devise a language, an ethical paradigm, which spoke to and for the inhabitants of Middle America— the new urban-oriented middle class struggling to forge an identity within a convulsive social order. A more accurate interpretation of this language will help to clarify the true meaning of the often quoted, yet frequently misunderstood, references to the small-town ethos; and it will offer a greater insight into the evolving meaning of community in the United States.

This study, then, investigating at length White's extensive written record, offers a further insight into the philosophy of one of twentieth-century America's most respected and well-read social commentators; of equal significance, it also offers a means, a case study with which to delve deeper into the increasingly provocative questions concerning the meaning of community, the power of rhetoric in our society, the relationship between small-town mythology and urban reality, and the evasive ideological construct by which that amorphous, widespread entity, the citizenry of Middle America, has attempted to measure and make sense of life in the twentieth century.

■ ■ ■

William Allen White was born in Emporia, Kansas, in 1868. He made his career in Emporia, and he died in his Emporia home in 1944, honored as a national citizen. Beginning about 1900 White was considered an increasingly prominent and respected spokesperson for a vast number of citizens who had arrived or were aspiring to arrive at the evolving middle ground of American class and society. White wrote hundreds of articles in popular magazines and erudite journals; he published over twenty fiction and nonfiction books; he delivered hundreds of speeches around the country. He aimed at middle-class audiences, and he was well-received. Newspapers frequently reprinted his editorials and, along with the magazines, ran hundreds of articles hailing the Emporian as a spokesman for "the people." Long before his death William Allen White had become a middle-class icon. The *Washington Post* memorialized in 1946: "He was a magnificent mirror of mid-America, a perfect facsimile of the best in middle-class culture as it developed toward self-expression and social consciousness."[2]

This observation by the *Post* points to an important aspect of White's popularity. White represented a transition in American society as much as he represented "the great middle class," a product of the transition. As White's influence began to extend beyond Emporia so "Main Street" seemed to stretch further across the nation. Author Hermann Hagedorn, presenting White with the Roosevelt Memorial Association Award in 1937, caught the essence of the change and the Emporian's relation to it:

> Along the crowded Main Street from Broadway to the Golden Gate, where daily a nation goes by—confused, complacent, angry, panicky, proud—a rotund man with a merry eye has for forty years gone up and down, talking . . . Main Street has been kindlier because of him, and safer; and his fellow citizens have understood better themselves, each other, their country and their dreams.

White stood for more than small-town homilies, and Main Street stood for more than one-stop provincial thoroughfares. Both symbolized the rise of the middle class, the extension of a set of evolving societal norms and cultural values across an ever-broadening middle girth of the nation. The country had changed, and White had changed with it. He understood the transition from a provincial, nineteenth-century society in the throes of industrialization to a cosmopolitan, corporate, twentieth-century urban order with a predominantly middle-class social structure. He understood and dealt squarely with the hopes and anxieties inherent in such a societal transformation. He seemed to transcend the transition. As a nineteenth-century provincial Kansan who had become a twentieth-century cosmopolitan American, he appeared to embody the best of both worlds. He knew this and capitalized upon it, modeling his persona and his philosophy with this transition in mind.[3]

White was a character—of sorts. He presented himself as a sartorial ragamuffin, a cracker-barrel country editor, an early-twentieth-century period piece. Yet he was more than a country yokel, and the public knew it. White was a high-level Republican power broker, particularly influential in Kansas, who projected a persistent if not always effective voice into national councils. He was an acquaintance and friend of presidents from McKinley to FDR, and he was especially close to Theodore Roosevelt. He was a provocative social, political, and cultural critic. In the guise of a simple country editor, White spoke authoritatively to current public concerns.[4]

Only since his death has White been misinterpreted as the defender of small-town America, barricading the past from the onslaught of the twentieth century. Certainly in his day he occasionally would be typecast as such, and in rare moments, in reactionary lapses, he did fill the bill. The most glaring performance was seen in his virulent opposition to Al Smith's presidential bid in 1928. Just four years earlier White had carried the progressive banner in a nationally hailed, futile candidacy for the Kansas governorship, crusading against the Ku Klux Klan resurgence in the state and nation. In this campaign, exuding optimism, the William Allen White the public generally knew showed his real colors. White was the perennial and practical optimist, a foremost progressive spokesperson, touting a tolerant middle-of-the-road philosophy, enjoying life as part of, not in spite of, the twentieth century. He spoke for small-town values, but most people surely understood his argument as he intended it—as a metaphor. It would have taken some effort not to do so. At different times, as his fancy dictated, White would claim that Emporia and its way of life represented communities ranging from one thousand to a million citizens. He threw the figures fast and loose, but he was dead certain about the message. So too, apparently, was his ever-expanding audience.[5]

White seemed to carry about him an oddly conjured aura of dynamism and timelessness. While in ways he harked back to a more individualistic frontier era, he represented, too, the twentieth-century imposition of that era's values upon the nation. One commentator noted in 1927,

"White stands out as one of the leading figures and builders of a prairie civilization that is gradually assuming the common American shape." White and the modern Middle West had become synonymous to many as that amorphous region's values became a twentieth-century norm. John Finley, editor-in-chief of the *New York Times*, wrote in 1938,

> It is impossible to think of the Middle West, or the American small city, or the homely virtues, or independent journalism, without thinking of William Allen White . . . If we could believe that the whole Middle West was something like Will White and that the rest of the country was something like the Middle West, one could be perfectly confident as to the future.[6]

White did all he could to convince the American public that the country was in fact something like the Middle West and like himself. It was not a futile effort. Walter Lippmann believed it: "For as long as I can remember when anyone wished to find out or was advising someone from abroad how to find out what was the American view at the heart of the Nation and in its purest form, he turned as a matter of course to William Allen White in Emporia." Walter Winchell agreed: "William Allen White assumed that, since Kansas is the geographical heart of America, he was specially equipped to interpret America's soul. In this he was largely correct." For White the future of the country was, as John Finley hoped, safe in the Middle West. It was particularly safe in Emporia. He saw Emporia as a model community, a paragon of swelling middle-class, Middle American values. To make his point, he rhetorically transposed Emporia into surrounding Lyon County, into Kansas, the Middle West, the West, and the nation; Emporia could represent Western civilization around the globe. White championed a greater twentieth-century community, no matter the geographical base, founded upon rock-solid virtues that one might find in Emporia or any idealized American small town. His statements to this effect are innumerable, but one stands out amongst the rest. Swept up in the European crusade in 1917, White traveled to France on a Red Cross mission. In 1918 his half-fictional account of the experience, *The Martial Adventures of Henry and Me* was published. The book portrays the journey across the Atlantic. The ship and its passengers represent Emporia, and a small-town spirit is omnipresent once landed in Europe. White later explained: "Now of course Emporia was only put in as a symbol—a symbol of all America—all middle class, with no particular beginnings . . . and with no pride of ancestry, but a vast hope of posterity." "Emporia," in White's view, would make the world "safe for democracy."[7]

■ ■ ■

Here, then, is the small-town metaphor. White's role as a spokesperson for developing twentieth-century, middle-class values came to be epitomized in his own caricature of Emporia, Kansas. Emporia could be all
things to all people. It represented the past and the future. It stood for
communities of all shapes and sizes. Above all it represented the ideal of
community life in an increasingly impersonal world. This would become
White's preoccupation for forty years and his greatest attraction for the
American public. Community was his most powerful message, and community was his technique, his medium, to reach into the hearts and minds
of millions of citizens.

Community had become the concern of an emerging middle-class
majority and a common denominator for a nascent Middle American
ethos. The ideal of the small town came to embody this new ethos, and
William Allen White came to be one of the great propagandizers for
Middle America. Both as an ideological construct and as a rhetorical
device the concept of community for White evolved out of his early
involvement in the Progressive Movement. In ensuing years he developed
an increasing sensitivity to the communal tensions within a developing
urban society and a highly adept manner of addressing those tensions.
Three scholars help to grasp the relationship between the development of
White's role as a national spokesperson, his sense of concern over the
meaning of community, and his use of the small town as a rhetorical
device. Daniel T. Rodgers, Thomas Bender, and James Oliver Robertson
look at community from complementary perspectives. Taken together they
help us to understand the important roles the idea of and the rhetoric of
community have played in twentieth-century American culture, the root
and strength of their appeal, and White's relationship to them.

Daniel T. Rodgers in his seminal historiographical survey "In Search
of Progressivism" suggests that by understanding groups of ideas, and
more important their effective conveyance, we will have a means to decipher progressivism. He points out that after decades of study "some typical
progressive profile, coherent political agenda, or, at least, definable ethos"
still eludes historians. Rodgers argues that some sort of progressive ideal,
if not a single ideology, must have existed, for despite diverse interests, millions of individuals considered themselves a group, called themselves progressives. In search of "the ideational glue" which held together these
individuals as progressives, Rodgers looks toward the rhetoric of the
period. He argues that within the rhetoric, encompassing broadly shared
ideals changing over time as the clearly pluralistic nature of progressivism

itself changed, historians will finally locate the elusive meaning of progressivism. There was no single ideology but rather an array of rhetorical banners under which millions could gather to accomplish divergent aims at differing times. To grasp progressive social thought it is necessary to look at the language in new ways.[8]

The progressives seemed to have, according to Rodgers, "an ability to draw on three distinct clusters of ideas—three distinct social languages— to articulate their discontents and their social visions." One language was that of anti-monopolyism. A second stressed social bonds and the social nature of human beings. A third was that of social efficiency. The languages were not necessarily complementary, they had different historical roots, and they were in popular use at different times. Progressives used all three languages, as needed: "Together they formed not an ideology but the surroundings of available rhetoric and ideas—akin to the surrounding structures of politics and power—within which progressives launched their crusades, recruited their partisans, and did their work."[9]

Out of this fluid ideational environment William Allen White surfaced in the early twentieth century as a packager, as an adept distiller of ideas. Progressive Era reformers, Rodgers points out, "were made piece by piece, as unease and anger were channeled into vocabularies and techniques that were always in motion." White's understanding of the world about him changed and with it the techniques and vocabularies he used to make sense out of it. Here, in the roiling currents of progressivism, White first gathered together and learned to use the tools with which he would ultimately make his career as a national spokesperson for community.[10]

Rodgers contends that anti-monopolyism characterized the earliest progressive approach to reform. As White entered the progressive ranks just after the turn of the century he spoke the language of anti-monopolyism. This view of society and the language associated with it was still strongly influenced by the late-nineteenth-century concern with the autonomous individual. White saw society composed of a distinct minority of plutocrats, fat with greed, opposed to everyone else—the tens of millions of working people and a much smaller middling group with no clear characteristic except an unfortunate disinclination to govern. Under the tutelage of Theodore Roosevelt, White flailed the vested interests, trying to arouse the middling group out of its lethargy, speaking up for the rights of a vague "common man" to his fair share within the commonwealth.[11]

During the first decade of the new century anti-monopolyism waned, replaced by a marked concern for social harmony. The interest in "the autonomous economic man, the autonomous possessor of property rights, the autonomous man of character" gave way to a "rhetoric of social cohesion." In accord with this new way of looking at the world, White became less concerned with the malefactors of wealth and more concerned with surveying a broader expanse of social, economic, and political maladies. He began to divide the citizenry less and less into opposing groups of autonomous haves and have-nots, emphasizing instead a greater community of shared interests, a broad commonality needing to work together to eliminate society's inequities. The president, representing the greater community, was managing a bevy of problems. All good and all powerful, Theodore Roosevelt, for White, embodied the hope for a harmonious social body. White's first use of the language of community, purportedly representing the interests of an enveloping greater community, was clearly political in inspiration. One of Roosevelt's greatest publicists, White came to realize the rhetorical potential of this language. He soon would capitalize, as well, upon its malleability.[12]

After Roosevelt left the White House and William Howard Taft moved in, White became convinced the president now stood as the chief obstacle to the needs of the people, the common good. He turned the language of social cohesion against the administration. In the 1912 Republican insurgency campaign with Roosevelt, White tried to rally a national citizenry to the cause of the greater community against a reactionary government. Suffering defeat in 1912 and a devastating Progressive Party loss in 1914, White reviewed his thinking regarding this greater community and retooled his technique and his vocabulary to deal with it. He concluded that this community was best represented by a newly emerging middle group in American society. For the first time he identified a "middle class" whose members shared the broader social concerns of "all the people" but were more endowed with the right to rule, and to lead—they were the truly progressive element in society. Perceiving that the immediate fortunes of the Progressive Party and any long-range progressive reforms lay within the power of this group, White began specifically to address its concerns.[13]

As the Progressive Party disintegrated and as the fervor of progressivism burned out with world war, White continued to speak to the issue of social harmony, the needs of the greater community, and the more particular needs of the middle class. He adapted his thinking to the postwar order, and he adjusted his technique and vocabulary to reach his middle-class audience. He became increasingly preoccupied with the idea of community itself; he interpreted social tension, economic disorder, and political unrest purely in terms of problems of community—middle-class problems of community. The middle class expanded and contracted in accord with White's changing sense of the political, economic, and social obstacles to be overcome in creating the ideal community, in achieving social harmony. Before the war he had identified the middle class as a prosperous citizenry congregated in smaller urban centers, particularly strong in the Middle West—the key to Progressive Party victory. In the twenties, with the dramatic increase in the standard of living, he expanded his definition of the middle-class community to include struggling Middle Western farmers and aspiring workers across the country who might live in cities of hundreds of thousands. He began increasingly to identify the greater American community as middle class in nature. As the economy cracked in the 1930s, and as it became obvious under intense economic pressure that the middle class was fractured and turning on itself, he worriedly contracted his definition, identifying a higher strata, the upper middle class, as best representing greater middle-class community values and leadership. With the Second World War and the recovery of a more harmonious domestic order, White declared middle-class America triumphant, with the upper and lower strata working together again, nationally prepared to set the postwar social, political, and economic agenda. A materially secure, unified middle class would in the postwar years anchor a greater middling community at home and abroad.

It was, hence, the idea of social harmony that most impressed White, the ideal to which he committed himself for over forty years. Fully involved in Progressive Era politics, social thought, and writing, White reflected the evolution of successful technique and vocabulary, which, Rodgers argues best, explains the dynamism of progressivism. White also reflected the continuing relevance of those techniques and vocabularies beyond the Progressive Era. Having grown to understand and effectively address issues of social cohesion in the headier years of progressivism, White adapted his thinking to the "problem of community," the increasingly complex issue of maintaining semblances of community life in an urban society. In so doing he demonstrated an astute understanding, as well as a marked sensitivity, to a perplexing twentieth-century social concern. The problem of community provides further insight into the power of the language of community and more particularly into the appeal of small-town rhetoric for an emerging Middle American populace.[14]

The problem of community is analyzed by Thomas Bender in his study *Community and Social Change in America*. Bender argues that community, while often associated with "visions of the good life," also evokes fear: "Modern Americans fear that urbanization and modernization have destroyed the community that earlier shaped the lives of men and women, particularly in the small towns of the American past." Sociologists and historians have only exacerbated these fears with studies referring to erosion, decline, breakup, and eclipse of community. Bender reexamines this problem and suggests a means to clarify the meaning of twentieth-century community for the public and academia.[15]

Bender traces the beginning of concern with the problem of community to the last half of the nineteenth century. He sees a "bifurcation of society" that occurred when centralization of authority and massive changes in transportation and communications fundamentally altered the social structure: "Growth in the size and complexity of local life combined with important losses in local autonomy encouraged people to identify community with certain of its parts rather than with the whole." Increasingly drawn into metropolitan orbits inhabitants saw outside political and economic forces transform long-established social institutions. Community ways of conducting life became delineated from metropolitan ways. It was troubling as roles, statuses, and personal identities changed.[16]

The public was understandably disturbed, but in fact Bender argues that the evolving twentieth-century social structure contained within it vital, adaptive elements of the old patterns of community life. Individuals were not really so dangerously adrift in a new world. It was simply a matter of establishing new bearings, adapting old ways to new ways in a more complex environment. To explain the social changes occurring a German sociologist, Ferdinand Tönnies, in 1887 developed a typological theory known as *Gemeinschaft* and *Gesellschaft*. *Gemeinschaft* and *Gesellschaft* contrasted ideal models to study social change. Tönnies interpreted *Gemeinschaft* as a type of social cohesion based upon personal and exclusive family, kin, friendship, and neighborhood ties. *Gesellschaft* he associated with the more competitive environment of the city where individuals of necessity established more artificial social relationships. Tönnies saw a trend toward a predominantly *Gesellschaft* culture but one incorporating strong elements of *Gemeinschaft*.

Bender believes Tönnies's theory remains viable. He rejects urban sociologists and modernization theorists who contend that aged communities collapse and older patterns are totally subsumed in a *Gesellschaft* culture. Tönnies's original theory offers a means of comprehending and appreciating the resiliency of community in twentieth-century America. New patterns replaced old, but older patterns of community clung to and integrated themselves within the new social order. "The task of the historian," writes Bender, "is not to write the obituary of community, but rather to discover its changing role in people's lives." He suggests studying institutional patterns of behavior, the mix of *Gemeinschaft* and *Gesellschaft* in people's lives, and changing beliefs, "the changes in meaning" that people gave to "the changes in the structure of social relations."[17]

William Allen White was intimately in touch with these changing institutional patterns of behavior and changing beliefs regarding community. His world consisted of constantly expanding and contracting local and trans-local social, political, and economic networks. White's role as a social commentator, in Emporia and beyond, sensitized him to what Bender calls the "ongoing tension between communal and non-communal experiences in the daily lives of men and women." He was acutely conscious of changing patterns of community, of a changing social order. He came out of the Progressive Era speaking directly to this issue, trying to put the problem into words. White never used the terms *Gemeinschaft* and *Gesellschaft*, but he clearly understood the conflict and translated it into a more commonly understood language. He chose to identify the middle class, with its unique shift in "role, status, and identity" and its rise to dominance in American society and culture, as representative of the new order. He in fact spoke to individuals in all walks of life, all classes, all communities, recognizing the growing pervasiveness of middle-class values. He addressed a variety of what he termed middle-class issues: immediate social, political, and economic problems and the more general cultural concerns of individuals caught up in widespread societal changes. White was in the mainstream of changing *Gemeinschaft* and *Gesellschaft* patterns of living, flowing with them, not working against them. No spokesperson for a past order, no believer in community collapse, White had a contemporary perspective, trying to lend a hand, to build a new order.[18]

White was constructing a belief system suited to the new patterns of living he saw about him. He perceived a vast Middle American ground developing, transcending traditional communal bonds, a greater community made up of equally important lesser communities. He sought to define an ideal middle-class enclave within this panorama. It was homogeneous in population and values. It had no particular bounds or regional identification and was intricately tied to other communities and the greater community. If it had to be tagged, middletown would do, and not incidentally the Lynds' Middletown did fine. Robert S. and Helen Merrell Lynd's classic studies of Muncie in the 1920s and 1930s revealed this small Indiana city to be, in the words of one scholar, "an interpenetration of two opposite kinds of living, thinking, and feeling . . . an isolated, homogeneous, sacred, and personal community . . . and . . . the heterogeneous, secular, and impersonal community that we find approximated in cities."[19]

In the same way that Muncie had served the Lynds as a demographically ideal American community, the model also served White. He saw many Middletowns across the national landscape, and a vast, growing number of Middletowners. He did not identify his model community as

Middletown—for him it was Emporia. Emporia represented the new belief system and served well to transmit it. In his editorials, his speeches, his magazine articles, his essays, and his books, White spoke a language of community. He used Emporia to reach out to the citizens of Middle America, the middle class and those aspiring to it who lived in larger urban communities, to help them make their way in an evolving social order. In Emporia, in the rhetoric of the small town, White caught an evocative experiential quality of community to which millions could relate. Bender makes the point:

> Americans seem to have something else in mind when they wist-
> fully recall or assume a past made up of small-town communities. This
> social memory has a geographic referent, the town, but it is clear from
> the many layers of emotional meaning attached to the word "commu-
> nity" that the concept means more than a place or local activity. There is
> an expectation of a special quality of human relationship in a commu-
> nity, and it is this experiential dimension that is crucial to its definition.
> Community, then, can be defined better as an experience than as a place.
> As simply as possible, community is where community happens.[20]

White made it "happen" in Emporia. Grasping the changing meaning of community, the altered patterns of human relationships over space and time, White set up a dynamic metaphor. He presented Emporia as a small town, a middle-sized city, even equating it at times with New York City. Its basically homogeneous population was increasingly classified as middle class, white Anglo-Saxon Protestant in origins and values, and strongly influenced by greater societal forces. For White Emporia came to represent the best of *Gemeinschaft* patterns of living embedded in a *Gesellschaft* world. It was styled the archetypal middle community—middle-sized, located in the heart of the Middle West, in the middle of America. Emporia represented the best in American life, or, at a minimum, its homogenized potential. It was "too good a town": too good, White futilely pleaded, to elect a Ku Klux Klan mayor in the 1920s; too good to give into the foibles of twenties Babbittry, which it all too often flaunted; too good, White was gratified, to elect Al Smith president; and in 1939 and 1940 White contended Emporia was too good a town to allow Hitler to overrun the British Isles. Emporia was, quite simply, as White well knew, too good to be true; but it was a formidable rhetorical device with which to speak to a good many people.[21]

White had captured in Emporia a powerful metaphor to speak to the changing meaning of community in twentieth-century American life. In using it to epitomize a greater Middle American community, he con-tributed to a significant, evolving twentieth-century system of belief.

Middle America, and the relation of the small town to it, is analyzed by James Oliver Robertson in his work *American Myth, American Reality*, a study of the development of American belief systems over the past three and a half centuries. Robertson argues that myths serve as mechanisms by which people integrate and resolve contradictory beliefs, or at least hold them in a tension which is not uncomfortable; myths are "the means by which visions and ideals are combined with reality." These are dynamic mechanisms:

> Myths are accretions of many stories and many images which transform themselves in new circumstances and differing realities. Myths always represent the past—the tradition, the social ideals, the imperatives of explanation and behavior—to the present. In each of them there is a specific core of logic. And they die, they become meaningless, they become "myths" (in a pejorative sense), instead of logical explanations, when they cease to provide imperatives.[22]

Robertson sees the idea of the small town as a myth offering a logical explanation for life in an evolving Middle American community: "The myths which have given vivid images, controlling metaphors, and substance to what Americans believe community to be are the myths of rural, small-town, agrarian communities." The small town represents to Americans a homogenization of values, a melting pot of individual interests and backgrounds, of families, classes, nationalities, and races. It provides all individuals with the opportunity "to move, to rise, to change, to progress, to succeed."[23]

In order to retain its logic, the idea of the small town changed over time in accordance with the changes in the greater society. As America in the twentieth century became predominantly middle class, with its strength lying in cities, in industries, and in corporate bureaucracies, a new ethos and a broadened conception of community arose. Robertson writes,

> The use of "middle class" by Americans is of the same order that "middle America" or "Middle West" is. It does not signify the self-contained, middle order of a structure with lower and upper orders—as it does for Europeans. Rather, it is much closer to the view the Chinese have traditionally had of the Middle Kingdom. For Americans, the "middle"—whether middle class, Middle West, or middle American—is a large, solid, geographical center of almost limitless extent. Around and beyond it are other, haphazardly arranged areas of varying, but entirely peripheral, importance.

Of necessity the archetypal small town grew into the boundlessness of Middletown:

Rural communities were full-scale participants in American progress. The visions of elm-lined streets, big front porches, white paint, and picket fences were able to transform themselves to accommodate automobiles in the streets, machines in the homes and the barns, "science" in the agriculture, corporations sprawled across the nation, and mobile, dynamic, progressive, improving individual Americans.

This progressive small town represented the new "middle" developing in American society—the center, the consensus, the amorphous silent majority. More than a geographical locale, it designated the ideal of community life in a greater community, the bonding of neighbors across the countryside. Synonymous with the middle class, with the Middle West, with Middle America, the small town became "the American community writ large, a reflection of every real community in America . . . homogeneous and proximate; therefore, in the logic of the myth, classless, democratic, and equal."[24]

The emergence of Middle America was reflected in the development of a new cultural dichotomy, replacing the nineteenth-century rural-urban conflict with a Middle American–cosmopolitan division (cosmopolitanism best represented by New York, Chicago, and Los Angeles). Middle America saw itself as the mainstream. It depicted its values in the transformed image of the small town, now any size Middle American community. "Ordinary" city life, carrying all the traits of the idealized small town, came to be the standard, and "big" city life, the abberation. Robertson cites the 1973 observation of journalist Peter Schrag, which catches the essence of the new American norm:

> Every time you flew across the country or looked at the ads on television, the vision returned: Down there was the real America, on the wheat fields of Kansas, in the small crossroads towns with their helpful banker and their friendly Mutual of Omaha insurance agent, in the shopping centers where the farmers congregated on Saturday afternoon and the women came to have their hair set, in the new developments of Topeka or Quincy or Macon or Rapid City, neighborhoods clustered around cities of twenty thousand or seventy-five thousand. . . .

Robertson concludes: "it is still possible for people who dwell in all but the largest cities (and many of those, too) to retain the mythology of rural community—much transformed—as the logical explanation of their urban lives."[25]

There emerged in the twentieth century a Middle American ethos. William Allen White was a contributor to this development—one of many who must be better understood. During the Progressive Era he learned to seek a commonality of interests through the use of rhetoric. He came out of the era a prominent national spokesperson and addressed himself to a growing audience of middle-class Americans concerned about the changing meaning of community in their lives. In the 1920s, underscoring this concern and capitalizing on his association with small-town America, White secured his position as a spokesperson for community in America. He used the small town to offer an explanation and solution to the problem of community: all America could be content, could learn to live in an array of reasonably sized middle-class communities, all part of a greater American community, a harmonious, homogenous blend of *Gemeinschaft* and *Gesellschaft*, of middling all-American values. In Emporia White had a metaphor reflecting the dynamism of the language and techniques he learned earlier, tailored to the changing meaning of community in America. He used the rhetoric of the small town to speak to, of, and for Middle America.[26]

Small-town rhetoric sheds light not upon the small town but upon a vast, emerging middle ground of American society. It reflects the dynamism of progressivism, of the idea of community, of the middle class, and of Middle America. Understanding the use of the small-town metaphor helps to grasp the true nature of the evolving social structure and the belief system tailored to it. It helps explain how people dealt with social concerns and cultural problems in a rapidly, radically changing society. The rhetoric of the small town, far from hindering the development of a new order, in the final analysis spoke for it.

CHAPTER TWO

The Progressive Promise I

Portraying the Idyllic Community

T HE FIRST WORLD WAR proved to be the watershed in William Allen White's life. The Kansan had made a huge political and philosophical investment in progressivism. Having ridden the crest of the progressive wave, he found himself in mid-life having to adjust to the backwaters of postwar reform. As a young man White had set out upon three career paths: In 1895 he purchased the decrepit *Emporia Gazette* and took up the task of establishing the newspaper's financial solvency and editorial integrity. He developed his hand at fiction, over the years turning out an extensive collection of socially relevant short stories and novels. Meanwhile, White emerged as a political broker, wielding considerable power within local, state, and national party councils. By the outbreak of European war in 1914, the Kansas journalist, through his widely reprinted editorials, the political and social commentary he wrote for national magazines, his popular fiction, and his political machinations, had become one of the foremost progressive reformers in the country.

In the 1920s the difficulty of balancing multiple careers of necessity gave way to a more restrained but singularly important public role. White's fiction and reformist politics suddenly became old-fashioned in the "New Era." Abruptly, he abandoned literature. He continued to exercise leverage within the Republican Party, but realized he no longer carried the weight of the prewar years. Left with the prosperous *Gazette* and a huge magazine audience, White traded on his fame as a reform combatant to establish his credentials as a sensitive national spokesperson with a respected Middle Western base. The Kansas journalist assumed the posture of a conciliator, an arbiter of conflicting social and cultural interests, and he rose to be a folk hero.

As with so many changes in the postwar order, White's New Era role had been long in the making. Still, the war stood as a significant turning point in his life. Initially adverse to American participation, White became an enthusiastic convert to Wilson's crusade. He came to see the war as the consummation of the Progressive Era, the dawn of world peace, harmony, and community. It represented the culmination of his own life's work. With the denouement at Versailles he saw the most exciting and promising period in his own life, as well as that of the country, pass into an unexpectedly crass and trying era; it was, as he would recall in his autobiography, the beginning of "the downhill pull."[1]

The Great War, then, was not so much responsible for a change of direction in White's life as much as it signaled the end of the decade-and-a-half progressive heyday into which he had poured so much energy. All hardly would be downhill for the Kansas editor after 1918; the uphill climb itself had not been easy. The progressive years had been full of high hopes and a good deal of personal and political struggle. The postwar years, if less intoxicating, were calmer for White. Financially secure and generally healthy, with a single career to occupy his time, White channeled his reform impulse, enormous energy, and verve for life into the development of a practical social philosophy fit for new times and a much wider audience.[2]

Understanding White's postwar role as a national community spokesperson begins with tracing his prewar years and the shaping of his philosophy. The Kansas journalist had matured with the new century, easily adapting to the changing political, economic, social, and cultural order. Progressivism had flourished; corporatism was in the saddle; the middle class, new in composition, hopes, and fears, had come to prominence; an urban culture had risen to dominance. White's increasing concern with community and his success in speaking to the issue were direct outgrowths of his sensitivity to these developments. His early activity, his fiction, and the voluminous social and political commentary he poured out to the prewar press mark his philosophical growth and his nascent understanding of community.

■ ■ ■

Born in 1868, White grew up in El Dorado, in eastern Kansas. Vestiges of the Old West still hung about the small town in the 1870s and '80s, but the predominant spirit was seen in the "civilizing" aspect of frontier development—the re-creation of eastern community life replete with schools, churches, and prospering businesses and farms. As a boy White saw dream-laden wagons heading past El Dorado, carrying settlers westward to the lands opening on the Kansas High Plains. The experience of these pioneers would contrast sharply with the settled growth of central and eastern Kansas. White knew full well the tragedy that occurred in the high country: the bountiful early years followed by a decade of drought, insect devastation, ever-increasing debt, and final abandonment of the land. He always would consider western Kansas an alien territory, not really part of his own beloved Kansas.[3]

Distancing himself from the frontier calamity of western Kansas (and from the speculative mania which gripped thousands in central and eastern Kansas during the same period), White disassociated himself as well from the radical Populist politics bred out of the discontent of the 1880s and 1890s. His Kansas was Republican country. By his college years he had become a loyal constituent of the Party of Lincoln. Republicanism made sense to him: His mother outlived his Democrat father and impressed her ardent Republican beliefs upon her son. Both parents were reformers; Mary Ann Hatton White had been an abolitionist, and Allen White had shared his wife's commitment to women's suffrage and prohibition. In Kansas in the 1880s the Republican Party stood alone as the established, if short-statured, party of social justice. More important, the Republican Party stood at the fortress of Kansas political power; White easily grasped the advice of a mentor at the University of Kansas who told him to affiliate with the party if he desired influence in public affairs.[4]

Brought up in a civic-minded household, White had an early interest in political matters. At the new university in Lawrence he worked on a variety of newspapers and partook in college, town, and state politics. Leaving school early, he continued to gravitate to journalism and politics. He worked two years on the El Dorado *Republican* in the early nineties, bitterly lambasting the powerful Populist insurgency in the region. He left El Dorado to serve a short stint on the Kansas City *Journal*, and then he spent close to three years on Col. William Rockhill Nelson's Kansas City *Star*. The *Journal* was a reactionary, corrupt Republican organ; the *Star* was a progressive, fiercely independent Republican standard-bearer. White garnered much from Nelson regarding higher journalistic ethics and civic responsibilities, and he picked up a good deal from the *Journal* about the seamier side of Republican politics. Still, he learned nothing that seriously altered his conviction that the best interests of society were served by the Republican Party.[5]

White left the *Star* in 1895, determined to run his own newspaper. With the help of established political and banking interests, he purchased the meager inventory and scant subscription list of the *Emporia Gazette*. He and his wife, Sally Lindsay White, a lifelong personal and professional support, set up shop in June. White laid out his goals and ideals in his first editorial. He planned to stay in Emporia, to help it to prosper, and to make a name for himself beyond the town:

> In the first place, the new editor hopes to live here until he is the old editor, until some of the visions which rise before him as he dreams shall have come true. He hopes always to sign "from Emporia" after his name when he is abroad, and he trusts that he may so endear himself to the people that they will be as proud of the first words of the signature as he is of the last words.

He planned to perform all the community tasks incumbent upon a country editor, and he expected the "best" citizenry to help him cultivate public sentiment: "If the good, honest, upright, God-fearing, law-abiding people of any community desire to be reflected to the world, they must see that their private opinion is public opinion. They must stand by the editors who believe as they do." White discounted politics:

> It is a plain business proposition. The new editor of the "Gazette" desires to make a clean, honest, local paper. He is a Republican and will support Republican nominees first, last, and all the time. There will be no bolting, no sulking, no "holier than thou" business about his politics —but politics is so little. . . . The main thing is to have this paper represent the average thought of the best people of Emporia and Lyon County in all their varied interests.[6]

White's aim was to build a strong community newspaper and a platform from which he could broadcast his beliefs to a greater audience. He dismissed politics as "so little," but he really saw it as essential to creating proper public sentiment and a prosperous environment. He reveled in it in Emporia. While working to establish a permanent place for the *Gazette* in the town and surrounding county, White indulged in professing the virtues of dyed-in-the-wool Republicanism. In 1896, in the heat of the Bryan-McKinley contest and in the midst of a blazing Kansas summer, the town editor found himself entrapped on the street by a group of Populists. Angered and tongue-tied, he returned to the *Gazette* office and furiously wrote out an editorial, "What's the Matter with Kansas?" A stunning repudiation of Bryanism and Populism, the piece was reprinted in Chicago and New York and caught the attention of McKinley chieftain Mark Hanna. The Republican campaign committee widely circulated it, and William Allen White catapulted to national fame. The Emporian now had his greater audience.[7]

What White had to say soon changed dramatically. One year after the publication of "What's the Matter with Kansas?" the Emporian met Assistant Secretary of the Navy Theodore Roosevelt; he immediately fell under the future president's spell. The stand-pat country editor became a reformer. It took a few years for White's progressive stance to develop fully, but once it did, he threw himself wholeheartedly into the cause. It is difficult precisely to account for the transformation: Always a hero-worshipper, White was mesmerized by the charismatic Roosevelt. At the University of Kansas White had been under the tutelage of teachers critical of the social order. The Populists, despite his attacks, had evoked some sympathy from him. Raised in a reformist and Christian household, White surely would have been sensitive to the growing strength of the social gospel. In Emporia the editor and businessman had begun to sense clearly the relevance of reformist arguments. Finally, always politically abreast, White must have felt the swell of the progressive tide. Whatever the precise mix of factors might have been, Roosevelt's sudden rise to the presidency in 1901 drew White into the mainstream of progressivism.[8]

An intimate of the president and a ready publicist for him, White submerged himself in national politics. He was in regular contact with Roosevelt. At home he rose to head the powerful progressive wing of the Kansas Republican Party. His journalistic career skyrocketed as high-profile magazines such as the *Saturday Evening Post, McClure's Magazine,* the *American Magazine,* and *Collier's* sought out the opinions of the influential "pol," and newspaper syndicates contracted his reporting. White enhanced his reputation as a reform spokesperson through the publication of his short stories and novels. By the end of the Roosevelt presidency in 1909 the small-town Kansas editor had become one of the nation's most prominent progressives.[9]

White's progressivism was as muddled as that of many of his contemporaries. He campaigned for electoral reforms such as the initiative, referendum, recall, and the primary, all the while swinging his hefty club as a Kansas power broker. He advocated economic centralization and regional industrialization to defend against national hegemony; at the same time he praised agricultural and small-business individualism. The editor championed prohibition, and he defended the civil rights of minority groups. He was a tardy warrior in 1898 and 1917 and then in turn a chauvinistic crusader against the Spanish and the Germans. He believed in the power of the people, leveraged by the best people. He called for state licensing to limit the number of small businesses in his own community, favored one-newspaper towns, and railed against monopoly. Always ready to declare himself first and foremost a progressive, it was not easy for White, or anyone, to mark his reformist agenda definitively.[10]

As his power grew White drew criticism for juggling political alliances and for speaking his mind too openly. His maneuvers in Topeka over the years made a number of Kansas Republicans edgy. Nationally he incurred animosity as he joined the Republican insurgency in 1910, marched out of the party with Roosevelt in 1912, and struggled in 1914 to salvage the Progressive Party and as he reluctantly returned in 1916 with TR to the Republican fold. Meanwhile, to the colonel's own chagrin, to accompany all the marching and countermarching, White trumpeted praise upon the legislative accomplishments of the Wilson administration, and he heralded the Democrat president's neutrality policy. Many could sympathize with the beleaguered Roosevelt: one Kansas politician exasperated with White's cantankerous irregularity once chastised him, "Bill White, sometimes I know just how your friend Roosevelt feels when he sees [his infamously troublesome daughter] Alice coming his way!"[11]

With American entry into the First World War, White's progressivism reached fever heat. Once committed to the cause he followed Woodrow Wilson every step of the way to Paris and toward what he and tens of millions of progressive crusaders envisioned as a "new dawn" in human relations. White readily acknowledged the battle to secure a new order would be rough and would take time. But he saw that great progress had been made at home, and he foresaw equal strides about to be made in Europe. People, he believed, were of two types—idealists and realists. The world had been revolutionized. The future now belonged to the idealists—and to America. Looking toward the peace conference he marveled, "It will be curious to see America, the world's hard-fisted practical money-grabbing dollar-worshipper of yesterday contributing her President as the leader of the idealists!"[12]

The world, of course, would prove not to be as revolutionized as White had envisioned. It was a bitter disappointment. The Kansan had undergone a radical transformation in perspective. He had thrown himself wholeheartedly into the war effort: He journeyed to France in 1917 as a Red Cross observer. He lobbied intensely to attend the peace conference as a delegate; failing in this, he sailed for Paris for a newspaper syndicate (and again for the Red Cross). While in Europe he prepared to meet the Russians as one of two U.S. representatives to the aborted Prinkipo Conference, an Allied attempt to bring the Soviet government into the peace talks. Returning home he fought hard for Wilson, the Treaty of Versailles, and the League of Nations. He denounced the Red Scare, arguing that the Bolshevik Revolution was a desirable adjunct to a reformed international order—it offered no threat to the United States. After years of parochial disinterest White had significantly broadened his horizons, now considering foreign affairs of utmost importance to himself and the nation. He saw it as imperative that the United States assume its destined role as the leader of a progressive world community.[13]

Community had become the key to White's entire world view. Growing up in El Dorado, establishing himself in Emporia, pouring energy into the improvement of his hometown and state, the editor knew the importance of community life. He projected this view onto the national and later the international scene, sensing the applicability of communal norms to a more abstract greater community. He had a knack for tapping into the essence of closer relationships and broadcasting them to a wider social stratum. Early in his career he incorporated the ideal of community into his fiction. At the same time he began to emphasize the idea in his social and political commentary, propagandizing for progressive reform in the nation's journals. In the first two decades of the twentieth century he grew to grasp the tremendously evocative power of the community ideal for Americans.

Community was a natural departure point for White as an aspiring writer and neophyte reformer. The small town was a time-honored literary device; multitudes of progressives campaigning for a kaleidoscope of reforms easily rallied to the rhetoric of social harmony. In fiction White portrayed comforting havens for troubled people. In journalism he explored the underlying meaning of communal norms for a nation rapidly becoming more industrial and more urban. Through fiction and journalistic commentary White developed a greater understanding of community and an ethical paradigm, the small-town milieu, to embody the hopes of millions of Americans. In the Progressive Era he first articulated the idea of community and sensed its rhetorical power; in later years, abandoning fiction and focusing solely on social commentary, he exploited it to the hilt. The story read well to a wide and sympathetic audience.

■ ■ ■

White's clearest and simplest expression of the community idea is found in his fiction. William Allen White was a popular early-twentieth-century writer. The importance of his fiction today, however, lies less in its literary merit than in the manner White used it as a medium to convey his reform philosophy. In the small-town metaphor that dominates his short stories and novels, White discovered an effective rhetorical device with which to envelop his message of progressive reform. White's literary intent never was simply to convey the joys of village life but to offer an expansive hope for a better world to all Americans in towns, cities, and metropolises.

Having read good literature as a child and having set upon a career in letters as a young man, it was natural for White to be influenced by the literary currents of the second half of the nineteenth century. He seemed intent, as did many authors of his generation, on writing "the great American novel." He came closest to this goal with the 1909 publication of *A Certain Rich Man*. The book was exceptionally well received by the public and the critics. *A Certain Rich Man* approached the aim of the great novel, which was to unify, to resolve conflicts and contrasts in the nation, and to develop an American character, an American place. While hardly great literature, *A Certain Rich Man* did reflect White's ability to pull upon a number of literary genres that each in its own way defined an aspect of American character and place.[14]

At base White was a regionalist. Ascendent in the late nineteenth century, regionalism was an attempt to locate the national identity within the composite sections of the country. For over twenty years, in short-story and novel form, White worked up a Middle Western character. Moving beyond regionalist purists, he sought to impose his section's identity upon the nation as a whole. It was hardly a difficult task: increasingly in the early twentieth century the Middle West was becoming a synecdoche for American values and norms.[15]

As a regionalist, White recorded negative as well as positive characteristics of the Middle West. He was not a young Ed Howe savaging the region nor was he a latter-day, aging Hamlin Garland romanticizing it into mythology. When he wanted to indict he could use bare-bones realism, even naturalist techniques. He tended, however, to emphasize the good over the bad, and to use realist techniques within a romantic structure, as did most regionalists. The courtly lover, the happy family, and the angelic-child figure always are present in White's work as he details their environs, society, and speech. Intent on conveying a positive image of the Middle West, White's romanticism tended to dominate his fiction.[16]

Within the romantic structure of his stories White embedded a powerful message. Vigorously campaigning for progressive reform, he incorporated into his regionalist perspective history and politics. White used history to portray the development of the Middle West, its manners and mores, and to emphasize the democratization of its people. Heavily influenced by Frederick Jackson Turner's frontier thesis, he conceived the region to be the seedbed of American reform, and he looked to it to nurture progressivism. He used politics to depict the need for reform. He drew upon the stock cast of the genre—young knights, bosses, distressed damsels, and designing dames—and moved them about on a corrupt political stage. The underlying literary theme was the quest for morality in an amoral world.[17]

What better force, then, than the ethos of the small town to cleanse an amoral world? White's most significant addition to his literary repertoire was the small-town genre. Drawing upon his own background and influenced by the work of writers such as Howe, Garland, Joseph Kirkland, and James Whitcomb Riley, White turned to the village to bear his message of progressive reform. The Middle Western small town came to be his model for national communal regeneration.[18]

At the turn of the century the small town still occupied a lofty position in American literature. It had come to stand for all that was supposed to be good and right in the nation. When the critics turned on it with a vengeance in the 1920s the target loomed large before them. Anthony Channell Hilfer in his study *The Revolt from the Village 1915–1930* explains the position of the rebels, "What they opposed was not an actual village existing in time and space but a mental conception of the village existing in the mind of a great number of Americans." The town differed from the farm and the city; it alone, in literature as in myth, stood for an elusive community sought by Americans caught up in a complex society. Small-town writers, arguing that the ideal really existed somewhere distant, possible of attainment, had long held a large public. Choosing the Middle Western small town as an exemplar for communal regeneration in the early years of the century, White knew full well the stature of the model.[19]

Leaning heavily upon the genre, White tumbled headlong into its pitfalls. What critic Ima Herron calls the "indispensable goodness, happiness, democracy, and heroism" of romanticized provincial life permeates his work. So, too, do "the gospels of conformity, thrift, industry, ... and boundless optimism. . . ." Still, White's work reads well. In 1906 he published his clearest evocation of the small-town ideal—*In Our Town*. Mark Twain wrote to White, "Howells told me that 'In Our Town' was a charming book, and indeed it is. . . . Pages . . . are qualified to fetch any house of any country, caste or color, endowed with those riches which are denied to no nation on the planet—humor and feeling. Talk again—the country is listening." *In Our Town* was good local-color work. Most of White's small-town literature packed a stronger charge. Hilfer points out that the small town often would be presented as a "refuge from the complications and intensities of life." Many novelists offered an escape "into the perfect community, the ideal 'Gemeinschaft' in which the class barriers and economic conflicts that jar actual human society are dissolved into a primal universal togetherness." White's work indeed offered *Gemeinschaft* but not as an escape; rather, it was presented as the progressive alternative within the modern order. White invited his readers not to join him in small-town America but to use the small town to cast reform upon their own communities and the greater community—to mold an American culture incorporating the best of *Gemeinschaft* within an emergent *Gesellschaft* order.[20]

Here, then, is White's small-town metaphor, the hallmark and strength of his literature. As his interest in progressivism intensified so, too, did his use of the small-town genre. Here lay the best definition of American character and place. Communal regeneration was the end, and the small town was the means to reach it. As White's recognition of society's problems broadened, his small town literally grew to incorporate his progressive remedy. He first used the small town as a reactionary device to excoriate the Populist menace within Kansas. He then expanded it to speak to the problems of industrial America. Ultimately it became America itself, a guiding beacon for all the citizens of one great Allied community. Fighting the conclusive battle for progressive regeneration in the Great War, the town, for White, soared to its zenith as a city upon a hill.

■ ■ ■

In *The Real Issue: A Book of Kansas Stories,* published in 1896, White first tapped the literary wellsprings of community. A collection of fifteen succinct and at times powerful stories, *The Real Issue* also was the Kansas editor's first substantial prose work. Coming on the heels of his meteoric rise to national attention with the searing campaign editorial "What's the Matter with Kansas?" the volume was a commercial and critical success. Realism and naturalism permeate the tales as White explores the vagaries of community life. Boyhood, business, politics, pioneering, and town development are all subjects for criticism, generally negative. White's primary interest in this work is western Kansas; he wants to uncouple the troubled region from the greater prospering state to which he has hitched his star.[21]

White makes the initial break, introducing "The Story of Aqua Pura":

> People who write about Kansas, as a rule, write ignorantly, and speak of the state as a finished product. Kansas, like Gaul of old, is divided into three parts. . . . Eastern Kansas is a finished community like New York or Pennsylvania. Central Kansas is finished, but not quite paid for; and Western Kansas, the only place where there is any suffering from drouth or crop failures, is a new country—old only in a pluck which is slowly conquering the desert.

White considers pluck admirable, but alone it cannot contend with the power of the desert to destroy civilization. Community must be built upon rock-solid virtues, not upon the shifting sands of extravagant hope. To draw the distinction between this wild land and civilized Kansas, White uses the naturalist's pen. In "The Story of Aqua Pura" he depicts a town settled in the flush of the mid-eighties speculative fever which swept across the Kansas High Plains. Aqua Pura quickly meets its fate as drought strikes the land. All the amenities of civilization brought in by its Ivy League and Inland University founders—the school, the library, the opera house, the new houses and businesses, the electric and water works, the new roads—come to naught in the desert sun. The citizens scurry back east, leaving one deranged founder behind. Years later the rains return; a five-day deluge, symbolic of the boom-bust economic cycle, washes the town. It is too late—left in the storm's wake are a lonely dead man and a town drained of its last speculative hope. The neighboring community of Maize, with its rough-hewn native element (and aboriginal name), survives to write the town's epitaph.[22]

Those who remain in western Kansas are a calloused and troubled lot. In a series of stories in *The Real Issue* dealing with Willow Creek, whose inhabitants bear a strong resemblance to realist Sherwood Anderson's famously gnarled residents of latter-day Winesburg, Ohio, White portrays men and women ravaged by an uncivilized environment. In "The Reading of the Riddle" White is scathing toward the town: "In Willow Creek where they scoff and higgle over sordid things, in Willow Creek the hard, the arid, the barren, they say—no matter what—but in and out of the narrow ways, turning the sharp corners with the rest, with tired feet, and timid, unsure hands, there goes a woman whose womanhood came to her as a dream—in the night." The woman is one of many repressed townspeople. Chief Clerk Hawkins, first appearing in "The Chief Clerk's Christmas," is yet another. Hawkins escapes Willow Creek but remains scarred by its engrained ways. White depicts Hawkins as an all-business, emotionless man who finally bursts forth his agony to his mother, only to endure her imminent death and a hasty retreat into his own spiritual entombment. Lonely, closed, and mean, Hawkins ultimately must confront the meaning of his life. In "The Story of a Grave" White takes the chief clerk to a tuberculosis sanitarium in the Great American Desert, similar to the one in naturalist Frank Norris's *McTeague*. Hawkins moves away from his fellow sufferers battling for their lives on the veranda—away from the skeletal vestiges of life—and finds a contorted happiness crawling out to a desert grave: "There they found Hawkins at the close of day, grim, repellent of feature, apart from his kind, alone in his very death. Men said it was a fitting end for him."[23]

This view of life as miserably scarred applies only to western Kansas in *The Real Issue*. White's stories of central and eastern Kansas in the collection, while critical of fraudulent boosters, narrow-minded businessmen, double standards of morality, malicious gossip, and restrictive small-town respectability, primarily portray a satisfying world. Life is stable, the people are fundamentally good, and the future is promising. The best example is located in "The Home-coming of Colonel Hucks." The old soldier is a town classic: a Civil War veteran, a pioneer, a lovable curmudgeon. After years of struggle and enterprise the colonel and his wife journey "home" to verdant Ohio. Disappointed with the old community which has gone to seed, the disenchanted couple returns to the grandeur of Kansas. As they gaze out of the railway window, little towns dot the landscape and opportunity abounds. This is truly home, where community lushly prospers.[24]

To secure a bountiful life, a finer community, was White's greatest concern. With the passing of western Kansas's climatic and Populist traumas, White directed his literary energy toward more fully embellishing the positive aspects of Kansas life. Severe realism and naturalistic technique give way to a still accurately detailed but romantically glossed portrait of community life as found in central and eastern Kansas. White sought to portray towns of commendable attributes and rectifiable failings. As he became concerned with progressive reform and the concomitant goal of community regeneration, the idyll and the ideal became irrevocably entangled.

The idyll is laid out in *The Court of Boyville* and neatly domiciled in *In Our Town*. A popular collection of short stories published in 1899, *The Court of Boyville*, projects into the small-town milieu an enchanted childhood full of pranks, play, evolving relationships, and youthful crises. The innocence and freedom of youth are identified closely with the town as both are set in a timeless, immutable state. While this world is impenetrable for adults, White in his concluding story makes it clear that the maturing boy can take much of the romance of the "town of Boyville" into the wilds of adult life.[25]

The romance is located seven years later in the anthology *In Our Town*. "It is 'Boyville' grown up," wrote one critic. In *In Our Town* White closely plotted the idyll:

> Ours is a little town in that part of the country called the West by those who live east of the Alleghanies, and referred to lovingly as "back East" by those who dwell west of the Rockies. It is a country town where, as the song goes, "you know everybody and they all know you," and the country newspaper office is the social clearing-house.

The town editor knows more than anyone and, as storyteller, depicts a snug community of homey but not provincial people. The folks in *In Our Town* rise above their failings and become generous, charitable, and merciful human beings. Here all are at bottom neighbors; no one is alone. The townspeople really are a family, enclosed, satisfied, and self-satisfied. Vices, biases, and idiosyncrasies naturally exist but not the uncivilized horrors found in *The Real Issue.* All can be and is worked out within the fundamentally classless, casteless community. Rules of life are to be followed; temperate and moral living is the maxim. Humanity is basically good, but all stray—and the community has the responsibility to keep townspeople in line. The worse violators pay the heftiest price for their sins—social ostracism. The town cleans itself up and always improves; the best citizens triumph as they banish liquor and gambling and build schools, libraries, and municipal works.[26]

The idyllic community in *In Our Town* ostensibly is apolitical; but White's interest always nested in politics. Indeed, five years earlier in 1901, White had published a collection of lengthy political stories. *Stratagems and Spoils: Stories of Love and Politics* was built around the theme that the political arena is a paradigm of life's struggle. The highest goal in life is to be brave, truthful, and kind. The political community, as the small town, had to be purged of its greatest sinners and forced to follow higher communal laws. Despotic plutocrats had overthrown popular democracy; public opinion was mocked; corrupt officials reigned in Washington. Reform had to be enforced but not too radically—demogoguery only exacerbated the evil. White's indictment was critically well received although its sales were mediocre. William Dean Howells hailed *Stratagems and Spoils* as "a substantial body of political fiction, such as we have so long sighed for." More was forthcoming.[27]

White prescribed "evolutionary progressivism" for an ailing republic. Human nature had to change. The world moved slowly, but inexorable progress clearly was at hand. People were working together; a majority opinion was developing; and rich and poor alike were seeking a better order. Caught up in Rooseveltian reform, White wrapped his political agenda within a rhetoric of human and communal regeneration. Foreseeing a victory of spiritualism over materialism and the rise of the common man into a broadened middle-class order, White set out to lay the grid of the reform state. Two novels, *A Certain Rich Man* and *In the Heart of a Fool,* profiled the ideal progressive community—the idyllic small town writ large over America and, in the end, the world.[28]

The evolution of human nature and of a community within the emerging progressive epoch is traced in *A Certain Rich Man,* published in

1909. A spiritually driven pioneer Kansas settlement, Sycamore Ridge, sends out its sons to fight the slavocracy, only to find itself caught in a backlash of postwar materialism. Increasing wealth and urban expansion are small compensations for individual degeneration and the atrophy of community spirit in Sycamore Ridge. The novel's protagonist, entrepreneur John Barclay, pushes on in Mammon's battle with the Christian spirit, exploiting fellow townspeople, building an empire of railroads, grains, and factories. Salvation is still possible as a mass movement begins to develop and public opinion crystalizes. In Washington a president, acting in the name of Godly progressivism, sets out to slay the malefactors of wealth. John Barclay suddenly sees the light, converts to the social gospel, and dies saving the life of a town outcast. All God's children, the mighty and the weak, equally victimized by their times, have come together to save Sycamore Ridge. The town stands as one as in olden days; so, too, can all of America.[29]

White had struck a responsive chord in 1909. Progressivism was peaking, as were the Kansan's reform efforts. *A Certain Rich Man* would represent the pinnacle of his literary career. The critics hailed the work and sales soared. The *New York Times* wrote that *A Certain Rich Man* "holds the mirror up to more that is truly native and characteristic in American life than has been reflected by any other storyteller who has essayed the task." The avant-garde *Craftsman,* a year after the book's publication, declared, "Everybody knows this book . . . for it grips the very roots of American life and shows the beginnings and growth of the great social and industrial problems that we are grappling with today." The *Nation* pronounced that this was no provincial novel: "Mr. White has shown a surprising power of relating his Sycamore Ridge to the national past, present, and future, and of making it mirror in some sort the developing character of the entire country." The *Graphic* concluded that White had made "the nearest approach yet to the great American novel, so long looked for." The *Outlook* concurred: "It is, above all, American through and through in its spirit, its intimate knowledge of every-day American life, its dialogue, its fun, and its pathos; it would be hard indeed to name a story of the last ten years that so positively deserves to be called a novel of American life." Theodore Roosevelt, not uncharacteristically, recognized himself in the limelight. On a safari in Africa the recently retired president concluded, "it is a real, and very effective, tract for the times. . . . I profoundly agree with the fundamental teaching of your book. It represents the major part of what I struggled for, what I had closest at heart, what I strove to accomplish, as President."[30]

Evolutionary progressivism, fictionally charted in *A Certain Rich Man,* followed a straight path toward a new dawn in human relations. Political and social progressivism as directed by politicians and diverse cadres of reformers across the nation, and as opposed by a multitude of entrenched interests, ran a decidedly more skewed path. Nine years after the release of *A Certain Rich Man,* in 1918, White's *In the Heart of a Fool* was published. The earlier novel embodied the spirit of the heady years of progressivism; the second possessed the eleventh-hour desperation of the reformist struggle. The wheels of industrialism had ground on, wealth had accumulated, problems remained unsolved, and resolutions were argued. Reforms had aided and hindered progress, and world war now eclipsed all other concerns. For White, as for many reformers, evolutionary progressivism suddenly catapulted onto a revolutionary world stage.

The Middle Western community of Harvey is the protagonist of *In the Heart of a Fool.* Towns, White informs his readers, are like people, formed generation by generation, layer by layer, each with a distinctive character. Harvey has forsaken its puritan past for materialism. Enriched by gas, oil, lead, coal, and zinc, the ungainly town has spread its pipes and rails over the surrounding countryside. The old town, elm-lined and tranquil, houses the entrepreneurs, comfortable and remote from South Harvey, the industrial wasteland. The workers of South Harvey live in degradation. The community has reached a crisis: divided between the rich and the exploited poor, it must make the choice between further materialist degeneration and Christian regeneration.

The workers of South Harvey have struck the mills. Their Christ-like leader preaches a nonviolent "religion of democracy," a call for Harvey's middle class to share its wealth and its security with the workers, to raise the wretched to its own comfortable standard of living. The hope of communal regeneration lies in establishing a higher quality of life for all the residents of Harvey and South Harvey, in resurrecting the old community virtues of neighborliness and kindliness. Materialism, however, has been so deified that the residents of Harvey are blind to communal virtue. Vigilante crowds are sent out to crush the strikers; they martyr the leader. An early prophecy in the novel rushes toward fulfillment:

> And so it shall come to pass that when the day of reckoning appears it shall be a day of wrath. . . . Then will the vicious poor and the vicious well-to-do, each crippled by his own vices, the blind leading the blind, fall to in a merciless conflict, mad and meaningless, born of a sad, unnecessary hate that shall terrorize the earth, unless God sends us another miracle of love like Christ or some vast chastening scourge of war, to turn aside the fateful blow.

Where Christian love failed to save Harvey, war succeeds: "Then the new epoch dawned; clear and strong came the call to Americans to go forth and fight in the Great War—not for themselves, not for their own glory, nor their own safety, but for the soul of the world. And the old spirit of America rose and responded." Swept up in the progressive crusade to save humanity, Harvey's battle has become part of a greater struggle. The divided city of Mammon, in its eleventh-hour of despair, has risen to be one city upon a hill for all the world to behold.[31]

In Harvey, as all across wartime America, White believed he saw the fruition of the spiritual destiny of the nation. The regenerative role of the saved community in the Great Crusade was summed up in *The Martial Adventures of Henry and Me.* In 1917 White and progressive Wichita editor Henry Allen traveled to France. In 1918 White published the half-fictional account of the experience: "So it really is not of arms and the man that this story is written, nor of Henry and me, and the war; but it is the eternal Wichita and Emporia in the American heart that we shall celebrate hereinafter as we unfold our tale." For White the war had become a tale of community as he knew it best. The Kansas progressive was inflated with hope, buoyed by a faith in America's promise, tightly tethered to Wilson's fragile crusade. The Allied world had entered into a great progressive "trust." A democratized order marched—countries, classes, and peoples joined together as a unified community, as Wichita or Emporia, as "a thousand replicas of Wichita and Emporia" back home in America, as Harvey. Watching the Allied parade across Europe, White believed he could see the progressive promise heading home.[32]

■ ■ ■

White's vision of Allied progressive community, the triumph of "the eternal Wichita and Emporia in the American heart," was heartfully received in 1918. Liberal critic Francis Hackett, reviewing *The Martial Adventures of Henry and Me* in the chauvanistic, reform-driven *New Republic,* wrote of White and Allen's pilgrimage, "It was their own old job in Wichita and Emporia, and they went to Europe with a firm conviction that the war was a colossal annex to their progressivism." In White, Hackett added, "You simply find an American who has at last carried Kansas to the planet, and espoused the planet on the terms of his long-held, authenticated morality." "It is," Hackett eulogized, "worth every drop of American blood."[33]

By 1919, however, the national mood as well as Francis Hackett's had shifted radically. Reviewing *In the Heart of a Fool* as the peacemakers machinated at Versailles, Hackett lambasted White's *magnum opus* upon which he had slaved for close to a decade as a severely tattered piece of propaganda cloaked in dated romantic garb: "Progressivism did well enough in a way and for a while. But where are the Progressives of yesteryear?" Hackett found particularly troubling White's vision of Harvey as a regenerated puritan community. Progressivism premised upon charity, mercy, and kindliness had become a mockery as nationalistic greed and acrimony reigned in Paris. Roosevelt's program, the Square Deal, mercilessly declared Hackett (Roosevelt himself had recently been buried), was dead.[34]

Hackett ended his review of *In the Heart of a Fool* with a plea to White:

> You are an artist. When you are not an ambassador or an editor or a reporter or a publicity man or a Progressive, you are an artist— sometimes, even, when you are one or all of these. But *In the Heart of a Fool* was not written with its eye honestly on the human object. It was written by the romantic Puritan, with propaganda behind it. Think of giving to stale propaganda what was meant for the great American novel!

Amidst the mounting disillusionment of 1919 White's progressive philosophy had become stale. So, too, evidently, had his fiction. Hackett was not alone in his criticism. Earlier the *Chicago News* critic found *In the Heart of a Fool* "about the dullest and most unentertaining reading that I have done in two and one-half years reviewing for this department." The brilliant Randolph Bourne was scathing: "Mr. White has become a sort of symbol of everything intelligent, progressive, 'folksy,' characteristic, in Kansas. The more I see of a mind like his the less I understand it." White took the notices to heart; save for one short story for the *Saturday Evening Post* in 1920, he never published fiction again. *In the Heart of a Fool,* ridiculed in the atmosphere of postwar cynicism, placed the seal on White's literary career; apparently it seemed, too, an aptly titled epitaph for his progressive philosophy.[35]

In the Heart of a Fool and its author were casualties of the times. Progressivism had borne it final fruit, and the harvest proved bad. For over two decades, White contributed to a powerful literary movement. Always focusing on community, and particularly on small towns, gradually bringing the expansive communities to the forefront of his work, White made his fiction resonate with the growing thunder of progressive reform. He utilized an effective metaphor for interpreting change in American society. He slighted issues and glossed over many problems. Nevertheless, his idyllic and his troubled towns reflected primary communal concerns of a good many people. Even in the end, verging into utopian visions of an ideal world community, White only projected what the vast majority of Americans anticipated in the Peace of Versailles. Francis Hackett, John

Dewey, Walter Lippmann, and a huge number of political and literary critics had only recently stood alongside White, envisioning puritanical, messianic hopes.[36]

White would take the literary lessons of the prewar era and apply them to his journalistic commentary for the remaining quarter century of his life. Despite attacks on the values and norms of small-town America, the vast majority of Americans tenaciously clung to their "village mentality." (So also did an impressive contingent of twenties and thirties intellectuals.) Having grasped the small town's evocative power in literature, White increasingly turned to it as a metaphor for interpreting social, political, and economic problems. In a language millions shared, the small-town Kansas editor continued to campaign for a regenerated American order, a broadly based middle-class society, tolerant, neighborly, and kind.

It was familiar terrain, for it was not through fiction alone that William Allen White had worked for progressive change. By 1919 the Kansas editor was a renowned social critic—he had long politicked as an informed American townsman for reform of the established order.

CHAPTER THREE

The Progressive Promise II

Politicking for the Ideal

OFFERING UP IDYLLIC COMMUNITIES in his fiction, William Allen White had sensed what appealed to readers' ideals. There was, still, a good deal more to his understanding of community in Progressive Era America than found in the simple portrayals of Willow Creek, Sycamore Ridge, and Harvey. In his social and political commentary White surveyed a vaster communal landscape. At first he held a limited vision of the "American community," a provincial Kansan's bird's-eye view. As his career developed and he became part of greater social, political, and cultural networks, the Jayhawker broadened his outlook. As he spoke to a wider public he found that the communal values and norms he grew up with in Kansas were adaptable, if not directly applicable, to a greater American community experience and its more complex array of problems. The nation was undergoing fundamental social, economic, cultural, and political change. It was in large part White's sensitivity to the changing meaning of community within an emergent new order, and his ability to speak to the issue, that made his social and political commentary so popular. It also helps to explain why his more simplistic fiction rang true to so many readers.

White's ability to reach out to a widely scattered audience and to speak effectively to its diverse concerns in terms of community first materialized with the distribution, by the hundreds of thousands, of his 1896 *Gazette* editorial, "What's the Matter with Kansas?" Written when his conservatism was, as he retrospectively surmised, in "full and perfect flower," the hastily drawn diatribe was an indictment of Populist political rule in Kansas. It was a rhetorical masterpiece, a portent of the young Kansan's future as a persuasive social and political commentator. While illustriously satirizing his political opponents, White articulated the communal values that were most dear to him and, as he must have sensed, to a good number of other people. Looking toward the development of a twentieth-century socio-economic order, he sought to plot his state's destiny, as well as his own, within its expansive bounds. "What's the matter with Kansas?" he queried. A century later the young journalist's answer still reads well:

> We all know; yet here we are at it again. We have an old mossback Jacksonian who snorts and howls because there is a bathtub in the state-house; we are running that old jay for governor. We have another shabby, wild-eyed, rattle-brained fanatic who has said openly in a dozen speeches that "the rights of the user are paramount to the rights of the owner"; we are running him for chief justice, so that capital will come tumbling over itself to get into the state. We have raked the old ash heap of failure in the state and found an old human hoop skirt who has failed as a business man, who has failed as an editor, who has failed as a preacher, and we are going to run him for congressman-at-large. He will help the looks of the Kansas delegation at Washington. Then we have discovered a kid without a law practice and have decided to run him for attorney-general. Then for fear some hint that the state had become respectable might percolate through the civilized portions of the nation, we have decided to send three or four harpies out lecturing, telling the people that Kansas is raising hell and letting the corn go to weeds.

Ridiculing the opposition, White in the end has stated what really matters with Kansas: respectability and civility rest more on his mind than corn. The underlying message is White's long-range concern with the reestablishment, after years of radical upheaval, of sound community in the state. The argument runs throughout the editorial: The nation is prospering, White charges, and "Kansas is not in it." The state is "losing standing" as the Populists frighten off people, money, and talent. Kansas needs "white shirts and brains" and "business judgment"; it needs fewer "of those fellows who boast that they are 'just ordinary clodhoppers, but they know more in a minute about finance than [conservative Senator] John Sherman.'" What Kansas needs, declares White, is population and wealth—"well-dressed men on the streets," "cities on the fertile prairies," and mills and factories.[1]

White's clarion call in "What's the Matter with Kansas?" was no herald to a bucolic order. He was interested in community development; he believed that meant industrial expansion and urbanization. The following year, with hopes of cashing in on McKinley prosperity, White renegotiated the case for Kansas before a national audience. Writing in the *Forum*, a respected journal of opinion, the ambitious journalist now caricatured the victorious Populists as conservatives. He pictured a staid Kansas community receptive to a new infusion of eastern money. Kansans were not men with "green ears, striped backs, and iridescent tail-feathers." They were more intelligent than the average American, and better read: Kansans owned more cabinet organs and watches, farmed with the latest machinery, and more often rode the railroad. Kansans were up-to-date—they understood the value of "slow, easy, and unpretentious growth"; they needed support to get back to work, to forget socialist fantasies; Kansans needed to industrialize, to enter the American mainstream. Harking back to Constantine, Rome's first emperor to embrace the cross of the Christian future, White prophesized, "By this sign, the sign of the village smokestack, shall Kansas conquer."[2]

White's continuing interest in an emergent industrial order, as well as his understanding of its incorporating character, is evident in a number of "travel" pieces he penned at the turn of the century. Beginning to look beyond the confines of his Kansas beat, White had set off for newly developing territories. He was a Darwinian, and he hailed a rugged new order. In 1897 he first found it in the Dakotas. In a lead story for *Scribner's* (the seventh in a series on "The Conduct of Great Businesses" published by the prestigious literary journal), the Kansas editor declared that the farmer was now a capitalist: he had brains, ran an efficient operation, and did little hard work. White based his proclamation upon his observation of bonanza wheat farming in the Red River Valley. Describing the giant enterprises in glorifying detail, he noted that they were modern plants where high-quality native laborers and transients, as skilled as mill workers, found good working conditions. Brawny, inefficient farming was a relic of the past. So, too, was the independent yeoman, disparaged as an artifact within a well-tooled new order. Within the excitement of the narrative, White neglected to detail that the yeoman had not transformed himself into the capitalist; rather, yesteryear's hero had been relegated to the new order's questionably well-tended laborer.[3]

In 1902 White found a similar incorporated wonder evolving in Idaho. In four installments in the *Saturday Evening Post* he reported upon the mining boom exploding across Thunder Mountain. White gloried in the miner's folklore, his legendary role in America's pioneer epic, and the excitement of the strike. Thunder Mountain, however, was part of a new epoch. It offered no golden future to the lone miner; this, proclaimed White, was a big business proposition. The diminution of the miner's role, fortunately, was of no great consequence: the rough-hewn mountain man, as other Americans, was evolving into urban man; he needed little money, reasoned White, for corporate America fulfilled all his needs—"creature comforts," education, and opportunity. The miner, as the yeoman, was supposedly well-cared-for in the twentieth century.[4]

This sense of an epochal dawn permeating White's turn-of-the-century work, the development of a more civilized, plentiful order incorporating all Americans, was most illustriously presented in two *Post* articles appearing in 1904. The magazine cover caught the grandiose vision: a yeoman overlooks a rising farming, mining, manufacturing, and trading empire. The saga is playing out in the Pacific Northwest. The *Post*'s illustrator, however, skewed White's viewpoint. While swept up in the grandeur of a pioneer epoch unfolding in the region, White in his articles discounted as in his previous analysis, the role of the individual. He saw man and civilization battling with nature and, with God's help, securing a foothold upon the land. From explorer through pioneer, settler, boomer, and finally to citizen, man was triumphant. But the farming, mining, and manufacturing within the region demanded capital; the individual could not go it alone. Great enterprises were necessary to develop the territory; civilization would blossom in the desert, riches would pour forth, and the communal needs of all would be served. The boom in the Northwest, as elsewhere for White, had become a story of capital—not men. The finished product would be a greater common good for all America's citizens.[5]

In the early years of the century the greater common good was fast becoming the dominant issue for White. It was not, he would argue, a matter of partisan politics, or of provincial jealousy, or of economic greed, but of common sense. It was clear to White, as he believed it should be to everyone, that the nation was entering a new age; the people were moving into one community. In back-to-back *Post* pieces written in 1902 the Kansan described the phenomenon, first from his own sectional vantage point and then from the national perspective. In "Ready-Made Homes Out West" he depicted a vast westward movement of home seekers. Times had changed: These settlers brought money—they did not come out of adversity. They were a new breed—not pioneers or speculators. The days of boom, scalawags, and costly experiments in money and lives had passed; lessons had been learned. These newcomers had come to stay in established communities, similar to the homes they had left behind. To White, this was simply one act in a larger drama. The entire nation was moving together and settling down, into what seemed like one large neighborhood. In "Uncommercial Traveling" he portrayed the American people gathering about "a common national fireside." Provincialism and sectionalism were giving way to an amalgamated socioeconomic-political order as individuals were "neighboring" across the countryside. Traveling, trading, and learning about one another, people were noting their similarities and overcoming their differences. The nation was melding itself into "a more perfect union."[6]

This was heady language, suited to a period in American history top-heavy with rhetorical hyperbole. The Progressive Era had arrived, and William Allen White had begun to run with the reformist pack. In their myriad guises progressives tangled with the problems of an incorporating order. While much of his early work was biased by his Western perspective and provincial boosterism, White, by the early 1900s, had begun to acquire a broader understanding of his society and could begin to address its problems. Importantly, he had met and been won over by Theodore Roosevelt. With Roosevelt's ascent to the presidency, the Kansas news-paperman began speaking a new language, a community rhetoric tailored to a refurbished socioeconomic perspective.[7]

From a politically conservative view of an incorporating society in which the good of the people was tended to by the vested interests, White rapidly evolved to a belief in a corporate order progressively regulated in the best interests of the common good, by the people. The gargantuan achievements of the nineteenth-century capitalists, in White's earlier sights, had eclipsed mythic heroes—the pioneering yeoman, the rugged miner, and the independent manufacturer. In their stead the entrepreneurs had created a materially endowed, if passive, national citizenry; but their machinations had led to trouble. The people had become spiritually cor-rupted, obsessed with materialisitic gain. Economic chaos reigned as corporate behemoths, small businessmen, farmers, and workers grappled for survival. The citizenry began to stir spiritually and politically. In White's newly enlightened view, there now arose another national hero, the common man. He was a fresh breed, not a nineteenth-century inde-pendent sort; this hero was a product of his age, an amalgam, representing the associated interests of an incorporated society. He spoke from a more moral perspective, thinking of his fellow men, of the common good, of the emergent national interest. As the rhetorical fortunes of the corporate giants dipped in White's estimate, the stock of this progressive common man soared to dizzying heights.[8]

With societal incorporation touching so many lives, the cause of the common man was a natural for the Progressive Era. Few rushed to his defense as swiftly as Theodore Roosevelt, and none so securely grabbed the leadership of this amorphous majority. Roosevelt spoke for the common man and his common good with great effect. And William Allen White spoke for the president. In the early days of the century these two men had found each other, a cause, and an enormous national audience. They seemed made for one another and for their constituency: a charismatic president; a young publicist eagerly awaiting his bidding; and an aroused citizenry anxious to register its "public opinion."[9]

■ ■ ■

Theodore Roosevelt was an exceptional public figure. Politically adept, he challenged the established conservative powers within the Republican Party and swung them through compromise into grudging support of his reform agenda. He was successful in large part because of his greater purpose: intent on arresting what he perceived to be the nation's post–Civil War materialistic debauch, Roosevelt aimed to redirect the country toward fulfilling its truer destiny, to lead the world to a higher spiritual as well as material plain. To meet this end he took to the hustings to reach out to "all the people," across party lines, disregarding meaner political skirmishes, advocating a lofty, inherently attractive message of spiritual regeneration. No novice, Roosevelt well understood the advantage of such a tack within a shifting political environment in which an unanchored public opinion held increasing sway. More important, he knew he was good on the stump, and he believed presidential leadership entailed education. He used his "bully pulpit," then, to speak to higher aims in the spirit of noblesse oblige and to promote his legislative agenda. He never succeeded in raising the people above their dearer economic interests, and he never achieved all he aimed to change; he could descend from the pulpit to the politicking pit, and he fell short of others' higher aims. But Teddy Roosevelt did catch the popular imagination and a huge number of votes.[10]

William Allen White shared Roosevelt's political views as well as the president's conception of himself as the public's foremost educator. A good communicator in his own right, White considered it his journalistic duty, too, to educate the public. Sensitive to the growing weight of public opinion, he set out to enlighten the people, to rally them behind Roosevelt and his agenda, for the salvation of the republic. With the president he shared progressive ideologue Herbert Croly's assessment of the brand of leadership needed to fulfill "the promise of American life":

> The common citizen can become something of a hero and something of a saint, not by growing to heroic proportions in his own person, but by the sincere and enthusiastic imitation of heroes and saints, and whether or not he will ever come to such imitation will depend upon the ability of his exceptional fellow-countrymen to offer him acceptable examples of heroism and saintliness.

Convinced that Theodore Roosevelt was such an exceptional American, White prepared to spread the word.[11]

Mass-circulation journalism had entered its heyday at the turn of the century, and the illustrious Kansas journalist, the friend of the fascinating new president, was in great demand. Seeing Roosevelt's natural constituency as an amalgamation of common people, White sought to identify the president with them by turning the Oyster Bay patrician into an exemplary common man. In White's words Roosevelt, too, became an amalgam, heroically embodying within himself and his political program the best characteristics and interests of the greater community. Theodore Roosevelt was, for White, truly "the great commoner" in a fashion William Jennings Bryan, the president's popular rival and great commoner of lore, could never be: Bryan was an anachronism, a representative of the independent man of the nineteenth century. Roosevelt understood his times: he stood as the prophet of a new order. He spoke to and for the rising, independent-minded middle majority of American society. In the image of the common man, White formulated a powerful identity for the president.

White's first mass-circulation pronouncement upon "the meaning of Theodore Roosevelt" to the American nation appeared shortly after Roosevelt's succession to the presidency. In 1900 White had started a series of political sketches for the popular reform journal *McClure's*. The first piece was on Bryan. White had praised Bryan as a powerful personality, but he had found the silver-tongued orator to be a political animal out of his depth in the twentieth century. Bryan, White contended, represented an older order, holding past values and perceptions; Bryan posed grandly, orated emotionally, and ultimately offered no feasible solutions to the dilemmas of a society becoming more and more industrialized. This was a new age, composed of divergent interests, classes, corporate entities, and aspirations. Extremist appeals to the people as if they held one base interest were now meaningless, and perhaps more to the point they were dangerous given *vox populi*'s proclivity toward socialism. Moderate appeals to the public's higher motives within a diversified greater community, in sharp contrast, were very meaningful: enter Theodore Roosevelt and a deeper understanding of the people and their needs within an incorporated society. In an article in *McClure's* two months after an assassin's bullet landed Roosevelt in the White House, White argued that Roosevelt was not political, he was a moralist. Roosevelt was clean, he had integrity, common sense, and most importantly he had drive. Roosevelt shared the aims of America's emergent common men; he would consult with them, and with his intensity he would accomplish much in the interest of all

Americans. Big changes demonstrably were afoot in the United States, and Theodore Roosevelt, alerted White, was prepared to lead the way.[12]

White continued his presidential analysis the following month in the *Saturday Evening Post*. What exact changes the president had in store for the nation were still unclear, but his approach was crystalline. White declared that Theodore Roosevelt was about to elevate politics. Occupying a higher moral plain than Congress, his party, and the national citizenry, Roosevelt recognized that the people were the key to his fight for the establishment of morality in government. Roosevelt wanted to raise the "national political ideal . . . to an astonishing degree." If the people treated him fairly, he would offer them this "new deal." He would speak to them, lay out the moral imperative of the hour, and they would respond. America as a nation had to return to first principles and stand above battling commercial interests as well as above a Populist-styled attack upon all groups. The nation, in all its varied interests, had to stand in common accord. The president, White declared, stood for the nation. He was listening to all parties, amalgamating all interests, representing the common good. Roosevelt's first annual address to Congress served as a prime example of his measured, constructive leadership. White wrote concerning it,

> And yet Roosevelt is not so cocksure as his firmness would make him appear. When he goes into a new subject he walks on eggs. His message, which reads off so vigorously, in the genesis was not Roosevelt's message. He sent out for information. He didn't write the message up "out of his head." There are some of a Western railroad magnate's ideas in it, and a suggestion from a steel trust originator in it, and some of a national labor leader's wisdom in it, and some of a great naval hero's ideas in it, a thought from an influential editor, a turn of a phrase from a magazine writer in it, a line of thought suggested by a renowned college president, and an economic principle laid down by a college professor, and a currency scheme evolved after talking with a successful Wall Street man. Yet the essence of the message is Rooseveltian, cosmopolitan, American. These qualities will show in the man and his policy. His administration will not be provincial nor personal, nor in a narrow sense partisan. It will come from all the people—not as a raw popular impulse, which is more often wrong than right, but as a popular impulse digested in a sober judgment by a sane mind.

Here was the consummate leader. Still, White warned the public not to deify Roosevelt as he could and would make mistakes. Turning about, White then punctuated the analysis with a conjectured epitaph to the nascent Roosevelt era: "'He Done His Damnedest—Angels Could Do No More!'"[13]

A year later, summing up in the *Post* "One Year of Roosevelt," White lifted the president to even loftier heights as the composite representative of the people, and not incidentally as the best candidate for 1904. Roosevelt, according to White, had battled the politicians and their allied corporate interests, with the people. "Roosevelt," he wrote, "is looming up as the great national leader, bigger than any party, the epitome of his times, the great American." The age had changed, but commercialism need not run riot over the nation's greatest interest, its moral rectitude. Roosevelt stood ready to guide the return to simpler, more righteous living within the complexities of the new order: White praised him:

> What is true of politics is true of society, is true of religion, is true of every department of human activity. In his New England speeches this August, Roosevelt spoke often of the humble virtues of family and civil life. There is no doubt that he sees the need in America for the return, in so far as civilization to-day allows it, to the simple life which made America sturdy and sane and brave a generation ago. His life as a father, as a husband, as a citizen, as a politician, and as a President has been simple in the extreme. And if he accomplishes no legislative reform, if he fails in every endeavor to set the world aright, the country cannot be cheated of that which is rather to be chosen than any law or any policy—the moving example of a plain, strong man, living, working wholesomely, in unpretentious, old-fashioned democratic simplicity.[14]

Here stands White's "Great Commoner," speaking to and for a greater community of interests and advocating a return to first and higher national principles in order to secure the common good, but importantly, within a new order. White wrote well; but was there any substance behind the rhetoric? In "Swinging Round the Circle with Roosevelt," written in 1903, White answered yes. He wrote that on his recent Western tour Roosevelt had preached tolerance, temperance, and brotherhood. He had denounced class lines and spoken out for charity and patience. He had not raised traditional, "beefy" issues such as the flag, the tariff, and the currency. Rather, he had spoken to decency, to the common citizen, to neighborliness. "The President," wrote White, "might well be called a revivalist, turning men from the avarice and wanton thoughtlessness and meannesses of this day and generation to those things which put men and nations in harmony with 'reason and the will of God.'" The president, in short, stood above all as a spokesman for social harmony.[15]

White was not simply indulging in rhetorical bluster, and neither was Roosevelt on the hustings. Roosevelt believed that "the people" were about to be torn asunder by rising class conflict. Divisive, uncontrollable economic interests, in his view, had led to a polarization of haves and have-nots. He feared that the extremes of left and right, represented by the likes of William Jennings Bryan and Marcus Hanna, offered no balancing remedies to right a threatened ship of state. Roosevelt saw himself, in the words of historian John Milton Cooper, "as a responsible conservative pursuing reform to stave off threats of revolution." He offered in his rhetoric as well as in his legislative agenda a course of moderation. In the name of conscientious leadership Roosevelt claimed to speak above discord, addressing the fundamental issue of social harmony. He beseeched all interests to join with him, to rise above selfishness, to think of the country's interest, of national unity. It was an enveloping rhetoric that spoke to a higher cause and served at the same time to rally diverse interests behind programs Roosevelt deemed beneficial for the common good and ultimately for the survival of the republic.[16]

Social harmony to Roosevelt and to White was the number-one challenge confronting the United States. Roosevelt stood before the people as a national arbiter, a grand harmonizer capable of leading the nation away from materialism toward a more spiritual order. America had plenty of wealth. It now was necessary in the name of social justice to ensure a more equitable distribution of the riches, to sacrifice individual self-interest for the greater national welfare. The nation as one great community needed to act decently, neighborly, to be at peace with itself. In reestablishing relations of old within a more complex order there lay a moderate solution to the dilemmas of the twentieth century.

Theodore Roosevelt and William Allen White could be distinguished as social progressives. There was more to their message of social harmony than a romantic return to olden ways—they had a down-to-earth reform agenda. Social harmony, they believed, could be achieved by securing a more decent life for all citizens. Social progressives sought justice more than control as a solution to social, political, and economic unrest. Traditional, moralistic, and Protestant, their idea of justice meant equal opportunity to achieve a satisfactory life: to be well fed and housed, to be educated, to lead God-fearing "Christian" lives. For close to two decades White campaigned with the president and on his own (and for another quarter century following Roosevelt's death), for a socially "just" legislative agenda anticipating the creation of a broad middle ground within American society where the bulk of the citizenry would rest materially secure and the republic would remain forever safe from internecine destruction.[17]

Following Roosevelt's resounding 1904 victory over Alton Parker, White increasingly spoke to social justice. Specific legislative goals abounded, but justice served as the point of departure to elaborate upon the larger concern of securing a socially harmonious greater community. The Roosevelt administration dealt with issues of anti-trust, railroad regulation, labor relations, consumer protection, and conservation. White additionally was concerned with expanding the regulatory powers of the states, restraining the political machines, and enacting municipal and electoral reforms. In pursuit of these ends he would attack the overzealousness of the muckrakers, the greediness of the plutocrats, and the "madness" of the Bryanites and the socialists. All, he determined, were immoderate, disruptive elements within the community. Such attacks were discounted, however, in regard to the greater message: all must get along; all must give. For all the crusade rhetoric it often sounded more like a plea not to careen off course, not to rock a shaky boat. Ultimately the Roosevelt administration and White stood for balance and restraint, for steering the middle course of slow, progressive reform. And in their view, the nation was heading their way.[18]

In the lead article for the *Saturday Evening Post* a month after the election, White enthusiastically anticipated the enactment of a broad social-justice agenda. He was convinced the American people had taken "equitable distribution" to their hearts. Fairness now loomed so large over the nation, it even dwarfed the president's generally insurmountable stature:

> Therefore the triumph of Theodore Roosevelt at the recent election means infinitely more than the personal victory of a man. Indeed, the fortunes of the President from now on are immaterial—except that he is needed as a leader during the few critical years while the new movement in American politics is taking solid form. But the tendency manifest in this election, to consider problems of distribution rather than those of the accumulation of wealth, is a strong, definite and permanent one in American politics. Theodore Roosevelt can give it great aid by merely living and working with the people during the coming four years, but the tendency has gone beyond him; it is in the heart of the people. Perhaps he had less to do with it than it had to do with his attitude. For the organs of publicity in this country—the reputable magazines, the great daily and weekly newspapers of high repute, the coming public men, Root, Taft, Folk, LaFollette, Bryan, Lodge, Knox, Leonard Wood, Jerome, Beveridge, Crane, Bailey of Texas, Butler of Columbia, Herrick of Ohio, and thousands of minor leaders of American thought, together with the spirit of the universities—reflect this conviction: the American problem is the problem of distribution, and not the production of wealth.

White argued that Roosevelt owed his victory to a better educated, more moral people, ready for change. The guiding maxim, thanks to the president, was no longer materialistic production as McKinley had advocated but the spiritually motivated distribution of an abundance successfully achieved. A great movement was afoot in the land. Roosevelt had offered neither radical demagoguery nor stand-patism but the middle road to sane, unselfish, constructive reform; a difficult transitional period in the nation's history had been bridged.[19]

The United States had set forth, White believed, toward establishing in the twentieth century a just order, a socially harmonious greater community. In an inaugural piece published in the *Post* he explained that America, owing to its laws, institutions, power, and wealth, stood at an unprecedented vantage point. A fair and intelligent people, just and moderate, was poised to demand an equal share for all hard-working and industrious individuals. A few months later, in the *Outlook*, a respected journal of opinion, he went on to explain that the people were moving closer to God—wealth was no longer the measure of right or wrong. The new criterion, he wrote in the lead article for the October issue of the genteel, New York–based *Atlantic Monthly* was "Thou shalt love thy neighbor as thyself." It was necessary to educate citizens further, to demand better wages and more of life's amenities for all Americans; the need was to nurture neighborliness, for the common good.[20]

All would not be easy. White spoke of a great battle still pending between the forces of spiritualism and materialism. His own state of Kansas served as an example of the materialistic quagmire and of the promise of spiritual victory. In "The Kansas Conscience," written in 1905, White depicted the fight in the state between a malevolent Standard Oil Company and a righteous citizenry. The immediate issue was regulation and the establishment of a state-owned, competitive refinery; the greater issue, according to White, was an un-American form of corporatism strangling a free people. The strength of the Kansans lay in their sense of community:

> . . . Kansas acted as any other American community would act having seen the truth clearly. Kansas is the unmodified American type. In many other states the large per cent. of urban population has in some measure veneered the original type. Men on salaries or working for wages have temptations to compromise with their consciences that do not come so strongly to men working for themselves. . . . Of the million and a half people in the state, less than two hundred thousand live in what, by any stretch of fancy, may be called cities. Even the three first-class cities of the state are large, neighborly country towns. The millionaires in the state may be counted on the fingers and toes of one man. And the number of paupers does not much exceed a score to the hundred thousand of population. The people are all well-to-do.

Seemingly anti-urban (and White could be at times), the principle message is one of equitable distribution. Cities in this piece metaphorically represent monopoly and constraint. Smaller urban centers and rural enclaves represent individual freedom and opportunity. The real question is not one of worker independence but of the diminishing chance for a better way of life, for a fair share of the American pie. Kansans knew better; they knew to look out for themselves and each other. If the American people would speak up, as had the Kansans, they too could be well-to-do.[21]

The issue came down to neighborliness. Really, White argued in the 1907 *American Magazine* article "Emporia and New York," Americans fundamentally were the same, cut out of the same native cloth. They shared basic likenesses; differences were minor. The most fundamental likeness was that of "social sympathy." Most Americans cared for one another, were ready to come to one another's aid. In Emporia, as in all of rural and small-town America, however, it was easier for people to express their social sympathies—it was a way of life. Unlike residents of New York and the rest of urban America, Emporians were more aware of and could sense their neighbors' needs. Smaller communities were more democratic, practically lacking in class and caste, teeming with equal opportunity. All deserved and received a chance. These were community values the nation needed to emulate. And it was possible in New York as in Emporia. It was possible in all the United States. Through the enactment of a more equitable distribution of the nation's wealth, social harmony would prevail.[22]

White was optimistic that the greater American community could be more socially sympathetic and could achieve the same sort of harmonious order found in Emporia and in Kansas. National regeneration, not provincial boosterism, was his primary interest; he made his position crystal clear in "The Partnership of Society," published in October 1906. The *American Magazine,* reorganized with White's help as a voice for moderate progressive reform, ran the piece as the lead to its inaugural edition. White forecast the imminent re-creation of genuine community in modern America; he placed his trust in the inherent social sympathy of America's common man. White traced mankind's historic struggle between individual selfishness, the "centrifugal force" of life, and justice for the many, the "centripetal force" of life. Selfishness in the past was represented by kings and priests and their ilk; today it was the plutocrats. Standing opposed to the millionaires, the "greatest failures in our modern life," were the poor, the masses, the workers—the common folk historically in touch with the highest purpose of life: service to humanity, not accumulation of wealth. In a society moving toward greater industrialization and urbanization the people instinctively grasped that they must be neighbors, as through all time the people had understood and prevailed. To prosper, civilization as a whole had to be more saintly:

> The spirit of social service is in the masses of all our people. One finds it throughout the land, among workmen who join unions, among farmers who put in their sick neighbor's crops, and country-bred people who come to one another's help in a thousand neighborly ways in time of trouble. The work that is done for money to buy comforts for the worker himself is but a small per cent of the work done in this world; it is the work done by fathers for their families, by mothers for their children, by neighbors for one another—all instinctively following the divine inspiration of social help—that has made our civilization grow and spread all over America.

Through cooperation in the past, through altruistic organization, the masses had found fellowship. They were prospering as never before, but they had to take care not to lose sight of their highest purpose:

> Little by little the people have gained political rights, and economic rights, and social rights. And the net gain for the poor has been that at the end of each succeeding century a day's work would bring the toiler and his family a few more comforts than a day's work brought his grandfather. To-day a day's work at the average American scale of wages will house a man and his family comfortably, clothe them decently, feed them wholesomely and well, give their child the opportunity to get as good an education as the richest man in the land can buy, furnish them with clean amusements, supply them with books and newspapers and give them a little leisure to reflect upon the meaning of life, that they may live to some purpose in the world. Many luxuries the poor man cannot have, but few comforts are denied him. By the poor man one does not mean the man whose poverty is abject, the result of his own deficiencies or of accident, but the average citizen whose life has another object than the possession of riches—the "poor in spirit" of the beatitudes.

The purpose for which people must live is one another. The social compact, White charged, must govern—not individualism, nor selfishness. A vast body of Americans was rising, not only in material well-being, but in spirit. Together, as one great community, organized for reform, it could secure the common good of the nation.[23]

White argued in "The Partnership of Society" that the time had arrived for the people to complete the Revolution of 1776 through the controlled evolution of the reform movement. He believed the nation had entered under Roosevelt an era of justice and righteousness, but much remained to be accomplished. Now there was to be a changing of the guard. The president was about to leave the White House; he had ordained as his successor William Howard Taft. White was not happy with the choice, agreeing that Roosevelt should leave but doubting Taft's commitment to the cause. As always, however, he did Roosevelt's bidding. In a pre-convention biography White gave his best to portray Taft as the man of the hour, prepared to usher in the progressive millenium. Taft was another exemplary common man, unique in that he would be the nation's first "suburban" president: here was a mix of rural and urban values, a no-airs American type, a businessman of a nameless middling class, representative of the changing order. He was, as Roosevelt, a man of ideals. In the contest between the plutocrats and the people, Taft would be fair and courageous; he would move the nation toward a more equitable distribution of the wealth. A "hewer of wood," Taft would hone all the jobs begun by Roosevelt, and not embark on anything new. Judge Taft was what the craftsman ordered; he would carry the moderate Rooseveltian reform movement to its judicious end.[24]

But Taft simply was not Roosevelt; nor was he a credible pretender. A year earlier in a *McClure's* piece, "Roosevelt: A Force for Righteousness," White had once again deified the president as a progressive fundamentally beyond reproach and virtually irreplacable. In summing up the Roosevelt reign, White claimed that with the president honesty, fairness, and justice had triumphed in the land. Roosevelt was an average, common-sense man who had reached heroic proportions as a spiritual leader and teacher: "his whole being is of native mud, but it is of the kind which under pressure and heat easily turns to marble and becomes immortal. Washington, Lincoln, and Grant were made of similar stuff." Taft never had the spiritual "stuff" of such greatness in White's estimate—under the excessive pressures of the next four years, the new president would prove to be materially all too common for the likes of the Kansan.[25]

Initially, White remained optimistic. In a series of articles published in 1909 and early 1910 in the *American Magazine,* he laid out his vision of a people caught up in a secular reformation. All effective progress, he argued, was accomplished only through organized, national efforts. America was heading toward equitable distribution of its vast wealth. Reform was binding the nation together into a true union, as men of all sections having seen the truth met together, searching for the common good. The need now was to spread the word further:

Laws will not make us a free people; presidents and governors will not make us free; courts will not make us free. "Ye shall know the truth, and the truth shall make you free." . . . The upper grades of our common schools and our high schools and our colleges and universities are turning out millions of men and women who are giving their lives to society unselfishly as teachers and preachers and farmers and doctors and lawyers and mechanics and merchants, whose chief thought is not for money—men and women who form the bulk of the well-housed, well-clad, well-fed prosperous body of the people neither rich nor poor.

For the first time White identified this growing, national progressive constituency as "the middle classes." These were Americans of a new order: educated, well-off, just, and prepared to secure the same for everyone else. An amorphous group, with much work to be done, its accomplishments were nonetheless clear: The political process had been democratized through such measures as the direct primary, initiative, referendum, and recall. Capital had been harnessed through government regulation. And perhaps most emblematic, the cities had been saved. America's urban centers were becoming models of social harmony, overcoming problems of class and caste. The twentieth-century metropolis represented the success of progressivism. The nation stood on the verge of the millenium:

And now for ten years there has been a distinct movement among the American people—feeble and imperceptible against the current during the first few years of its beginning—a movement which indicates that in the soul of the people there is a conviction of their past unrighteousness. During the five years last past that movement has been unmistakable. It is now one of the big self-evident things in our national life. It is called variously Reform, the Moral Awakening, the New Idea, the Square Deal, the Uplift and by other local cognomens; but it is one current in the thought of the people. And the most hopeful sign of the times lies in the fact that the current is almost world-wide. The same striving to lift men to higher things, to a fuller enjoyment of the fruits of our civilization, to a wider participation in the blessings of modern society— in short to "a more abundant life"—the same striving is felt through Europe and among the islands of the sea, that is tightening the muscles of our social and commercial and political body.

The United States, in White's eyes, was about to consummate its own social-justice revolution, and so too the world's. A great community, middle class in nature, harmoniously organized as one, was prepared to bestow the blessings of a materially and spiritually rich society upon all humankind.[26]

While White prophesized the coming progressive millenium, trouble was brewing closer to home. William Howard Taft, White painfully concluded in 1910, was a Judas to the cause. Instead of representing the interests of the greater community, the president had taken his stand with the reactionary elements of society. In another series of articles in the *American Magazine,* appearing throughout the difficult political winter of 1910–11, White began to stake out his position with the Republican insurgents —those reform voices increasingly resistant to the Taft administration's conservative tilt. He tagged the insurgents as none other than the "people," the "masses," the "common man," the "average man"; they were representative of a national movement, a worldwide movement taking power for the common good. He saw a momentous battle dawning. The nation had entered an historic era as it moved forever from crassness and materialism towards a reformed twentieth-century order. The middle classes had risen to replace the unnecessary and disproportionately rewarded and praised nineteenth-century captains of industry. In "When the World Busts Through," White charged that there was no stopping a change for the better for the average man. The insurgents stood with the people, in the middle of the road, temperately leading the way. The conservatives, with the president, were blocking the progression. They had to move aside.[27]

The insurgency led to the 1912 split in the Republican Party. The president, as it turned out, was not about to be budged aside, particularly by Theodore Roosevelt. White had written in May 1912 of the insurmountable task of holding the party together if either the incumbent Taft or the insurgent Roosevelt was to be nominated. In his article "Should Old Acquaintance Be Forgot?" White declared there was little choice. Taft was an amiable, passive sort of man who had betrayed his predecessor. Roosevelt had assumed that as a capable overseer, Taft would carry his reform program to completion. Unfortunately, as Taft had taken the path of least resistance by agreeing to Roosevelt's plan, so once in office he gave way to the established, anti-Roosevelt party hierarchy. White charged that corporately aligned Taft had overseen the reactionary, materialistic dismantlement of Roosevelt's progressive achievement. This was unacceptable. When Roosevelt, in White's view, subsequently was robbed of the nomination in Chicago, the Kansas national committeeman and convention power-broker joined the Roosevelt walkout. White was intensely active in Roosevelt's third-party "Bull Moose" bid, and for the next two years he tried to hold the new Progressive Party together; he gave his all to the insurgency. Years later he recalled the Progressive Party convocation as the high point of his life: "Looking back now more than thirty years, I can shut my eyes and see that Bull Moose convention of 1912, see their eager faces—more than a thousand of them—upturned, smiling hopefully, with joy beaming out that came from hearts which believed in what they were doing; its importance, its righteousness." He concluded: "It seemed to matter so very much, that convention of zealots, cleansed of self-interest and purged of cynicism. I never have seen before or since exactly that kind of crowd. I impressed it on my memory because I felt as they felt—those upturned, happy faces." Standing at Armageddon, battling with Roosevelt, the good stood together, for White, as one.[28]

And in the end, they stood alone. White correctly had foreseen a momentous battle dawning, but its outcome had a good deal more to do with *realpolitik* than with a conflict between spiritual and material forces. When the dust settled on election day, 1912, White could take solace in the victory of his second choice for the presidency, Democrat Woodrow Wilson. "Progressivism" had won. But White had to come to terms with the limits of the progressive constituency he had hailed as the coming force in American society. America hardly was one great, altruistic community; rather, it was composed of many communities of interest. Roosevelt had done exceptionally well in what came down to a two-man race with Wilson. He sparred with Wilson over economic and social matters, and he tried in his latter-day presidential style to champion the broader issues of class harmony, moderate reformism, and anti-materialism. The Progressive Party, however, based, in Roosevelt's view, on reform and morality, in the final analysis had little chance of victory. Wilson also stood for reform and morality, and he appealed to a greater number of interest groups. Morality and reform were never so much the issues for Americans: White and Roosevelt after 1912 were going to have to recognize that most Americans still had baser interests at heart. The battle between spiritualism and materialism within the greater community made for good rhetoric; but if social justice ever was to be a fully waged crusade, that occasion appeared a long way off.[29]

White did not easily give up. The cherubic faces he recalled at Armageddon were not figments of his imagination; he had written about such people for years. Middle class, economically secure, college educated, professionally aspiring—the interest of these people in spiritual matters over material may well have been real; certainly they paid an inordinate amount of lip service to the ideal. They were not, however, representative of the great majority of Americans. It was to take two years of hard work and the devastating Bull Moose defeat of 1914 for White to recognize that he, Roosevelt, and the moralistic Progressive Party constituted a distinct minority interest in the country. White then made an agile, rhetorical about-face to account for the political reversals. Having ridden the high tide of the Roosevelt presidency and the Republican insurgency, White had claimed that he and his fellow travelers spoke for all the people. In defeat, in reaction, he took a decidedly less tolerant view of the matter.

In "The Ebb Tide: Can the Progressives Come Back?" written in December 1914 for the *Saturday Evening Post,* White trimmed his reformist sails and redefined the "true" progressive constituency. Progressivism, he charged, politically had triumphed in the last decade; the people, unfortunately, had yet to arrive. The majority was coming into its own, into middle-class affluence and opportunity. Most individuals, nevertheless, still could not understand and embrace the real meaning of evolutionary reform. The greater community was still made up of warring interests seeking reform for individualistic material ends, disregardful of the highest purpose of an enriched, middle-class society: they could not see that there was plenty for all, and that all must be shared; individual happiness and social harmony could only be achieved through altruism. Realizing that his earlier perception of a materially endowed, spiritually saved majority had been wishful thinking, White now took a political scalpel to the emergent middle class. True believers in the progressive cause, he concluded, were middle class, but the entire middle class demonstrably did not believe. The average folks, the masses, the common people formerly included in the enlightened majority, took on new status: these people were crass, in need of further enlightenment. Those who had stuck with the Progressive Party were the only fully arrived middle-class citizens. Where the Bull Moosers lived, and voted, lay America's future. This was the most important lesson of the election:

> Practically the only thing really proved by the recent elections about the Progressive Party is that it is, as it stands, a middle-class party. It polled its best strength in the home wards of the smaller towns—towns of from five thousand to fifty thousand inhabitants; and in those wards, where wide lawns and shade trees and comfortable houses and happy families give color to the social structure of the community, the Progressives polled a heavy vote, and in many cases carried those wards rather decisively.
>
> In those wards live merchants, chief clerks, doctors, lawyers, the high-grade mechanic, the superintendent, the railroad conductor and engineer—the poor plutes of the Socialist catalogue—the college professor, the preacher and the small capitalist. . . . All of them are seekers after light and many of them are "Godsakers"—persons who, according to Mr. H. G. Wells, are forever crying, on hearing of the wrongs of others: "For God's sake, let's do something about it!"

Here, in small-town America, the middle class had arrived—here lived the righteous prepared to lead the nation to its salvation. Representing the best elements and long-term interests of the greater community, these

Americans who had voted Progressive had to remain active, to choose issues and battle sites, to win the hearts, and the votes, of the emergent majority. The Progressive Movement would survive even if the party died. The battle between spiritualism and materialism would continue, and the highest principles in the end would triumph:

> These tides in politics and business, and in all social activities, represent the growing and waning of popular attention. The crowd's mind is a child's mind—it cannot concentrate its attention long on one object; but through all the tides that wash the shores of time, where the child is playing, always it holds fast to the good and stores it up for the race. Nothing vital is ever lost.
>
> Men come and go; movements rise and fall. The people forget faces—they forget slogans—they forget parties and the issues of the day; but always, from the slow, resistless current of life that streams by this vale of tears, we take the good and let the worthless pass.

White had not given up hope. The children of the middle class would come of age, and national progressivism in all its glory would reign triumphant.[30]

For all the paternalistic rationalizing, it all nonetheless looked bleak after 1914. William Allen White and the others clinging to the remnant of the Progressive Party were wandering in a political wilderness. The Republican Party, from which most had deserted, once again was in firm conservative control. The Democrats, meanwhile, were proceeding to enact most of the 1912 Bull Moose platform. In "The Republican Party," written in July 1915, White emotionally plotted his position as he juxtaposed the goals of his party to those of the Democrats and particularly the Republicans. The Democrats were directionless, unenlightened as to true progressive ideals, he argued. His old party, on the other hand, knew exactly where it was headed—backwards. Crassly materialistic, the Republicans were concerned solely with individualistic accumulation, offering only the grossness of consumption as a sop to the masses. They had become the party of negation, with no interest in a humanistic agenda. The Progressives, with little hope of survival as a party, still had destiny on their side, White parried. They retained their principles: "Ours is a creed of faith—not negation. We preach the gospel of the eternal 'yes.'" He pointed to progressive legislative victories and defensively argued that the Progressives were not millenialists: they did not expect perfection; they simply believed that the people ultimately would turn from the materially obstructed low road of the established parties and take the higher road of altruism. It was simply a matter of time—more than they had reckoned.[31]

Time, however, was running short, and White knew it. As early as 1911 he had observed that the only real threat to the long-range success of the Progressive Movement was war. After August 1914, he referred periodically to the diversionary problem of the European conflict. But from the trough of political defeat the war began to take on new meaning. The battle in Europe began to tower as an opportunity to bring the Progressive Movement to its just end. White was slow to rally to the side of the interventionists, but once enlisted he became an ardent warrior. He took Wilson at his word—the crusade rhetoric was familiar. Here was the opportunity for a righteous people, freed of selfishness, to lead the way as a single-minded community to a new world order. Here was the historic chance to resurrect, in one fell swoop, a truly progressive community.[32]

Military matters never held much interest for White; he wrote just one article from 1914 to 1918 dealing with the nuts and bolts of the war effort—a U-boat piece in 1917 for *Collier's*. He wrote more relating to the war cause. These commentaries were a product of his journeys to France as a liaison for the Red Cross and as a syndicated reporter covering the Versailles Peace Conference. The conference ultimately would be a story of postwar disillusionment; the articles from the field were prime crusade documents. White gloried in middle-class victory as he directed most of his attention to the missionary army. In "The Doughboy on Top of the World" he depicted the occupying soldiers as morally pure, representative of a righteous middle-class society back home. And here was a world receptive to America's blessings. Writing in "The Highbrow Doughboy" of the educational opportunities provided for the soldiers overseas, White pointed to a significant lesson lodged outside the army's schools:

> Now a most important feature of the educational work of the A.E.F. [American Expeditionary Force] University was not in the catalogue. It was the town of Beaume—an old French town that was built in Roman times. It is a beautiful town, typical of the best that is France. More than Paris it carries the spirit that made France the savior of the world in the great days of September, 1914. It is a decent middle-class French town with no poverty and small riches among its people. In the long, narrow streets or under the old lindens of its lovely boulevards kindly French people greeted the American boys, not as a broken people whose hearts are in mourning, not in a shattered civilization such as the Americans saw in the wrecked towns of northern France, near the battle-front. These citizens of Beaume in an organized community, surrounded by things they and their ancestors have loved for a thousand years, presented a newer and happier aspect of France to the soldier students than they had been used to seeing.

Here, for White, were the spoils of war. The middle class of Beaume, as of the United States, organized into one community, represented the best, the world's salvation. In Beaume White saw not the shattered civilization of the past nor cosmopolitan Paris; rather, he found the enlightened brothers and sisters of those decent folk who had clung to the progressive torch back home—the old Bull Moose contingent living in America's small towns, "neither rich nor poor," preaching "the gospel of the eternal 'yes.'" The citizens of Beaume heartily welcomed the emissaries of the new progressive order. To Beaume, the American Promise had come home.[33]

■ ■ ■

With war, and now peace, a momentous opportunity had dawned fully outshining the hopes of 1912. In a message of thanksgiving in November 1918, before leaving for the peace conference and France, White spoke to his fellow Emporians of the significance of the moment. "The season," he proclaimed, "is one of great worldwide rejoicing, as for something lost that is found." Still, his feelings were mixed: "For to make the world better we must conquer ourselves—our own greed, our own selfishness, our own tyranny."

> And unless the great war has made us all feel the pull of brotherhood in our hearts, unless we all feel that we are willing to compromise the vast differences which men must have living in civilization, unless we are willing to submit to some injustices for the larger justice to our neighbors, then we shall soon have the same old world. But this is a season of almost Messianic hope. That hope in the heart of humanity indicates a new vision in the heart of humanity, which would seem to foretell a better day for the world. And for this hope, even though it shall not be entirely realized, for the hope that foretells a new heaven and a new earth, which sooner or later shall come, we should give our thanks today. For the hopes of one age have been the realities of the next. And because this hope today is fair, we may know that tomorrow will be also fair.

Having cautioned against expecting too much, White set off for Europe fully prepared to see the consummation of a new world order.[34]

Perched once more at Armageddon, White would see the nation shy from embracing its destiny. His prophecy of a harmonious order would fall far short of fulfillment as the nation conservatively retreated into the twenties "New Era" and as the international community failed to reach satisfactory accords. Nevertheless, preaching to his townspeople of regeneration, of the triumph of the selfless community, White in 1918 spoke what had become a relevant, distinctively national language. For close to two decades a mass movement, encompassing diverse legions of progressives, had swept across the political landscape. Public opinion had become a potent force, the media had grown in influence, and a national dialogue of reform had developed. Theodore Roosevelt was the most important single factor in the emergence of this dialogue. Many have questioned his reform credentials but few have denied him credit for making progressivism the paramount issue of the day. Roosevelt in particular spoke of social harmony, unfurling a rhetorical banner under which millions comfortably could gather. Sharing Roosevelt's politics, appreciating the power of public opinion and the media, William Allen White, too, took up the rhetoric of social harmony; he studied its meaning, refined its terms, and ultimately helped to establish it as a viable lexicon within the national discourse.

Russel B. Nye in his classic study, *Midwestern Progressive Politics,* challenges both Roosevelt's and White's contributions to the Progressive Movement. While acknowledging Roosevelt's key role in establishing a national dialogue, Nye takes both the president and his publicist to task as ideologically compromised reformers, opposed to the purer Middle Western progressive of the La Follette ilk. Yet surely as important as any progressive wing or ideology was the development of a language by which diverse groups of reformers, lobbying for parochial concerns entangled within a cosmopolitan web of competing interests, could communicate. Both Roosevelt and White grasped the importance of such a discourse and, significantly, sensed the relevance of social harmony to millions of men and women caught in the throes of change. White went further than Roosevelt and most of his contemporaries as he tackled the knotty issues of middle-class identity and the meaning of community within the evolving twentieth-century order. His social perspective was deeply rooted in Nye's politically "pure" Middle West—from it he developed a practical definition of class and an appealing set of communal values. His slightly anti-urban bias, his emphasis upon common sense, and his concern for the common man and small-town values spoke well to the needs of an emergent middle majority seeking some semblance of harmony within a heavily urban, industrialized society.[35]

Grappling with the subtleties of social harmony within a trying period of social change, William Allen White—townsman, novelist, political activist, and national commentator—had developed by the end of the Progressive Era a serviceable language of community. He was well prepared for the New Era. In the 1920s he offered a sophisticated interpretation of the social order cloaked in Middle Western simplicity. He found an even more receptive audience than he had had in the reform era. Ensconced as the Sage of Emporia within a contentious national community, White sent out a message of social harmony which struck home to millions of Americans.

CHAPTER FOUR

Fashioning the Model American Community

F OLLOWING THE GREAT WAR, William Allen White's nurtured use of the small town as a rhetorical device and his interest in broader questions of community served him well. Swept aside by politicians and literary critics as old-fashioned in the rush of the New Era, the aging progressive settled back in as the country editor of Emporia, Kansas. The town proved to be an advantageous post from which White could monitor, as he frequently observed, "the passing show." The *Emporia Gazette* editor hardly was on the sidelines. The twenties were years of great activity and personal success for White. During this period he secured his position as a national spokesperson: he acquired a reputation as a tolerant, yet critical, observer of the American scene, generally above discord, speaking for a greater harmonious order. He continued to write a great deal: He won a Pulitzer Prize in 1923 for his *Gazette* editorial "To an Anxious Friend," a widely applauded plea against the repression of free speech; two years earlier his editorial "Mary White," written in anguish following the death of his sixteen-year-old daughter, had attracted immense national attention. White regularly contributed political and social commentary to the national magazines and an occasional essay to a scholarly journal. He began, as well, to write biography, completing a study of Woodrow Wilson in 1924 and the first of two studies of Calvin Coolidge a year later. In 1926 White helped to found the Book of the Month Club; he would be a member of the editorial board for the remainder of his life. As the Kansas editor's fame increased, a host of social, political, and charitable enterprises eagerly sought and generally received his well-publicized support. In the postwar decade, Progressive Era–reformer William Allen White had metamorphosed into the popular Sage of Emporia.[1]

The Sage appeared to the world to be a mixture of personalities, a composite of 1920s Americana—a good-natured Babbitt and a sophisticated cosmopolite. Comfortable at home in Emporia, White enjoyed watering the lawn, reading in his porch hammock, shopping on Commercial Avenue, and passing the time with his neighbors. He was at ease speaking before his fellow Rotarians, discussing shared business and civic concerns, and boosting the hometown. He and his wife, Sally, regularly entertained neighbors while hailing a steady stream of famous visitors into their large house on Exchange Street. The Whites' circle was expansive: The couple made a home, as well, far from the confines of Emporia. Their interests were far flung and their tastes urbane. Friends, associates, work, and rest drew them out of Emporia six months a year. They wintered in the Southwest and summered in Colorado. White would return to write glowingly of the cultural riches and excitement found in watering holes such as New York, Washington, and Paris.[2]

This combination of provincial neighborliness and cosmopolitan urbanity proved attractive to friends and to his reading public. Popular novelist Edna Ferber, writing in 1925 of the Whites' famed hospitality, caught the appeal:

> The White family will call for you at the station, and return you to it. As you step off your train some one steps on it who is being farewelled by the Whites. As you board it twenty-four hours later there descends from it someone who is welcomed by the Whites . . . your twenty-four hours will be a mellow blend of roomy red brick house, flagged terrace, lily pond, fried chicken, books, ancient elms, four-poster beds, hot biscuits, front porch, old mahogany, deep-dish apple-pie, peace, friendliness, bath-rooms, Kansas sky, French peasant china, and the best conversation to be found east (or west) of the Rockies.

The White household appeared to enclose the best of two distinctive cultures: an old-world stability, calm, and compassion popularly assumed to be preserved in small-town life; and a reassuring familiarity with the hurly-burly of twentieth-century metropolitanism. Here was a comfortable environment within which one could easily and lucidly converse upon the parochial and germane problems of the world.[3]

By creative extension, in his writing White similarly portrayed Emporia to the rest of the country as a mix of provincialism and urbanity, as a perfected composition of *Gemeinschaft* and *Gesellschaft* in a perplexing world. In this manner he brought meaning to his isolated position as a country editor, and he gave form to his thought. In the postwar era it became important for White to decipher the meaning of community in American life. As he looked about him, what was wrong with America, as well as what was right, seemed to lie in the problem of community—in the changing structure of social relations within and across communities. He was quick to recognize that there was no singular American way of life, but he argued that there were certain desirable, broadly based communal traits to be nurtured within a complex society. Emporia offered not the answer but a direction. The primary need was somehow to remain neighborly within an increasingly alienating world. Presenting Emporia as a harmonious blend of *Gemeinschaft* and *Gesellschaft,* White could speak for the enduring hopes, if not always to the more parochial concerns, of many Americans. White's language of community proved to be as comforting and as popular as a stay in the big red brick house on Exchange Street.

In the 1920s, then, White's long-term concern with social harmony, his developing sense of an idea of community, and his feel for a language of community came to be attached to Emporia. He had dallied with the small-town idea for years in his commentary, using it to convey an ideal of social harmony. In literature he vigorously had courted the town as a metaphor for idyllic communal values. Now he fully engaged his hometown as a rhetorical device to address the wide ranging problem of community in American life. White identified himself and his thought with the small Kansas community. Social harmony could be achieved in America, in all American communities, as William Allen White and his town had achieved it. "What's the Matter with America?" White would query in the 1920s; nothing, he would answer, that could not be located and resolved in "Emporia."

■ ■ ■

White's concern with deciphering the meaning of community in American life was no solitary enterprise in the 1920s; nor was he alone in using the small town to shed light upon the problem of community. Sinclair Lewis, Sherwood Anderson, and a legion of literary rebels lambasted the hypocrisy of small-town life while Zona Gale, Dorothy Canfield Fisher, and cadres of supporters rallied to defend village ways. H. L. Mencken, in his vitriolic attacks on the emergent cultural norms of the "Booboisisie," found an easy mark in America's smaller towns and cities. Presidents Harding and Coolidge tried to link themselves and Republican virtue to small-town values; and in 1928 Herbert Hoover battled Al Smith in a campaign that came down, for millions of voters, to a choice between small-town Republicanism and urban Democracy. By the third decade of the twentieth century the small town (and small city) had become an alarming symbol of disquiet over the changing patterns of life in a highly industrialized and urbanized society.[4]

Perhaps most representative of the interest in the smaller town and city as a symbol of the problematic cross-currents engulfing twentieth-century American life was the publication in 1929 of the popular and critically hailed sociological work of Robert S. and Helen Merrell Lynd, *Middletown: A Study in American Culture.* In their pathbreaking research, the Lynds found 1920s Muncie, Indiana, to be caught in the throes of change. Muncie was a small, developing, industrial city within which the Lynds could still perceive multitudinous traces of small-town life; it was a city which they believed they still legitimately could tag with the quaint pseudonym of Middletown. For the Lynds Muncie was, in short, a perfect example of the problem of community in the United States—a town bobbing midstream between the powerful cultural currents of *Gemeinschaft* and *Gesellschaft.* In Muncie, the Lynds believed, lay America's dilemma and, significantly, its salvation.[5]

In many ways, what the Lynds were trying to use their sociological expertise to say with Middletown, so, too, William Allen White was attempting to use his rhetorical expertise to say with Emporia. The Lynds and White were setting up models, throwing into relief the problem of community, in the hope of suggesting a solution to the debilitating tug-of-war between *Gemeinschaft* and *Gesellschaft* that was hampering American life. In the work of the Lynds, and particularly in the thought of Robert Lynd that most influenced the Middletown study, lies an opportune insight into White's work and thought regarding Emporia.

While *Middletown* ostensibly was undertaken as an objective study of changing community in twentieth-century America, Robert Lynd in fact was intent on demonstrating a way out of what he perceived to be the fundamental dilemma of a broadening middle-class society committed to a vacuous set of values and norms—the unfortunate by-product of the immense material production of the nation. The problem was undisciplined consumption—consumption for consumption's sake—a process whereby vital, traditional communal patterns of living were being consumed along with automobiles, washing machines, cigarettes, sermons, and whiskey; a process whereby, in the now-classic words of the Lynds, "more and more of the activities of living [were] coming to be strained through the bars of the dollar sign."[6]

Robert Lynd saw Americans caught in a vicious cycle. His brief was not against an industrial- and urban-based economy but rather against the consumptive ethos which it had come to nurture. The huge size and power of the productive interests had led, in his view, to the fragmentation of community life with a concomitant loss of active and meaningful communal control over many of the community's own affairs. This loss, coupled with the increasingly passive focus on goods to fulfill one's needs in life, had led, in turn, to an abdication of individual responsibility for working out the social, economic, and political problems arising out of the complexities of twentieth-century life. The end result was a tendency by individuals to leave decisions affecting their lives and the life of the community to those with size and power, and to find meaning in life, and to fill the void once occupied by community commitment, with a growing number of goods. The importance of the individual as a contributing member of society had become lost in a vast, and ultimately meaningless, marketplace, and so too had the community.

Lynd believed people still had the power to halt the debilitating progression. It was incumbent upon them to rise up, exercise their will, and break the cycle. They had to be reeducated to make meaningful choices in life, to shun unnecessary goods, and to participate in community affairs; they had to reassert substantive control over their own destinies. Originally intending to enter the ministry, Lynd had believed in the necessity of spiritual and social leadership of an inherently good people caught in an oppressive environment. Losing his faith in God, Lynd turned from preaching a predetermined course of change to parishioners to teaching the limitless possibilities of choice to citizens. He believed that through an understanding of modern society one could help people to face facts and think through their problems, to intelligently find their own way to a more fulfilling existence. Having shifted his focus from the spiritual to the cultural realm, Lynd transposed the old battle of spiritualism and materialism into a conflict between *Gemeinschaft* and *Gesellschaft*. Individual salvation had become a matter of community. Individual regeneration could be accomplished by moving away from irrational, self-indulgent pecuniary habits, from *Gesellschaft* patterns of living, toward rational, selfless, cooperative participation in the life of the community, toward *Gemeinschaft*. Herein lay real fulfillment and a society truly rich in its freedom to tackle its own problems in its own way. Meaning in life could be recaptured, Lynd believed, with the reinstatement of the old virtue of service to society: the meaning of life lay in community.

In undertaking the Middletown study Robert Lynd harbored no bucolic illusions. He recognized that *Gemeinschaft* inexorably was giving way to *Gesellschaft,* but he did not accept the notion that all the older patterns of living necessarily had to cave in to a new order. Unlike Robert Park and the influential Chicago school of sociologists, Lynd turned away from the ethnically mixed, large cities for his understanding of social development, away from the seemingly inevitable advance of *Gesellschaft*. Lynd looked for a vanishing locale where *Gemeinschaft* remained a clear alternative within a domineering *Gesellschaft* world. He sought an atypical, traditional, Protestant town, a model visibly demonstrating the potential of retaining vestiges of *Gemeinschaft* within a rapidly evolving *Gesellschaft* culture. And so Robert Lynd turned to Muncie, to Indiana. to devise a case study which might serve as a beacon to enlighten people, to redirect them from their pecuniary interests to the worthier social aims of community.

Lynd's choice of Muncie reflected his Middle Western upbringing, his bias toward town life, and, possibly of most importance, his faith in the "substantial type of American" found in the Middle West—native born, Protestant, with a long tradition of democratic participation—as opposed to the acquiescent, foreign-born workers of Eastern cities. In Muncie there were few blacks, immigrants, Catholics, and Jews. The citizens, in Lynd's view, possessed the democratic will and intelligence to take matters into their own hands in the best *Gemeinschaft* tradition, to contend with the great economic, political, and social forces infringing upon their lives, and to turn those forces toward the consummation of higher communal ends at home and abroad in the land. Muncie, as other communities across the nation, was under seige. But here, in the heartland, Lynd believed he could demonstrate the possibility of rallying a proud, resilient, and capable people into the vanguard of social progress; through education and conversion to a selfless ethos, salvation was possible for the greater American community, as it was possible for Muncie. Indeed, Robert Lynd believed that in an idealized "Middletown" lay America's last hope to form a viable, twentieth-century communal order investing the best of *Gemeinschaft* within a *Gesellschaft* world.

William Allen White shared this belief. In fact, White shared a good number of ideas with Robert Lynd. Like Lynd, White held no brief against a robust economy churning out a plethora of goods for a broadly based, middle-class society. He shared the sociologist's concern over the fragmentation of American life; and he despaired over a corruptive, consumptive ethos eating away at a once sound, more morally correct commitment to the greater community. White, too, believed matters could be turned around: an inherently good people needed to move away from self-indulgency toward participation in the life of the community in order to solve shared social, economic, and political problems. White also had switched sights from the spiritual to the cultural realm. Once he had recognized that the progressive-charted road to Armageddon was not about to be taken, he began to speak less of the great impending battle between spiritualism and materialism and more of the everyday skirmishes between older and newer ways of living. And like Lynd, White believed the people needed leadership: he saw himself, as a local editor and a popular national spokesperson, using his ken of modern society to teach people, to open their eyes to their real problems, and to find their own best way to a better world by reasonably working together. Service to society had to be the highest goal; the end product would be individual fulfillment within a richer community life.

Trusting in the people to make their own decisions, White, like Lynd, placed the bulk of his faith in the native-born, Protestant, democratic Middle Westerners whom he knew best. Where Lynd found Muncie to be a prime sociological model for Middletown, White found Emporia to be a prime rhetorical model. This purportedly atypical, traditional hamlet, blending old ways and new ways, demonstrated the potential of retaining some form of *Gemeinschaft* within an evolving *Gesellschaft* world. In Emporia intelligent citizens were capable of cooperatively contending with the economic, political, and social forces infringing upon their lives; Emporians were capable of turning those forces to higher communal ends. In the heartland, in Emporia, lived a people willing to work together, prepared to establish a socially progressive city upon a hill.

As Robert Lynd, then, through *Middletown* intended to reeducate Americans in communal ways, so, too, White had plans for Emporia. Vanishing small-town habits, and most importantly a selfless ethos, could be regenerated across the country as the virtuous citizenry of Emporia held to the core. So White, through the twenties, thirties, and early 1940s, pictured Emporia to the nation.

Closer to home, of course, the battle against selfishness was less decisive, and communal victory more dubious. Emporia, as Muncie, evinced the problem of community as much as any possibility of its resolution—both towns were more typical than either White or Lynd had imagined. Emporia "potentially" could harmonize old and new ways; White had his work cut out for him. Nevertheless, the editor of the *Gazette* intended to make Emporia a workable model. His town could be fashioned into a better community.

■ ■ ■

Throughout the 1920s the news, editorial columns, and advertising of the *Emporia Gazette* typeset a community caught between *Gemeinschaft* and *Gesellschaft*. A sophisticated newspaper for a community of ten to fifteen thousand residents, the *Gazette* reflected its owner's sensitivity to a small community's intense preoccupation with itself and its growing awareness of its relationship to the outside world. Before the First World War the *Gazette* primarily carried local news and advertising. After the war community affairs took up the same amount of space, but national news and advertising received considerably greater emphasis. Within the *Gazette*'s six to twelve pages, published Monday through Saturday, 1920s readers encountered the traditional spread of local news and announcements, regional reports, and farm notes. More prominently they faced up-to-the-minute Associated Press news stories and wire-service photographs featuring Hollywood starlets, European royalty, and the latest criminal sensations; New York society notes, national sports coverage, and syndicated special-interest series; reviews of the arts, as well as commentaries upon the latest fashions and fads sweeping the country; and, starting in 1920, despite Editor White's reluctance to lower his standards, the nationally circulated "funnies" graced the pages of the *Gazette*. Whether it was a city election or the Coolidge-Davis-La Follette race of 1924, a local real estate scam or the Teapot Dome scandal, a county murder or the Fatty Arbuckle trial, the high-school basketball victory or the Dempsey million-dollar gate, the new county road or Lindbergh's flight to Paris—the *Gazette* covered its expanding beat fully and fairly, keeping Emporians well informed of their close-knit world along with the increasingly familiar environs beyond Exchange Street.[7]

Within the *Gazette*'s daily editorial page—running from an inch of commentary to six lengthy columns—Editor White might discourse upon one to ten wide-ranging topics, offering, as he did in the news pages, a sampling of his take upon the cross currents of modern life. Most editorials were written explicitly for the *Gazette;* on occasion White would reprint or excerpt portions from his syndicated newspaper and magazine articles or from his recently delivered speeches. The editor often passed judgment on local, regional, national, and international political affairs. He praised the civic contributions of Emporia's bankers, churchmen, and women's groups; he bewailed the town's "low-brow" attraction to the movies—not in keeping with Emporia's reputation as "the Athens of Kansas." One day White might print an articulate declaration of his own or a prominent educator's social philosophy and follow up the next day or in the next column trading professional barbs with an editor from Iola, Kansas City, or New York. Boosting Emporia with the pep of the heartiest "good fellow," "'ol Bill" regularly lodged in his columns stinging critiques of a debased commercial order. He sympathized with the labor struggles of Emporia's workers, and he wrote erudite analyses of national and international labor and capital conflicts. Constantly worried over reaction at home and saber-rattling across Europe, White campaigned in the *Gazette* throughout the postwar years for a lasting peace based upon reason rather than force, be it within Klan-infested Emporia or Fascist Italy. Every year he editorialized upon the change of seasons: autumnal harvests, curbside elm plantings, and flowering spring gardens received their due; and day in and day out, he noted the deaths of Emporia's bums and its philanthropists, as well as the nation's loss of its luminaries. Whether it be Rudolph Valentino or Charles Eliot Norton, Samuel Gompers or Frank Munsey, Woodrow Wilson or Henry Cabot Lodge, or Andy Armstead, Emporia's "colored policeman" of twenty-seven-years' standing, all the world's citizenry seemed to find a place in the editorial columns of the *Emporia Gazette*.[8]

Emporians, clearly, had at their disposal on page four of the town's only substantial newspaper an insight into William Allen White's view of the passing show. If the subscribers cared to read the editorial page, it was not difficult to catch the drift of the editor's thought. While White gave himself plenty of intellectual leeway—on occasion critics disposed of it as tomfoolery—to tell the truth as he saw it at the time, while he admitted his views shifted in reaction to changing events and personal whims, and while the odd editorial could wildly stray into overt racism or chauvinism, for the most part he stuck to a moderate mainline of opinion. Seeking to locate "the inherent good" in people, White's biases gravitated to the interests of what he considered to be the "best" elements of society—the professionals, business people, educated clerks, well-heeled farmers, and skilled workers. Believing in the worthiness of the democratic impulse of the people, his ideal citizenry in the *Gazette* editorial columns tended to be white, Anglo-Saxon, and Protestant, adhering to what White perceived to be mainstream American values and norms. These citizens White saw as middle-income earners, residents of a middle-sized, quintessentially American community, and most important, they were securely lodged within the middle class or they were actively aspiring to join its ranks. Amongst these individuals White looked for what he deemed to be a progressive expression of social cohesion. He looked to these citizens to open their doors to all Americans, to allow the dispossessed a chance to fulfill what he still believed to be the American promise—entry into a middle-class society of true equality, within a land rich in opportunity for all its inhabitants to occupy a broad middle ground of material comfort, higher education, and secure, self-respecting work. In his editorials, year in and year out, throughout the 1920s, White eagerly worked to arouse those he considered to be well-to-do—to shake them out of their apathetic state, to inspire a sense of social solidarity. In so doing, he expected they could fill a moral void in their own lives and within American life.

At base, White was a democratic elitist. As in the suddenly bygone days of Theodore Roosevelt and the Progressive Movement, while caring for the welfare of all Americans White looked within Emporia of the 1920s mostly to those, as in 1909, "whose chief thought is not for money—men and women who form the bulk of the well-housed, well-clad, well-fed prosperous body of the people neither rich nor poor." These were the paragons; these were the leaders. In his editorials White claimed to speak to their intelligence; he sought to offer them an escape, a means to turn away from themselves and postwar crassness and once again to look toward their fellow men and women. He believed he offered a groaning board of possibilities—be it by participating in the local "Y" drive, aiding flood victims of a neighboring community, supporting progressive legislation in Washington, or demanding League of Nations membership—a healthy means for the good folks of Emporia to give of themselves for the good of all.[9]

Where it would all end, White did not know. Where the good men and women would take the community, he was not sure. But he did know, as he emphatically made clear in the editorial columns of the *Emporia Gazette,* this was the right route to a better community, to a more just world at home and abroad. Throughout the 1920s, surveying the local, national, and international scene, White used the *Gazette* to help Emporians find their way—to fashion a model American community, to take the lead in America's passing show.

■ ■ ■

Following the Armistice of the First World War, William Allen White spoke to his fellow Emporians with great optimism regarding the postwar order. Editorially tracing developments in Washington and Europe and reporting from Versailles during the winter and spring of 1918–19, White cautiously anticipated Woodrow Wilson's success in securing his treaty and a League of Nations. He wrote in "The Second Coming of Wilson," from Paris in late March 1919,

> Just now [Wilson] is having the fight of his life; here in the conference, and there in America. The old world of Nationalism, of individualism, of laissez faire at home and abroad, the old world that was not its brother's keeper, is battling for its life. It will be a long fight; this is merely the first round. This decade will not settle it. The new idea, the idea of social democracy, of international responsibility, of the genuine brotherhood of man will not spring full-panoplied into power. It is an epoch's fight. And today America, through its President, is the chief defender of the new faith.

For the crusading Kansas editor, a new era in human relations aggressively dawned.[10]

White was heavily preoccupied with the treaty and the League of Nations question throughout 1919 and 1920. He was equally concerned with domestic matters. If America was to lead the way within a new epoch, it was imperative that the nation get its own house in order: social democracy began at home. While White spoke of a long fight, and while he recognized the immediate difficulties for the League in the United States, he really reckoned upon an early and a decisive victory for justice upon the home front. The new faith, epitomized for White by Wilson's messianic posture at Versailles, was decidedly old-line progressive in nature. And it was a hero of yesteryear, Theodore Roosevelt, to whom White looked to lead the charge into the new era. In November 1918, White rushed to capitalize upon the Republican congressional victory; he wanted to develop a "thorough-going progressive policy" for the party:

> There is just one Republican leader who can develop that policy, and that leader is Theodore Roosevelt. He may not enter the promised land of the presidency; that is really unimportant. But he is the only Moses who for the next eighteen months can formulate and put through a policy of progressive reconstruction. We are not going back to the old order. The railroads never will be what they were a year ago; labor will not be sold again in the open market; the society of nations never again will be a freebooter's paradise. Price making of necessities like wheat, meat, fuel, and cloth will never again be left to speculators on exchange. Life for the average man after this war will contain more than it held before of creature comfort, of civilized amenities. But these things will not happen automatically. They will happen only if the Republican Party in majority in Congress rises to an appreciation of its great duty. If it fails to appreciate its responsibility, then the Democratic party will come into power for a generation as the liberal party of this Nation.

Savoring a triumphant return to party power of the "prodigal" progressive Republicans and encouraging a Roosevelt run for the presidency, White looked forward to the 1920 campaign.[11]

Contending that an "economic revolution" was in the offing after the war, White argued that only the Republicans could meet "the new needs of the new nation":

> For in the Republican party are the constructive minds of the nation. The Republican party is the dynamic force of America. It always looks forward and not backward. It attracts minds full of optimism, not of despair. And when it has choked the life out of the profit hogs of one sort and another, who have dominated its party organization from Wall Street for the past decade or two, it will be again the great party of the great aspiring common people that it was under Lincoln.

But Roosevelt was dead by 1920, and the aspiring common people turned not to progressive Republicanism but to Warren Harding, who had other business in mind. In an ironic turn of events the economic revolution White predicted did occur, but it proved to be of an unexpectedly crass and popular nature. White found himself philosophically out of step with the people—and out of power within the Republican Party. Hard on the heels of Harding's smashing victory, he despaired in the *Gazette:*

> Today we are living in a hard boiled world. The joy of sacrifice is gone; the vision of brotherhood is departing. Nations have shown their greed, and statesmen have been unashamed of raw cunning. Whole peoples have been seduced into crass selfishness, and the receding wave has left all the ugliness and selfishness, and fear and gloomy terror that haunts the human heart in secret exposed in indecent indifference.

It was Armistice Day, and White wondered for what end had the world sacrificed so much "blood and treasure": "How long, O Lord, how long shall we wait upon thy coming!"[12]

The Harding administration, of course, proved to be a political disaster for the reformers. White had little to say for the president and his policies; occasionally he rallied as the administration supported a progressive measure. Upon Harding's sudden death in 1923, the editor drew out a short eulogy to "a leader who had piloted [the nation] through the stormy sea of reconstruction." While aware of the erupting scandals, White generously concluded with an unintentional prophecy, "His name in history will stand out among the presidents."[13]

History would soon judge Harding harshly, and so, too, would White. The *Gazette* editor, however, reflecting the interest of his readers, had become more riveted to the president's successor and the gloss of the New Era and less attentive to the leaden underside of "the Republican Ascendancy." Giving Coolidge his fair due as an honest and tested leader, White futilely warned the president and his coterie of an impending popular progressive reaction; finally, clearly errant, he resigned himself to the "unbeatable" reign of "Coolidge Prosperity." From the 1924 Republican convention in Cleveland he tried to explain to Emporians the meaning of the new order. Reporting upon the demise of business-controlled back-room politics and "the sloppy, noisy, fatuous crowd of 'whoopers-up' that one sees in the hotel corridors and around the convention," he depicted a more fashionable style representative of a new day:

> The general impression that one gets of the convention and its crowd is a Rotarian impression. Busy young gentlemen in fairly well cut clothes and nobby straw hats, better than decently neck-tied, who are putting spirit

and snappy pep into the proceedings. The whisper is gone. Orders come from Butler's room, the Coolidge manager, with a certain tone of authority as from the general superintendant's office or the head of the sales department.

Sales—it all seemingly had come down to goods.[14]

After the election, in a Thanksgiving message to his readers, White eyed a world across the board cashing in on "good times." Surveying Emporia and its environs he declared in Bryanesque tones: "Kansas has never had such a year for material prosperity. Great crops and high prices have come together for once in a lifetime. Farmers are paying their debts and the farmers' creditors in the towns are paying their debts, and money from the soil—the great source of wealth—is flooding Kansas with riches." Looking further abroad he sounded a McKinlesque trumpet:

> The nation is enjoying a prosperity which recalls the good old times before the war. Every form of business is speeding up. Industry, agriculture, merchandising—all are running on top speed and full time. Labor is making splendid wages. Capital is getting large returns. Every one is at work. Every dollar hunting an investment is finding a place to earn a fair return. The business of making money and making prosperity is in fine condition. The American people never before have had such an outlook for the good things of this earth.

Around the world White noted a similar preoccupation with materialism. He rationalized the waning interest in social reform: "Slowly the world is moving forward—as fast as it can, with the people as they are. Progress is coming as rapidly as the hearts of men will let it move." He concluded, scanning the new order, that the people were not much interested in his brand of progress:

> The forces which are interested in justice, rather than prosperity, are in eclipse. This is not their day. Justice will come along, lagging in a decade or so; maybe sooner. But this is no time to hamper progress by splitting hairs about justice. When everyone, high and low, is tramping on his neighbor to get to the trough, there is no sense in planning out an equitable route and a fair line-up. The sting of injustice must come before the demand for justice will appear in this country. As it is, we are satisfied and happy. The devil taking the hindermost, really hasn't much fodder for there is no hindermost. When the cramp comes in the times, justice will cry out. But it has not come. We are all happy—and too prosperous to care much what happens to the other fellow. The under dog has a fairly good slop route, and no one talks of taking him to the pound. So we are all in good humor.

Complacent, apparently with no time for splitting hairs over justice, William Allen White along with the majority seemed to have become mesmerized by the glitter of the new era.[15]

But the glitter was on the surface, and White had not blindly affixed rose-tinted glasses. In February, 1925 he snapped:

> America in these days under the influence of the motorcar, the movies and the radio is getting a lot more economic abundance than spiritual pabulum and moral sense. So we are growing a population more and more permeated with blatant, dull, noisy, cheap half-wits who take propaganda of clever designing-greedy-guts in high places with well concealed motives!

Losing his confidence in the wisdom of the people, Editor White warned: "More and more is democracy in danger all over the world by reason, not of the machinery of autocracy, not because the people do not rule, but because they do!" In "The Cock-Eyed World," written half a year later, he despaired that the leaders in America (as elsewhere in the world) simply represented the public will:

> With the ascension of Calvin Coolidge to the presidency came also his kind to leadership all over America. The whole country since 1920 has been flooded with replicas of the Coolidgeian type. Governors' chairs are filled with stern, masterful, patient men who believe in the divine right of capital to rule the various commonwealths. Mayors, district attorneys, constables—all reflect the mood of the American people. In another day the land was noisy with the rush and clamor of 10,000 little Roosevelts, and a myriad of miniature Wilsons hurrying about establishing justice and putting capital in its proper place in the scheme of things. They were not imitators. They came before Roosevelt and Wilson. If anyone was an imitator, it was the greater leader of the hour.

In a materialistic age the people had become a tarnished commodity, and so too had the nation's leadership.[16]

By the end of 1925 White wearily concluded the Progressive Era had come to a close. Whether he looked abroad, toward Washington, to the statehouse, or into his own backyard, the writing was on the wall. He urged his fellow townspeople to consider "the Emporia situation; after all this is an average town." He queried: "Who in all this man's town so far as The Gazette scouts have been able to ascertain, gives a tinker's red rosin dam what happens in this country if it doesn't happed [sic] to him? We answer sadly, no one; not a dad-burned soul."

> So far as we have been able to figure it out if thieves broke into the government and stole the gold dome of the library building at Washington, and filled it full of Liberty bonds from the treasury depart-

ment, then took it over to the White House, had it frozen solid and chunked it off for sale to the multitude there would be no important Emporia protest.

A month later, White memorialized his old friend Theodore Roosevelt. It had been seven long years since the colonel had died:

> In those seven years civilization has begun to show the tremendous change which the new century is working in the hearts of men. In those seven years many ideas that Theodore Roosevelt stood for during the climaxical years of his life, have been pushed aside for new issues. The old order has gone. The cause of social and industrial justice is not a vital cause in this modern world.

The new century no longer recognized Rooseveltian qualities: "For he was a man; brave, with drama in his daring; far-seeing, with a world vision in his eyes; big-hearted with magnanimity in much that he did. He stands out largely for what he was, for the size of his aspirations, for the sturdiness of his soul." This modern world, in contrast, adhered to money, goods, accumulation, and to a new rule. A year later, White tallied the ethical cost of the new order: "America has snowballed the material things of this earth into a vast accumulation of wealth and its evidences. But have we kept faith in spiritual things?"

> Where are the spiritual leaders of a world that needs faith worse than it needs steel and copper and oil and timber and phosphate? What are we doing toward the peace of the world except to look after ourselves and the main chances for ourselves? With all our leadership in machinery what are we doing for peace and goodwill among men?

Sadly the editor surmised, "them as has 'gits'—and 'gits' it in the neck."[17]

In an editorial written the same day as "'Them As Has Gits,'" White further indicted the leadership that a craven people had demanded and received in kind. He parsed "The President's Message" to Congress which ran "true to form": "Probably no other American who ever occupied the high office of president has ever delivered a message so full of facts and figures and so utterly lacking in emotion and that constructive vision which makes for leadership in times of change and stress." The editor called to justice the citizenry who would tolerate such a chief executive:

> The people of America have evinced no interest whatever in the emotional side of politics since the defeat of Woodrow Wilson. The American people are static. They are living under the burden of some terrible spiritual inertia. They are back in Grant's administration. They wish no change. They desire no betterment in conditions. They are overwhelmingly for the order that is.

The president, White determined, had struck the keynote of the age with a "message which might have been written on an adding machine." In short, "Democracy never was better vindicated than in the calling and election of Calvin Coolidge. Democracy is getting exactly what it wants in the way that it wants it. The few insurgents, kickers and idealists, among whom the writer is which, have a mandate from the American people to go way back and sit down until it hurts." In an era devoid of "change and stress," White concluded, "They also serve who only sit and wait."[18]

■ ■ ■

White would have to wait the decade out for a progressive political renaissance, for a more desperate era of "change and stress" which would call forth another Roosevelt, "brave, with drama in his daring." For the duration he was not content to sit. An era of unprecedented material comfort was omnipresent, replete with the more subtle stresses of changing manners and mores, and shifting associations. White felt compelled to comment. He found the new era to be both troubling and promising. White was not offended by changing mores, but he was bothered by the discounting of morality amidst plenty. In an editorial written in November 1922, he came to the defense of the excesses of the young—"the jungle dance, the petting parties, the all night shindy and the parked coupe." Youth, he declared, "is not to blame for its jazz joy." White criticized the elder generation:

> The war gave a lot of us an opportunity to pin on tails and climb into the trees. The profiteer who sandbagged his neighbors, the patrioteer who kukluxed his enemies, the desk soldier who swanked around afternoon teas while his betters were were [sic] dying, the politicians [sic] who let the drums do his thinking and the guns do his talking, the war worker who let his emotions govern his conduct and wasn't particular which emotion was running his behavior—all these let down a lot of bars that have kept society in bounds for hundreds of years. So there was more or less running hog wild upon the once prim laws of orderly society.

While condemning selfishness, White still hailed the revolutionary material progress engulfing and tempting the nation. The automobile epitomized the wealth of the new era. In 1925 the editor marvelled in "The Gas Buggy": "All America is buying cars. In the last 25 years this country has produced 24 million automobiles. . . . To buy and run these automobiles Americans have spent more than 40 billions of dollars." This was good:

America and the American people have become greater because of
the automobile. We would not step back to the mode of life 25 years ago
if the 40 billion dollars was showered down upon us with 7 per cent
interest. The motorcar industry has furnished remunerative employment for hundreds of thousands of workers. It is responsible for the
expansion of the oil industry with its army of employes [sic], and it has
fathered the good roads movement in the United States. The automobile
has put us 50 years ahead in our highway program.[19]

Still, it was all very disturbing. The goods were fine; the selfishness
associated with the goods was debasing. Looking about, White could only
hope the great material expansion would somehow pull people together.
The highway program was important, especially for a state like Kansas.
Automobiles and good roads were drawing Kansans into the prosperous
mainstream of twentieth-century American life. In 1923, writing of the
impending experiment in transcontinental air mail service, Editor White
noted:

Emporia is nearer the world today then ever it was before. . . . And
the nearer people are to one another the better they understand one
another. Hatreds and fears and suspicions arise largely through distance
—distances of race or class or geographical locations. As we obliterate
distance we bring fellowship into the world. The railroad, the telephone,
the radio, the airplane, are greater Christianizers than all the churches
and preachers.

In material expansion, then, lay the promise of consolidation and with it
the possibility people might think less of themselves as they moved "nearer
and nearer" their fellows. The goods could deliver an answer of their
own to the problem of *Gesellschaft*. Material plenitude could re-create
Gemeinschaft.[20]

Through the early postwar years that were strained socially and economically, White wrote scores of editorials in the *Emporia Gazette*: He
traced the battle of the farmer to hold on to his wartime profits; he
recorded the struggles of the labor movement; he analyzed the problems
facing the depression-plagued interests of capital; and he articulated the
position of a developing consumer sector of society caught in the middle,
hearing "a chorus of capital on one side and a chorus of labor on the other
shouting 'The public be damned!'" Postwar consolidation became White's
battle cry; he came to the conclusion that to survive in a complex urban-
industrial society individuals must organize. People, indeed, were edging
closer to one another, finding security along new lines of middle-class
association. Ultimately, White contended, the entire society was moving,
grudgingly, toward one large association of mutual interest. In the vision

of an emergent, selfless middle-class community, the aging progressive found relief amidst the vicissitudes of the New Era.[21]

"Association," indeed, had become the trademark of the era. Everywhere White looked he saw encouraging signs of progress, of people moving "nearer and nearer" to one another within a trying world. Writing in July 1919 of his mixed feelings over the radical Non-Partisan League's recruitment activities amongst Middle Western farmers, White protested that his gripe was with the group's leadership, not with its premise of strength through association: "The farmer is too much an individualist. He is too suspicious. He is too much inclined to think he can beat the game of life with his own brains, when organization is the only key to success in the modern world." The maxim held true across the board for all Americans. Writing the same day of the need for regulation of the meat-packing industry, White noted that the packers were "allied with the millers, with the railroads, with the bankers" into "'one big union'—a union of capital." They were "dead right" to organize. In turn, "'one big union' of labor" justifiably arrayed itself against the capitalists. The public, the consumers, were finding as well their own brand of safety in numbers: "There will be eventually in this country—at least by the end of the century, three of these 'one big union' combinations: One of labor, one of capital, and one of the public, which is a little of both." Within such association White perceived great promise. In an era of massive, consolidating, and conflicting interests, lay the possibility of fulfilling the greater common interest— equitable distribution of the national wealth. White looked to the federal government as the arbiter of the overwhelming national interest, ensuring the security of all Americans. The "greatest" of the new combinations, he declared, "will be the American government. It is to be boss on this continent."[22]

White's, and others', long-range view of the coalescing of such powerful combinations would prove to be prescient. Of course, White himself had a more pressing progressive axe to grind, especially in 1919. Yet whether he advocated his own immediate political agenda or sought long-term social goals, his editorial perspective throughout the tough years of the early 1920s remained consistent: He saw great changes occurring in American life. Aligning out of self interest along broad associational lines, Americans were slowly moving toward a community of singular interest. Agriculture, capital, labor, and the public needed to see this, to work together, to give as well as to receive. Constantly drumming away at this issue White tried to depict the emerging common interest. The nation was plunging headlong into an era of great abundance. All could and should have plenty. Looking to the rising worker as the greatest exemplar of the new age, White explained to Emporians amidst the industrial strife of late 1919 "What Labor Really Wants":

> High wages have brought labor into a different standard of living. High wages have distributed automobiles, moving pictures, middle-class amusements, middle-class comforts and luxuries, and middle-class aspirations in the working man's home. They have changed the wage earner's heart. He is not satisfied any longer to be a wage earner; he wants to be a partner. And he will not be satisfied until he is a partner.

A time of reckoning had arrived. It was imperative to offer the workers not only goods but a seat in management: "It may be right, or it may be wrong, but we might as well make up our minds as middle-class citizens of a middle-class republic, to look the situation squarely in the face. The workman has come up into the middle class; he is demanding middle-class partnership of society." The hour had arrived, White believed, to give the worker due respect, to fully welcome him into the middle class—the moment had come to offer him not only goods but a guarantee to oversee their equitable distribution. The time had arrived to associate as equals.[23]

White had been speaking of the "partnership of society" since Bull Moose days. To his astonishment he began to see it roughly emerge within the "consciousless" prosperity of the Coolidge era. No matter that the government was not "bossing" matters in a progressive manner, nor that the worker remained outside the boardroom, a middle-class society was in the making. Americans, in his view, had divided into huge interest groups and had grappled their way to good fortune. After the election of 1924 and the inauguration of Coolidge Prosperity, White spoke less of battling groups and more of the fruition of the Great American Middle Class. Looking again to labor, by 1926 he could speak of the skilled worker as having reached some form of material equity if not full partnership within the new order:

> Everywhere are evidences that the man who works with his hands as a skilled mechanic is getting more out of life than his father got. Schools are filled with workingmen's children, and colleges also. Wherever workmen are congregated long ranks of motorcars are parked. New additions in every town, beautiful additions with lawns and trees and modern houses filled with what once were luxuries and now are comforts are occupied by workingmen and their families.

The worker had arrived—comforted as a junior partner into a middle-class addition. "Poverty in the United States," White surmised, "is gradually passing into song and story. . . . the man who works is entering his millenium."[24]

Entering the millenium was one matter; resting secure within it was another. White remained troubled by the refusal of the established order to grant the workers anything more than goods: the nation had yet to achieve a full distribution of justice. White was forever defining for his Emporia readers the meaning of a just, middle-class society. Class divisions, he declared in 1920, exist in the United States: "no one who examines our social and economic fabric can deny the fact of classes." But Americans of all classes, he went on to explain, deny the fact: "We have put it out of our consciousness." The nation was dominated by the middle class—politically, economically, and culturally—with an ever-increasing flow of workers aspiring to and entering its ranks. The middle class, he argued, was the victor of the war and slowly but surely was spreading its riches. The United States, White declared, "is tremendously middle class." Nevertheless, there were problems. A more equitable distribution of the nation's wealth was evident; an inequitable distribution of power represented a grave challenge to the new order. The classes remained engaged in a struggle to control this evolving middling society. Ceaselessly campaigning for the rights of labor, White beseeched the labor movement's leaders not to politicize their cause through class-aligned parties. Applauding the achievements of the nation's entrepreneurs, he warned the capitalists to hedge their greed and compromise their opposition to organized labor or reap a whirlwind of class warfare; and while singing the praises of the emergent middle-class majority, he as often chastised it as a selfish body ready to side with the wealthy against the needy, fearful of losing its social prerogative. There was, White determined, a mean edge to the nation's bounty—it was almost as if a more equitable distribution had been inadvertently achieved. A just society would make equality of position the first priority, from which all riches, material as well as spiritual, would flow. To attain abundance for all, to permanently eliminate poverty, to secure a truly middle-class society the people needed to respect the mutual interest of all citizens to more than goods: a common brotherhood was in order. The nation, White concluded, prided itself as middle class; unfortunately, it all still seemed a bit "cheap."[25]

■ ■ ■

White, hence, found himself in the 1920s hailing material progress and fearing spiritual declension, trusting in harbingers of consolidation and querying continuing division. It was all rather bewildering; and so he spelled it out day after day on the editorial page of the *Emporia Gazette*, telling the truth as he saw it at the time. White was quick to recognize great discrepancies within the commonwealth—equitable distribution of the national bounty was no fact of life in the 1920s. Still, like so many pundits, he was taken by the fact that an increasing majority of Americans seemed to be finding material well-being within their grasp. In 1926 he explained to a Socialist correspondent "what we mean by the ever recurring phrase in our editorial columns about 'the equitable distribution of wealth.'" The *Gazette* did not mean "the exact and continual re-division of wealth so that everyone always would have precisely the same amount of wealth." "The distribution of wealth is gauged not by money nor wages but rather by the rewards of labor in terms of material comforts—housing, food, clothing, leisure, education, and family life. Gauged thus the distribution of wealth in America is much more approximately equitable than it is anywhere else in the world." White went on to sugarcoat a good number of material differences still extant within the American social order, differences which in less apologetic moods bothered him a great deal. Nevertheless, differences had begun to appear to be more a matter of degree than of well-being itself. For the first time the great nineteenth-century dividing line between the "haves" and the "have-nots" seemed to be within crossing distance; the American people were approaching a twentieth-century middle ground within a materially reconciled middle-class order. If the nation, in White's view, would only raise its consciousness to match its standard of living; if the increasingly well-off would take less stock of their own good fortune and a fuller measure of the welfare of all others as a worthy goal; if those who had moved into the middle ground would move to establish an even more equitable distribution of life's comforts and opportunities, all would be more spiritually as well as materially secure in one another's abundant middling company. For White "middle class" meant respect for others as well as the fulfillment of the needs of others; this too was within reach, but few seemed to take notice. He was the last to sugarcoat this fact.[26]

One commodity, then, in short supply in the 1920s was selflessness. "Hatreds and fears and suspicions" based upon "distances of race or class or geographical locations" remained; but, White believed, Americans could overcome their differences as they moved into the broadened middle class. A moderating middle ground was open to them. White pointed to Emporia. This town was no middle-class haven, but it had come, White declared, about as near as any American community had come to bridging the gap between selfishness and selflessness. In this close-knit community laborers, businessmen, and professionals, whites, blacks, and Mexicans, men and women, young and old, and country and city folk mingled. Problems existed, but with the problems there stood a recognition amongst Emporians of the higher moral obligation to improve their neighbors' well-being. This materially blessed community as a whole was moving toward a communal salvation. Over and over in the *Gazette* White pounded out the message:

> Emporia is a pretty decent town; not as decent as it should be, for it has its social lepers and its unpleasant haunts, but on the whole a clean, honest, [*sic*] where men live equitably and peacefully and industriously. Generally speaking a man gets what he earns in Emporia, and mighty few people earn what they do not get, or get what they do not earn. That is one of the major tests of a community or of a civilization. There are no town factions, and nothing to quarrel about. Everyone pulls together. We have a strong community spirit and it works for the good of individuals by making them work for the town. Nothing helps a man so much as to devote several hours a day to the common good. Emporia is the kind of a town where every man lends a hand and not a hammer. We have learned to labor and to wait. And it pays.

In Emporia, White propagandized, the fulfillment of the American promise was close at hand. He was determined to move the community forward toward its just end.[27]

The rhetoric could seem overblown, but for White the message was not inflated. He knew the real Emporia was no halcyon haven of decency, honesty, and equitable distribution. This was not the issue for him; Emporia was moving in the right direction and had what it took to become an ideal community. Emporia stood as an atypical community: the town retained an old-world closeness and a recognition that it was part of a newer world. *Gemeinschaft* and *Gesellschaft* mingled in Emporia along with the citizenry on Exchange Street; Emporia stood as an example of the advantage, and the opportunity, of retaining neighborly relations within an alien world. Emporians had within their grasp the answer to the twentieth-century problem of community. White was intent upon convincing Emporians and the rest of America how good community life could be in the new age.

Emporia in the 1920s did appear, in many ways, to stand at a junction between two worlds. Demographically it seemed a throwback to the nineteenth century. The town, as surrounding Lyon County and the state of Kansas generally, was made up of a homogeneous, predominantly native-white citzenry. The foreign-born population of Kansas had peaked at 13.3 percent in 1870 and thereafter had steadily declined: in 1930 4.3 percent of close to two million Kansans were foreign-born. The vast majority of these immigrants had come from northwestern Europe. Migrants from other states had come from the Atlantic seaboard by way of New York, Pennsylvania, Ohio, Indiana, Illinois, and Missouri. Non-whites in 1930 made up 4.7 percent of the population: blacks constituted 3.5 percent while "other races" including Chinese, Japanese, and an increasingly large influx of Mexicans made up 1.2 percent.[28]

Still, while Emporians may have looked like nineteenth-century old-stock Americans, their way of life was hardly a throwback to an earlier era. Close to 40 percent of all Kansans were engaged in agricultural occupations; as many other Kansas towns, Emporia served as the hub of a large agricultural hinterland. Emporia, however, was not simply another farm town. The Santa Fe Railroad had invested millions of dollars to establish the town as a division headquarters. Emporians benefitted from the presence of two institutions of higher learning: the Kansas State Teachers College and the Presbyterian-affiliated College of Emporia. The self-proclaimed Athens of Kansas was no cultural oasis, but it did attract a respectable parade of touring performers: Anna Pavlova, Ethel Barrymore, Paul Whiteman, Harry Lauder, Hugh Walpole, and the St. Louis and Minneapolis symphonies, amongst a host of others, were to stop in Emporia in the twenties. Years of steady growth and a sudden population burst in the second decade of the new century had led White in 1920 to boast in "The Passing Decade" that prospering Emporia and its fourteen thousand residents had vaulted into the twentieth century:

> The passing decade has seeen [sic] a marked change in the American country town. Emporia is only typical of the best of those towns, wherein people are learning to spend money on the pleasant things of life. Ugliness of various sorts is slowly disappearing. The community spirit is growing. . . . A broader and broader section of the community is coming into an economic status which demands better things.

In White's lexicon Emporia, with the best of America, was becoming middle class.[29]

For the editor of the *Emporia Gazette,* however, middle class meant more than increased earnings, and he made sure Emporians knew it, too. As good middle-class citizens, Emporians demanded better things not only for themselves but for their fellow citizens. This was the essence of "community spirit." White continued on in his inventory, in "The Passing Decade," to tally ten years of communal progress. The list of accomplishments was extensive. It ran from the new high school, the country club, and the new suburban addition to the new YMCA and YWCA buildings; it sped through twenty miles of paved streets, sidling by the street cars and over the sewer extension; it hustled along to the new garages, by way of the improved Commercial Street store fronts, toward the "score of handsome residences and hundreds of beautiful comfortable bungalows and rebuilt houses." Not to be missed were the three new movie theaters, three new banks, the loan companies, and the mortgage companies; nor did it short-cut the Welfare Association and the county hospital as it hailed the inno-vative commission form of government overseeing the town's good fortune. It all added up to an enviable booster's list, but White believed a good deal more was written into the record than material progress. This community exemplified a new, twentieth-century American spirit:

> When it is considered that these things are not mere counters in new population, but are indications that the present population is living better, the real value of the gain is seen. The change is vital; it seems to prove that a deep social change is coming into American life. We are increasing our taxpaying class; we are decreasing our poor. We are dis-tributing better than the world ever saw wealth distributed, the earnings of the social unit.

The community, with deeply engrained, old-fashioned neighborly effort, had arrived, as one, into the mainstream of American material and spirit-ual progress. Emporia exemplified the American community spirit.[30]

In addressing his town White tried to amalgamate both sides of its character—and his own. He was a great booster. The YMCA and YWCA, the pretty gardens and elm-lined streets, the professional women and the Rotarians, the College of Emporia and the Kansas State Teachers College, the Santa Fe and the railway union—all received White's enthusiastic sup-port in the *Gazette* news columns and editorials, not to mention a large measure of his time and money. Ultimately, however, White was really much more interested in raising Emporia's moral sights than he was in boosting commercial sites. In 1921 Emporia faced the prospect of an oil boom—the great lubricant for towns to slip into the twentieth-century urban big leagues. It was exciting for the town and for White. In "The New Well," the editor warned Emporia that a lot more was at stake than a rich field close to town:

> The clash between the old town and the new one will be of interest. Oil came to ElDorado, and absorbed the town completely. Oil came to Wichita and Wichita overwhelmed the oil completely. Emporia is larger than ElDorado and smaller than Wichita. But it is hard-boiled in the belief that it is better to have a decent town than a big one. If oil comes, it will bring as neat a little contest of ideals as ever came into a Kansas community—and may the best man win.

There was little question who White was backing. The contest between old-world decency and new-world largesse, however, never took place as the oil revenues eluded Emporia. But, as White swelled in an editorial three and a half years later, decency had to have been the victor—carefully built civic ideals meant much more to Emporians than carelessly boomed civic development. Linking his own position to the idealistic ethos of the town, he explained in "An Editor and His Town,"

> An editor can build up his community only by preaching unselfish citizenship. The booster, the boomer, the riz-razzer who screams in headlines about the glories of the town gets nowhere. But the editor who, by his own practice as well as his own preaching, stands for decent things and encourages unselfish citizenship, glorifies giving and frowns on taking, has a constructive attitude which is sure to help his town. He may not bring more people in; that is as fate wills it. But he certainly can make life better and happier and broader and more comfortable for the people who live in the town. It is better to have 10,000 people living equitably and happy than to have 10,000 people growing fat upon the toil of 90,000 who live lean and sordid lives. The Gazette is printed in a community where there are 13,000 people, without a pauper, with every man at work, without a millionaire, with as many telephones as there are homes, as many automobiles as there are families, as many schools as the children need, as many books in the library as the public will read, with a municipal band, a bath tub in nearly every house, no home-made crime. The people in our jails come to town to get there, and we haven't an able-bodied person in the poor house.

Emporia, in White's brief, approached spiritual as well as material victory. In 1920s America Emporia was a middle-class community that worked—even if an outsider, not to mention a good number of Emporians, might question where the line was drawn between fact and fancy.[31]

■ ■ ■

Fact and fancy—White knew exactly where to draw the line. Rhetoric had its place; so, too, did hard truth. Emporia worked; but it could work harder. White often took his town to task for its shortcomings: discrimination against Mexican-Americans; ugly storefronts and disheveled gardens; crass, "low-class" taste in leisure entertainment; "boozing" in well-to-do suburban "Pepville"; stingy contributions to community drives—all and much more received the editor's stern attention. With the jeremiad always came the call: Emporia was, above all, a decent community, striving to be better; it had to try harder. Both the town and its editor would be put to a severe test in the early 1920s. Emporia's decency and White's commitment to the communal ideal ran up against a challenge cloaked in the garb of the Ku Klux Klan. The town took a body blow; the editor might well call the contest his finest hour.

In the spring of 1921 the resurgent, Georgia-based Ku Klux Klan launched a national membership drive. Under the banner of "100% Americanism," "Kleagle" recruiters crossed into Kansas, ostensibly to sign up Protestant patriots adhering to old-fashioned morals. Capitalizing upon postwar economic, social, and cultural disruptions as well as latent prejudices against blacks, Jews, Catholics, and foreigners, the financially astute organizers brought into the secret society an estimated forty thousand Kansans at ten dollars a head in membership fees. The "Invisible Empire" quickly materialized as a powerful political force in the state.[32]

The Klan made an early recruitment stop in Emporia. In July 1921 White confidently took its measure in the *Gazette*, "It is to the everlasting credit of Emporia that the organizer found no suckers with $10 each to squander here." By April 1923 Emporia had elected a Klan mayor. The following year both the Democratic and Republican parties nominated gubernatorial candidates sympathetic to the Ku Klux Klan. Wishing to garner as many votes as possible for their statewide tickets, the party leadership disingenuously claimed the organization was not an issue in the fall campaign.[33]

During the immediate postwar period White had despaired over reactionary and radical developments in the United States and overseas. He had spoken out early and forcefully to halt the Red Scare; he had condemned Bolshevism and militarism in Europe; and he had been quick to target the Italian Fascists as "Kluxers." In December 1919 within the maelstrom of the Red Scare, he ruminated:

> We are given to fads and fashions in this country. Vast crazes overwhelm us. A year ago it was the flu; two years ago it was Hun baiting; three years ago it was keeping ourselves out of war; four years ago Belgian relief; six years ago it was "social and industrial justice." Just now it is seeing Red. Always our crazes have a basis of common sense, but we are such a big country that the psychical momentum of a hundred million people makes us mad. We fly the track and go shooting into the booby zone at a tangent.

Now, with the Klan so close to home, White saw little sense in what was swirling around him. This craze had shot off the track and landed right in his own backyard; it collided with all that he believed in. He kept running anti-Klan editorials in the *Gazette;* as a result he became a subject for editorial attack by the Klan. White himself was not free of racial and religious prejudice; he did believe, however, that all people had a right to speak their minds and a right to fair opportunities to progress in American society. His biases were mild for his day and his fundamental faith in the constitutional order of society was strong. He could not tolerate the uncivil state of affairs rooting in his own town, and in Kansas. In May 1922, he innocently addressed himself to the Klan, adroitly explaining his position in "The Ku Klux Klan Again":

> The *Gazette* has nothing to gain by fighting the Klan. It is nothing to the *Gazette* one way or another, except that this paper feels that good will in a community is better than ill will, that friendly, open, neighborly relations are better than secret and hateful ones, that the Christian religion is a religion of fraternity, and not of jealousy, hatred, malice and suspicion. Except for those things the *Gazette* has no interest whatever in the Ku Klux Klan.

White's interest in community had run headlong into the Invisible Empire.[34]

The breaking point for White was the gubernatorial contest of 1924. Having seen his hometown and his beloved Kansas infected by the Klan, it seemed too much when his purportedly progressive Republican Party refused to take a stand against rabid reaction. During the summer he lobbied friends and associates to take up the cause of harmony, to run an independent third-party campaign on a strong anti-Klan platform, to advocate reason over force, to speak to the intelligence of the people, to educate the voters to express their democratic will—in short, to make a race for the sake of the community. None would take up the standard; in September White decided to forsake his lifelong reservation against seeking public office and make the run on his own. Except for the briefly infectious bite of the campaign bug, he had no interest in overt political power. More than the governorship of the state was at stake. For White, his faith in the people and his vision of a just society based upon mutual respect were on the line. On September 20, 1924, to the chagrin of the Republican state organization but with the support of some influential party members, White rallied to his own cause and announced his candidacy for the governorship. He hoped to capitalize on his reputation, contacts, past campaign experience, and his command of the language to clear the air. Despite the efforts of the two major parties the Klan was an issue, and he was going to make a campaign of it in Kansas and beyond. For White the Klan was the only issue that mattered: he wanted to set the record straight in Kansas and the United States regarding the meaning of community in America.

The campaign proved to be the most public and dramatic stand of White's life. Beginning in late September, in his Dodge touring car with his son Bill at the wheel and his wife, Sally, occasionally at his side, candidate White hectically travelled the state. He turned what aimed to be a dull, suppressed contest into an exciting, emotion-laden race with the Ku Klux Klan the fundamental issue. White addressed not only his own candidacy but the races of two other anti-Klan Republicans—the next attorney general and secretary of state would exercise key votes as members of the Kansas Charter Board determining the legal outcome of a lengthy battle over the corporate status of the Klan. Late in the campaign White expanded his platform to include a number of progressive reform planks, but his issue was well taken by big crowds and plenty of local, state, and national reporters. In the national press White received criticism and praise for his stand. The *New York World* ran a superb Rollin Kirby cartoon featuring a rifle-toting, corpulent William Allen White chasing a cowardly gang of robed Klansmen across a Kansas pasture. It was entitled "A Real American Goes Hunting"; White proudly ran the cartoon in the *Gazette*.[35]

White had a field day with the nomenclature of the Klan. In a speech tracking the Republican Party's gubernatorial nomination of Ben S. Paulen, he regaled his audience:

> The gag rule first came into the Republican party last May. A flock of dragons, Kleagles, cyclops, and furies came up to Wichita from Oklahoma and held a meeting with some Kansas terrors, genii, and whangdoodles. . . . A few weeks later, the cyclops, Kleagles, wizards, and willopses-wallopuses began parading in the Kansas cow pastures, passing the word down to the shirt-tail rangers they were to go into the Kansas primaries and nominate Ben Paulen.

While making fun of the "Kluxers," White hammered away at a serious message. The day before he announced his candidacy he ran an editorial in the *Gazette* celebrating the anniversary of the adoption of the Constitution. The nation rested, as did Christianity, upon the Golden Rule. The Constitution guaranteed both justice and self-respect to all Americans: "Charity, religious tolerance, neighborly give and take, political compromise, and the high aspirations of far-seeing men all are provided for under that constitution and its amendments. It has instituted in America the rule of reason and law rather than the rule of force." Now there stood opposed to the Constitution "an ignorant minority, a bigoted minority, a shallow minority that wants to solve all problems by ukase and decree." "There is nothing," White admonished his readers, "so dynamic in life as neighborly affection." It was time, he argued, to stand by reason and the Constitution: "Unless we approach our serious problems sanely, kindly, patiently and with a deep faith in the unswerving purpose of God and a corollary faith in the essential goodness of common man, we will get nowhere, and the work of the fathers who established our constitution is bound in the end to come to naught."[36]

White never let up; he was determined to draw the Invisible Empire out into the open and destroy it. In announcing his candidacy he protested this infestation:

The issue in Kansas this year is the Ku Klux Klan above everything. The Ku Klux Klan is found in nearly every county. It represents a small minority of the citzenship and it is organized for purposes of terror. Its terror is directed at honest, law-abiding citizens, Negroes, Jews and Catholics. These groups in Kansas comprise more than one-fourth of our population. They are entitled to their full constitutional rights; their rights to life, liberty and the pursuit of happiness. They menace no one. They are good citizens, law-abiding, God-fearing, prosperous, patriotic. Yet, because of their skin, their race, or their creed, the Ku Klux Klan in Kansas is subjecting them to economic boycott, to social ostracism, to every form of harrassment, annoyance and every terror that a bigoted minority can use.

The Klan, White elaborated, was a "nation-wide menace." But its Kansas presence was more difficult and pertinent to understand:

Kansas, with her intelligence and pure American blood, of all states should be free of this taint of bigotry and terror. I was born in Kansas and have lived my life in Kansas. I am proud of my state. And the thought that Kansas should have a government beholden to this hooded gang of masked fanatics, ignorant and tyrannical in their ruthless oppression, is what calls me out of the pleasant ways of my life into this distasteful but necessary task. I cannot sit idly and see Kansas become a by-word among the states.

There was only one conclusion: the word must go out that Kansas knew where to make its stand: "So I feel that I am walking the path of duty in going into this race. I ask my fellow Kansans to come with me and to stand with me for free government and the righteous guarantees of our constitution, to all its citizens." The issue, clearly, was a matter of the highest order: the issue was sound community.[37]

White had undertaken a hefty challenge. Entering the contest late, with virtually no organization, and depending upon his own financial resources, he never really had a chance. He did succeed in running a successful campaign highlighting his fundamental conception of community in American life. He came in third, garnering 149,811 votes; the Democratic incumbent received 182,861 votes and the Republican victor, 323,403. While losing the governorship, in all likelihood White's candidacy did secure the election of the anti-Klan charter board members (which ultimately would deny the Klan its coveted legal status). But White's greatest victory was in clearing the air, as he had intended from the beginning. Believing he could educate the people, he trusted that an exposé of the Klan would bring the people to their just senses. Surely his campaign did not eliminate hatreds, fears, and suspicions amongst Kansans. But by bringing the issue into the open, in all its ugliness, he forced the voters and the parties to come to terms with the Klan presence in Kansas, to publicly if not privately renounce divisiveness, and to rally to the ideal of community. White had made his communal vision the issue, and he forced Kansans to declare, however reluctantly, for harmony. In the final count, this represented a greater reward for White than the statehouse.

During the campaign, Editor White had summarized his interpretation of the election as he asked, in the *Gazette* in "Forward or Backward," which way Kansans were prepared to move. Idyllically plotting the state as "a parallelogram of prosperity," he declared,

> These people are the most civilized people in the world. They have more of the material comforts, which make the white man's civilization, than any other 2 million people on this planet. Steam, electricity, the schoolhouse, and the printing press have produced a citizenship here which is better housed, better clad, better educated, than any other 2 million people in the world. Moreover, they worked out with the heritage of 2,000 years of Christian civilization, the most equitable government in the world.

The question came down to whether or not "utopian" Kansas, where there were "no rich and no poor," was to progress in a neighborly fashion to further the advantages of its twentieth-century middle-class citizenry, or was Kansas to squander its magnificent heritage upon senseless hate? "How can we do that if every neighbor is at his neighbor's throat, criticizing his religion, scanning his skin, demanding for birth certificates before beginning the day's work for Kansas." What sort of society, White demanded, did Kansans and the nation want? After the campaign, the Emporia editor, at least, could rest assured he had broadcast his answer: a society where individuals gave of themselves, where service was the highest goal, where all reaped rich communal rewards.[38]

By 1927, less self-assured Kansans had come to the conclusion they too, at least, did not want the Ku Klux Klan in their community. White's campaign of exposure indubitably had contributed to the organization's demise. Still, in 1924 the Klan had achieved a majority of seats in the state senate and a sizable representation in the Kansas house (Governor Paulen in the end steered clear of the Klan). The national decline of the organization, as well as financial scandals involving the Klan in Kansas and a revulsion in the state against its violent tactics, resulted in a heavy defeat for the Klan in the 1926 election. The final blow came in January 1927 with the legal ouster of the organization. Reaction was hardly a dead issue; but White could declare with justifiable pride after the 1926 election that Kansas had turned an important corner in 1924 when he had forced the Klan into open battle. "The Ku Klux Klan in Kansas," he pronounced, "is a busted community." "It could be done in any state where the decent element will exhibit courage and hard work." Kansans, he determined, were on the right track again.[39]

■ ■ ■

For White the Ku Klux Klan presence never so much was an issue of black versus white, Jew versus Protestant, or native versus immigrant. The issue for White as for the Klan was what sort of community did Kansans—did all Americans—endeavor to create. For White community in the twentieth century meant overcoming old divisions and animosities to forge a common bond within a middle ground of affluence and mutual respect. The twentieth century—the "machine age" as he came to refer to it—offered a challenge, but with the growth of a broad middle class it offered as well its own unique solution to the problem of alienation within the complexity of mass society. He offered a positive message: he called it neighborliness, and he idealized its existence in Emporia and Kansas. The message was hardly provincial. White's idea of community had little to do with small towns; nor was it limited to Kansas's parochial social concerns. Community had to do with changing values, not with size or place. Community, White long argued, was a national concern.

In countless editorials in the 1920s dealing with explicit communities, White clarified, well beyond the "busted" Klan and increasingly artificial rural-urban distinctions, what he had in mind when he spoke of community. Naturally, as a small-town newsman and local booster, he was quick to knock the competition: ever competitive with nearby Kansas City, he waved a chastising finger at its metropolitan "sloth and indolence and sin"; he poked fun at "little" Ottawa's provincial ways, and in turn printed the small burg's pointed retort—a stinging critique of Emporia's own brand of pretentious urbanity. White was ready to hand out the kudos as well: Wichita, "the quintessence of Kansas," frequently received his praise—prosperous and unaffected, "Wichita," he pronounced, "is our kind of folks." Behind the editorial posturing always lay White's concern with the quality of life to be found in any town or city. In 1921 he compared Emporia with the big guns of American community:

> Emporia has not as many folks as some towns in this country—and we may as well name names—New York is one, Chicago possibly is another—but man for man we've got 'em backed into the ropes. Man for man, we live better, eat more regularly and have a wider bill of fare, drink less booze, keep out of jail more regularly, and get home earlier of nights than either of our above named rivals. Also we are more neighborly. ·

The tone was jocular, but the bottom line was boldly etched: towns and cities, one from another, differed little in White's communal perspective except as one measured the material and moral well-being of the residents.[40]

New York was White's great urban foil. He surely loved the city: he visited often for business and pleasure, and he sang its laurels as the commercial and cultural fountainhead of the nation. In many ways New York, he claimed, was "Hickville on the Hudson," just another Duluth, Boise, Kansas City, or Emporia, with its fair share of Babbitts; but there was one essential difference: New York in all its crowded greatness also was divided by class, race, and religion; tainted by extremes of wealth and poverty; and absorbed in self-indulgent sins. In 1922 the Kansas editor reviewed "one of the most charming sketches published recently," English author Rebecca West's "Impressions of America," which appeared in the *New Republic:* "It takes just such an article as this to reveal to us foreigners out here in Kansas what a wonderful 'city' America is." After trailing along on an exhaustive tour of exotic, sweeping, and towering Manhattan, White had had enough:

> All right, but when Rebecca West gets through seeing America, we Kansans want her. We have no Broadway skyscrapers, no Broadway lights, but we have a prairie and a sunset, and we manage somehow to find in them our beauty, art and religion. We have no Assyrian quarters and Chinatowns, but we have our Main streets; no millionaire homes, but five room modern bungalows.
>
> We Kansans are foreigners to Rebecca West's America. We have no Gypsy cellar-home picturesqueness. We are not picturesque, we are too plain, too practical, too new, to be picturesque. Our five-room bungalows may not always be related to art, but they are hygienic and livable.

"Rebecca West," White advised, "would learn all these things if she would only come and discover Kansas as she has discovered America." White was not angry. He suspected Rebecca West, underneath the charm, knew what he and a good lot of others knew: "After all, we have a hunch that she is only kidding the New Yorkers of New York—God pity them—they think it is America."[41]

Beyond the great metropolis, White confidently asserted over the years, lay the real America—in the heartland. America was not a city; but it was not a small town either. If Rebecca West would have ventured west of the Hudson, White would have had her discover a quintessential American place somewhere between the city and the small town—somewhere like Emporia. In the same manner that New York was no longer simply a city but had come to stand as a symbol of cosmopolitan, metropolitan culture, so Emporia with a good deal of aid from William Allen White was coming to stand not so much as a small town but as an alternative way of life to that of the city. Smaller, more homogeneous communities, predominantly and practically middle class in values, White remonstrated, more fully and satisfactorily represented American culture.

Emporia in the 1920s, along with its most famous citizen, began to receive a large amount of national attention. Newspapers in Kansas and the Middle West, in New York, and even in Paris carried stories about the town. Magazines like the *Ladies' Home Journal, Hearst's,* and *Collier's* featured Emporia in their widely read pages while Walt Mason, the *Gazette's* erstwhile cracker-barrel poet, broadcast syndicated paeans to small-town life (from his new home in Southern California). A visitor in 1923 summed up his impression of the town for *Collier's,* noting that all Emporians appeared to belong to a church, to be prohibitionist, and to be decent, clean, and orthodox. This was a town "waging war for righteousness":

> It is waging war for Conscious Goodness, and I think few Emporians will dispute the statement that Emporia is consciously good. One might almost say that it is smug, that it feels its virtuous oats, that it points with pride to its morality as against that of even Ohio or Indiana or Illinois, and that it is incomparably superior to New York or San Francisco.

Most of all, this paragon of Middle Western righteousness, observed the writer, was democratic.[42]

Commentary reflecting upon Emporia's brand of democracy were not always so laudatory. In August 1925 the sophisticated weekly humor magazine *Life* featured a full-page cartoon entitled "An Impression of Emporia, Kansas," drawn "By One Who Has Never Been There." The cartoon features Main Street intersecting with Main Street, both roadways spotted with wheat shocks. Unpredicatable tornados hover on the horizon. Jails occupy three corners, two police officers are gunning down an outlaw cigarette smoker, while another lawman remarks upon the noose awaiting an incarcerated "desperado," "caught red-handed wishin' fer a glass of beer." On the fourth corner stands the "Temple of Virtue," established by "Vox Populi" for the "Society for the Suppression of Every Little Thought." Close by sits the shop of one of the town proprietors, "Wm. Allen White." The editor of the *Gazette* was not amused; in "Emporia and New York" he shot back, noting the picture should have been titled: "'Emporia, Kansas. As Seen by Carnival Men, Managers of Shows with Barelegged Chorus Girls, Sunday Air Circus Promoters, Bootleggers and Cigaret Peddlers using the Braille System.'" He was not finished:

> New York probably rejects the Emporia attitude to that burg because it is not constructive criticism. But after all, what can you say

constructively of a place where everything—love, joy, peace, beauty or light—is on a meter! In New York the Irish run the politics and religion, the Armenians run the rug business and the agony works, the Jews run the banks and the theaters, the Italians run the food and the crime; while the poor dubs cursed with more than a generation of Yankee blood run their legs off for the one sweet boon of keeping their pants on.

Outraged, White launched one last salvo:

> A fine place that—to criticize Emporia for making a town where an American citizen can live without having to divide his substance with a lot of crooks, grafters, come-on men and hijackers of one sort and another. Emporia may not have so many people as New York but such as they are they are not bossed, busted and booted all over the place by a lot of brass collars.[43]

White's vituperative reaction was uncommonly telling. Generally he was a good sport about Emporia, trading barbs with the best of them and generously reprinting critiques of the town. But when his ideal was directly attacked a raw nerve seemed to be hit. In *Life* the New York "highbrows" had gone too far. Emporia was more than a main-street crossroads. White had carefully nurtured, for public viewing, an idyll of twelve thousand decent, middle-class Americans whose idea of a good community—democratically expressed, not suppressed—was one that enhanced the quality of life of all its citizens. Emporians were plain, practical folks, busily building "five-room bungalows" and a "hygienic and livable" civilization. Predictable moderation was their motto and the common good their standard. Emporia was a small town in name only. *Life* had misrepresented all that White and his town had come to stand for; he could not let the slander pass unchecked.

"Emporia and New York" displayed a number of latent prejudices White generally kept under wraps. It was not really representative of his more fundamental instincts. It did throw into relief, however, the underpinnings of his view of American community. He was ready to welcome all races and creeds into his "town," but in return he expected their assumption of a white, Anglo-Saxon, Protestant cultural ethos he termed "middle class." More representative of White's views was his much more tempered response to the controversy triggered by Sinclair Lewis's 1920 publication of *Main Street*. Well into the middle of the decade the *Gazette* pages were open to an array of interpretations of community in twentieth-century America: Wire service stories carried home to Emporia the attacks of religious groups upon the Jazz Age evils of Gotham. Articles and editorials singled out for emulation model, middle-sized communities dotting the American landscape, and pointed out the attractions of big-city life. Writers such as Duncan Aiken were reviewed. In *The Home Town Mind* Aiken indicted small-town ways, associating the American village with Fascism, fundamentalism, ignorance, and prohibition. F. Scott Fitzgerald harangued "the middle border" for its provincial taste in reading. White had his own ideas regarding quality reading: he favorably reviewed the generous small-town fiction of friends such as Victor Murdock *(Just Folks)*, Dorothy Canfield Fisher *(The Brimming Cup)*, Charles M. Sheldon *(The Mere Man and His Problems)*, and Ray Stannard Baker (*Adventures in Understanding*, pseudonomously authored by David Grayson). White on occasion set forth his opinion as to what truly constituted "realism"; he dismissed the work of new lights Sherwood Anderson and Floyd Dell, and he praised the accomplishments of more traditional writers such as Edna Ferber, Edith Wharton, Willa Cather, and Zona Gale. Finally, he issued huzzahs for the criticism of the new literature by old-time village rebels Ed Howe and Hamlin Garland. Community was "hot" in the twenties, and the *Gazette* in its own middle-border fashion sizzled with the controversy.[44]

White's most revealing response to the debate over the meaning of community in modern America came in his review of *Main Street*, followed two years later by his assessment of Lewis's *Babbitt*. When the popularly esteemed defender of small-town America encountered the muckraker of Main Street, far from chastening the avenger for his errant ways White wholeheartedly embraced Lewis. He began his survey of *Main Street* with a backward glance down Emporia's own main street:

> Gazette readers for more than 25 years have wondered why this paper has cried out regularly every six months in all those years against the dried ulcers of tin corniced ugliness and vain pretense on the buildings on Commercial Street; why we always are for the bonds—no matter what the bonds are for whether for the municipal band, the public library, the paving, hard surfaced roads, the new High School building, the Memorial hall, the county hospital, the county home, the city market; why we have been for every subscription paper passed in town in a quarter of a century whether for the Y.M.C.A. building, the Y.W., the Welfare Association, with its new building, with its laundry, day nursery and sewing room for working women, for the new College building and the four manual pipe organ—now worth $25,000—for the park improvement, for the fair building, for the livestock sales pavilion; why we have been for enlarging the activities of the city government in every possible way. Well this is the reason—to bring a more abundant life to all the people of this town, to distribute the wealth of the town, by taxation and by gifts and otherwise, and distribute it more equitably, and thereby to bring beauty into what otherwise would be a sordid and impossible village life.

Having inventoried a quarter-century's progress in Emporia, White turned to Lewis's "great American novel," "the story of a woman's rebellion against the dreary mean ugly oppressive monotony of small town life in America." Here, he declared, was a commentary not upon progressive Emporia but upon the distance that the town, with the constant prodding of the *Gazette*, had placed between itself and the unsophisticated Gopher Prairies pockmarking the country. Lewis's indictment of heartland contentment and mediocrity was read by White as an approval of Emporia's achievement. Middle-class Emporia and other progressive communities, and the *Gazette*, must not rest on their laurels but strive for ever greater improvement. Here was Lewis's missive to America, "a highly noble aspiration for a finer, broader life on this continent":

> America is a bigger country and a better one for having produced a novel like "Main Street." . . . To write it is to be great; but to read such a book and consider it well will be something eternally to the credit of this country. And especially should Emporia read it—and all the thousands of Emporias in this country; towns that because they have left "Main Street" . . . think therefore that they have reason to rest and be proud. The journey is only well begun.

Sinclair Lewis, in White's opinion, stood with him in the vanguard of progress—together they urged middle-class Americans to join together in model heartland communities, to forge a better and greater American commonwealth.[45]

White's assessment that he and Lewis stood together on Main Street was not far off the mark. Mark Schorer in his authoritative *Sinclair Lewis: An American Life* portrays Lewis, the individual as well as the writer, as perpetually torn between his condemnation of small-town, middle-sized urban provinciality and his love of its many virtues. He demonstrates that Lewis, as White, stood in the mainstream of Middle America, clearly able to discern and to disseminate a popularly homogenized, evolving middle-class portrait. No less than White, Lewis sought to steer "a clear line between a surly proletariat and a stuffed plutocracy," wishing "to assure the middle class that the promise of American life lay in its best values."[46]

When *Babbitt* came onto the scene, White was beside himself with satisfaction that this great author so well understood the problems of America: "Sinclair Lewis who wrote 'Main Street' two years ago put a new phrase into the English language. 'Main Street' means something now that it did not mean before. Soon the word 'babbitt' will be coined into a new meaning. For Mr. Lewis's new book 'Babbitt' is a better, bigger book than 'Main Street' and should have more readers." Gopher Prairie, *Main Street*'s demographic protagonist, came in all sizes. Zenith, "one of our second-grade towns, of say, three or four hundred thousand people," was a seedbed of materialistic dissatisfaction—"Our urban life, whether in Toledo or Denver, Minneapolis or Buffalo, Sauk Center or New York, is jammed full of Babbitts. Babbitt is Main Street in tailored clothes. And the story of 'Babbitt' is a story that every American should read—a great philipic against the emptiness of this civilization." Middle-class Americans needed to be shaken. Lewis, White rejoiced, was "one of the major prophets of our times, a Jeremiah probably, but Heaven sent." Babbitt had lost his nobility—spiritually bankrupt, he futilely groped "through a sordid wilderness of substantial things, luxuries, pomps, honors, fastness, to find his lost soul." He did not recognize that his salvation lay not in serving himself but in worthy service to his fellow citizens, to his society. Here lay a fundamental lesson: "Students of our times in other eras must go to Lewis and his fellow protestors to understand what ailed us. 'Zenith' is the name of the city where Babbitt lives. History will call it and all its kind 'Nadir' in the epoch that followed the Great War. Lewis is the prophet of 'Nadir.' It will do no good to stone the prophet. It is better for us to repent and be saved." Middle-class America had to come home again, to a truer sense of itself.[47]

In both *Main Street* and *Babbitt* White had found Lewis overly harsh in his critique of heartland America; nevertheless, a great author had underscored a fundamental flaw in twentieth-century society. In looking to the heartland White grasped that Lewis joined him in seeing America's greatest hope lay in this region—in its smaller towns and cities, in its more homogeneous population, in its emergent middle-class culture. Lewis, White understood, did not focus on the hope: "if Mr. Lewis leaves nobility out of his stories we must remember that we are crushing nobility out of our lives." Still, inherent in his work was the call for a higher order. Accompanying White's review of *Main Street* in November 1920 was an editorial entitled "What Is a Good Town?" White declared to Emporia that some communities still retained "a highly noble aspiration for a finer, broader life" amongst the hustle and bustle and prosperity of twentieth-century life:

> A town is not judged by the number of people it contains, but by the way those people live. A town is really not the people at all, but rather their relations to one another. A town is its business, its public spirit, its churches, its schools, its play grounds, its community interests, its public toys, in the way of theaters, bands, pipe organs, orchestras, auditoriums, social organization. And a good town is a town where people may live, and live well after doing a good day's work with hands or brain or both, and enjoy the best things the town has to offer without considering whether their work is manual, mental or both. A good

town is a just town, a fair price town, and [a] well-kept, well housed [*sic*], well-governed, well-bred town. And in such a town, whether it be of 1,000 or 1 million, the number of people in the town is not important.

What mattered was mutual respect and fairness. A "good town" offered all its citizens an equitable share of the commonwealth. A good town, White believed, was middle class to its core.[48]

■ ■ ■

The issue, then, was not one of size—up to a million—but the more abstract one of character. A good community prided itself more on the quality of its group relations than upon the merits of its individual citizens. In the Middle West, White believed, communal relations had more of a chance to survive than in the larger metropolises of the East with their multifarious populations and greater extremes of wealth and poverty. In the nation's heartland the middle class purportedly thrived; here Americans had their best chance to prosper spiritually as well as materially. White, of course, recognized that divisions existed in his home territory, not to mention right in his hometown. But the ideal had a powerful draw for him, and he was not alone. It was this same idealized heartland appeal that had dictated Robert Lynd's choice of Muncie for the *Middletown* study. As White saw Emporia as a potentially "good" town, so Lynd had seen promise in Muncie. Here were antidotes for the maladies of Anytown, U.S.A., for Gopher Prairie, for Zenith, and ultimately for all of America.

White, Lynd, Lewis, and H. L. Mencken, too, spoke a common language. "Main Street" and "Babbitt" were fast becoming, as White had discerned, synonyms for an emergent Middle American ethos. Whether finding within this emerging middle ground in American society a cause for hope or despair, a growing number of twentieth-century commentators seemed to locate within its bounds a common denominator for, as the Lynds cited, "the gross-total thing that is Schenectady, Akron, Dallas, or Keokuk." Middle-class America in the twentieth century, with all its rambling parameters, was becoming associated with the equally ungainly Middle West. And the Middle West was becoming equated with life in a good town, whatever its size, as long as it was manageable, as long as it could remain communal, neighborly. No one had a specific town in mind; and what one connoted by the term "good" carried different meaning for an H. L. Mencken than for a William Allen White. Nevertheless, both did have in mind a way of living and thinking that they understood. They did share a rhetoric with which they could conduct a discourse upon the meaning of community in American life.[49]

In 1925, two months prior to publishing its unflattering caricature of Emporia, *Life* magazine carried on its cover a colorful illustration of a globe encircled by an archetypal Main Street. Replete with a five and dime, a movie house and a gas station, an opera house and a dry goods store, fraternal orders, false fronts, Model T's and bustling town folk, the picture captured the essence of a broad, Middle American consensus stretching from sea to sea, and overseas as well. White had intimated as much when he wrote of *Babbitt*, "These facts are part of the truth about our times, big universal facts as true on the Avenue Victor Hugo or Williamstrasse or Picadilly Circus as they are of American life." Main Street had become a universal way of life. *Life* hardly was sympathetic to the phenomenon, sniggering at it in its "Old Home Week Number." The radical *New Masses* was a good deal more blunt. In April 1926 White introduced the revived review to Emporia, reprinting a piece entitled "The Progressive Republican." The article was "mighty well done," he advised his readers, but way off base: "If you want to know the point of view of this group, here is a bit that you might try on your radio, or pianola or washing machine, or what have you":

> I know a man; he lives in the middle west, and he is a progressive Republican.
> He is a good man. Fat and kind, he sits on his porch in a big rocking-chair, and fans himself comfortably, sniffing the morning-glories.
> Nothing ruffles him; he is fat and sane. He is sad at times, but is practical, and a member of the Republican party, where things get done.
> Children love him; his wife worships him; his neighbors think he is the best neighbor in America.
> He sees only the good in life.

The article went on to reveal the underside of this life and laid full responsibility for it upon the front porch of Middle America. It identified the great numbers of dispossessed Americans: the weeping miners' widows, the painters rotting slow with lead cancer, the bakers burning with consumption; it called attention to the children working in the cotton mills and oyster sheds, "raped of life by the Republican party"; it painted a picture of a less commodious neighborhood housing eleven-dollar-a-week textile workers living "with their wives and babies in lousy, filthy, stinking rat-holes." White believed the *New Masses* sold short Middle America, the progressives, and possibly himself given the caricature. More important, he recognized he was in touch with a growing majority of Americans in a manner the magazine was not. He wagered the *New Masses* would fold in six months; in this he was wrong, but he was right on the money that his perspective of America was ascendent and the *New Masses,* as well as *Life,* represented a decidedly "minority point of view" of Main Street.[50]

After the war, figuratively stranded in Emporia, a political outcast and a literary anachronism, William Allen White found he fortuitously had landed in the center of a national debate over the meaning of community in twentieth-century America. He capitalized upon his position, building on his small-town journalistic reputation and his long nurtured interest in community, to establish himself as a spokesperson for Middle America. Identifying more fully than ever with Emporia, he made the town out to be a model community for all the nation to emulate—not so much a small town but an archetypal middle-sized, middle-class, Middle Western community. If Americans could bring themselves to act selflessly, in their best community interests, so many of their problems could be solved. Look to Emporia, and to folks like himself, he advocated, for national direction. Look to Main Street for progress and harmony. As those he identified as the country's "leading literary mentors," as Sinclair Lewis and H. L. Mencken, William Allen White, too, was a wordsmith of the first order, molding a language that Middle America could comprehend.

In the postwar era, personally, professionally, and philosophically, White had drawn up to the same Main Street junction as the nation. Assiduously plotting out for Emporians a good town, encouraging them to follow his lead, he was to argue to the country that here was community at its best: Emporia retained old neighborly ways while maintaining a keen perspective on a newer, more cosmopolitan world. Emporia offered inhabitants of all communities, of whatever size, an example of the benefits of keeping the interests of all citizens foremost—an example of the possibility of turning the vast riches of this new era to the advantage of everyone. Here was a community where the ideal was material and moral consensus; here was a community not preoccupied with consumption but with fairness—Emporians worked together for the common good; not abdicating individual or communal responsibility, Emporians endeavored to save their town and themselves through service to society. Situated in the heartland, in the middle of America, Emporia represented a comforting way station for a people speeding through the complexities of an incorporated, consolidated, and highly urbanized society. And it offered William Allen White a prominent platform from which to hail the passing show.

William Allen White. The young editor poses around 1895, about the
time he and his wife, Sally Lindsay White, purchased the *Emporia
Gazette*. (Courtesy of David Walker and Barbara White Walker, from
the William Allen White Library, Emporia State University.)

◀ William Allen White in a more casual pose, circa 1899. (Courtesy of David Walker and Barbara White Walker, from the William Allen White Library, Emporia State University.)

▼ White, the aspiring novelist, meets the dean of American letters, William Dean Howells, in Emporia, Kansas, in 1899. (Courtesy of David Walker and Barbara White Walker, from the William Allen White Library, Emporia State University.)

William Allen White, the well-established Progressive Era reformer, 1907. (Courtesy of David Walker and Barbara White Walker, from the William Allen White Library, Emporia State University.)

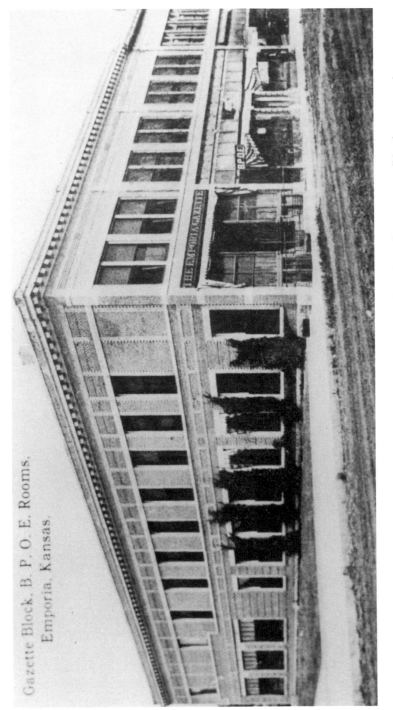

Gazette Block, B. P. O. E. Rooms.
Emporia, Kansas.

The Gazette block and B.P.O.E. (Elks) rooms in Emporia, Kansas. The "good roads movement" had yet to arrive. (Courtesy of David Walker and Barbara White Walker, from the William Allen White Library, Emporia State University.)

White at his *Gazette* desk, circa 1909. Theodore Roosevelt's portrait looms above. (Courtesy of David Walker and Barbara White Walker, from the William Allen White Library, Emporia State University.)

I can stand this if you can
Ben B. Lindsey

Denver June 10/10

Benjamin Lindsey and William Allen White. Two Progressive Era reformers take a stroll in 1910. Denver's nationally renowned Judge Lindsey inscribed, "I can stand this if you can." (Courtesy of David Walker and Barbara White Walker, from the William Allen White Library, Emporia State University.)

The White family poses with President Theodore Roosevelt and an unnamed visitor on the front porch, circa 1908. (Courtesy of David Walker and Barbara White Walker, from the William Allen White Library, Emporia State University.)

White stands with his hero, Theodore Roosevelt, in front of the Emporia home in 1913. They had recently lost the Bull Moose bid for the presidency. (Courtesy of David Walker and Barbara White Walker, from the William Allen White Library, Emporia State University.)

Three aging small-town Kansas editors and novelists. White, Ed Howe, and Victor Murdock gather together sometime in the 1920s. (Courtesy of David Walker and Barbara White Walker, from the William Allen White Library, Emporia State University.)

Four public figures gather together as the small town–urban controversy
roils in the mid-twenties: Sinclair Lewis, in the process of writing *Elmer
Gantry;* aspiring newsman and novelist William Lindsay White;
Reverend William Stidger of Kansas City, upon whom Lewis in part was
basing his searing caricature of religion; and William Allen White.
(Courtesy of David Walker and Barbara White Walker, from the William
Allen White Library, Emporia State University.)

White, shortly after declaring his independent candidacy for the governorship of Kansas, in Kansas City, Missouri, September 1924. (Courtesy of David Walker and Barbara White Walker, from the William Allen White Library, Emporia State University.)

William Allen White, the anti-Klan candidate, canvassing the women's vote. (Courtesy of David Walker and Barbara White Walker, from the William Allen White Library, Emporia State University.)

White took pride in Rollin Kirby's "A Real American Goes Hunting" in the *New York World*. (Courtesy of David Walker and Barbara White Walker, from the William Allen White Library, Emporia State University.)

Fellow reformer and novelist Upton Sinclair looks over the *Gazette* with Editor White, sometime in the twenties. Sinclair wrote, "To William Allen White, who is almost as saintly as he looks in this picture!" (Courtesy of David Walker and Barbara White Walker, from the William Allen White Library, Emporia State University.)

Henry Seidel Canby, Christopher Morley, William Allen White, and Dorothy Canfield Fisher judge Book of the Month Club entries sometime in the thirties. (Courtesy of David Walker and Barbara White Walker, from the William Allen White Library, Emporia State University.)

William Allen White and Albert Einstein receive honorary degrees at Harvard University in 1935. (Courtesy of David Walker and Barbara White Walker, from the William Allen White Library, Emporia State University.)

William Allen White poses in front of his house with former president Herbert Hoover in 1935. (Courtesy of David Walker and Barbara White Walker, from the William Allen White Library, Emporia State University.)

Kansas delegates Henry J. Allen and William Allen White at the 1936 Republican convention. White's inscription reads, "It seems that once there was a Jew and an Irishman!" (Courtesy of David Walker and Barbara White Walker, from the William Allen White Library, Emporia State University.)

Franklin Roosevelt sent White a cherished memory of his 1936 Emporia campaign stop. He inscribed, "For William Allen White—from his old friend who is *for* him all 48 months." (Courtesy of David Walker and Barbara White Walker, from the William Allen White Library, Emporia State University.)

ersonal

March 4, 1938.

Dear Bill:-

Here is the seersucker picture, duly inscribed by the sucker to the seer!

You are right about what happens when age creeps up on one -- but you and I are fortunate in having rather serene natures. I think even you could still smile after 85% of the daily press interpreters and editors and most of the radio commentators treated you twenty-four hours a day the way they treat me.

If you ever feel your nerves getting a little bit on edge, take up stamp collecting - it is never too late.

I am very happy that you have come through in such fine shape and I hope you will be in Washington this Spring.

As ever yours,

Franklin D. Roosevelt

William Allen White, Esq.,
The Emporia Gazette,
Emporia,
Kansas.

Roosevelt's note that accompanied his photograph. (Courtesy of David Walker and Barbara White Walker, from the William Allen White Library, Emporia State University.)

William Allen White in 1935. (Courtesy of David Walker and Barbara White Walker, from the William Allen White Library, Emporia State University.)

White in 1942, approaching "the end of the second act of this fast drama of the changing spirit of man." (Courtesy of David Walker and Barbara White Walker, from the William Allen White Library, Emporia State University.)

White enjoys a good laugh with fellow Middle Westerner and presiden-
tial aspirant Wendell Willkie in 1943. (Courtesy of David Walker and
Barbara White Walker, from the William Allen White Library, Emporia
State University.)

This photograph graced the cover of the Book of the Month Club's memorial tribute to William Allen White. (Courtesy of David Walker and Barbara White Walker, from the William Allen White Library, Emporia State University.)

Raising Middle American Barricades

Smith, Depression, and War

WITH A FIRM BELIEF in "service to society" William Allen White continued after World War I to address the greater American community as well as his own hometown. For the remaining quarter century of his life, through hundreds of articles and book reviews, collected essays and biographical studies, the Kansas editor used his small-town platform to speak to America's lengthening list of Main Street concerns. Particularly through national magazines such as the *Saturday Evening Post, Collier's,* the *Nation,* the *New Republic,* and the *Saturday Review of Literature;* and by means of regional and special-interest journals such as the *Kansas Magazine,* the *Santa Fe Magazine,* the *Rotarian,* the *New York Times Magazine, Vital Speeches of the Day,* and the *Yale Review*—White spoke to his perception of the communal concerns of America's emerging middle class. To the inhabitants of the nation's towns, small cities, and metropolises he offered encouragement that a semblance of traditional, neighborly relations could be and should be retained in a complex world; to the residents of a fast-paced national community the "Sage of Emporia" offered a refuge for a multitude of problems in the small-town ideal.

As in earlier years White would be on the spot—and increasingly in the spotlight—reporting and commenting upon the nation's news. The old Bull Mooser found it difficult to accept Harding and Coolidge. He was frustrated over the domestic stalemate faced by the progressives and their diminished strength within his own party. He placed his hopes on Herbert Hoover, as early as 1920 supporting him for the presidency, only to face the eventual debacle of his administration. Fully committed to an internationalist role for the United States, he despaired as successive Republican administrations shied away from overt cooperative initiatives. Most disheartening of all for White was the public's disenchantment with idealism.

Having begun during the Progressive Era to identify the middle class as the torchbearer of a new spiritual and material order, a greater American community, destined to lead the nation and the world toward a more equitable and affluent state, he could not reconcile himself to its postwar attitude. People had become immersed in materialism; carelessly abandoning two decades of idealism, middle-class Americans, White contended, were selling themselves short. Progressivism had given way to reaction, and the Sage could not abide the change.

Nativism and nationalism particularly rankled White, epitomizing for him the resurgence of ignorance and selfishness. Following the Armistice he battled A. Mitchell Palmer's promotion of the Red Scare and Henry Cabot Lodge's opposition to the League of Nations. Wrestling with the Kansas Ku Klux Klan was only his most demonstrable protest: in Massachusetts he rallied to the defense of Sacco and Vanzetti; and throughout the twenties he defended himself against such flag-festooned legions as the Daughters of the American Revolution, castigating them for blacklisting him as unpatriotic. And through the 1920s and 1930s William Allen White closely monitored events in Europe and Asia. He condemned reactionary tendencies and warned of parallel dangers in American society.

Concerned over the changing character of the national community, sensing that Americans were turning against instead of working for one another, White himself uncharacteristically succumbed to reaction in 1928. Active in the Hoover presidential campaign, the Kansan vehemently lashed out at the Democratic nominee, New York governor Al Smith. The attack revealed the underside of White's progressive philosophy and possibly the toll of a decade of political and social disillusionment. White, as most Americans, was a racist. He long advocated equal rights and opportunities for all people, all over the world, but he gauged equality in terms of Anglo-Saxon, Nordic, and Teutonic superiority, and he allotted an accommodationist role to lesser races. White also was anti-urban. He could accept the rise of a predominantly urban order but not the imposition upon the nation of a metropolitan and cosmopolitan culture. Accordingly, White's political biases for years had taken the form of portraying the Democratic Party as boss-ridden, enthralled by ignorant immigrants, southern autocrats, and generally unprogressive elements in American society. In 1928, as an ardent prohibitionist, White particularly could not countenance Smith. It all seemed too much—the "Happy Warrior" was leading a frontal assault upon White's world. Reform was necessary, but Smith, albeit a progressive, represented the wrong brand. Herbert Hoover, on the other hand, seemed a knight shining in all-American armor, offering a timely defense against the corruptive influences of the twentieth-century order. Hoover was an orphaned Iowan and a self-made million-aire. Selflessly he had saved postwar Europe from famine. As secretary of commerce he had been one of the few saving, progressive graces, of the Harding and Coolidge cabinets. As president he might return the Republican Party to progressive control—and White to political power. Hoover represented change, but change dictated by an older, less cosmo-politan, more temperate American commonwealth. For the Emporia edi-tor, a lot seemed to ride on the 1928 contest, and he did his utmost to ensure a victory for Hoover and for his own conception of middle-class America.

White's hopes for the Hoover administration and a renaissance of Bull Moose progressivism collapsed with the market in 1929. As the nation slipped into the grip of the Great Depression, White tangled with the knot of economic, political, and social maladies plaguing the nation. His con-cern over the evolving character of the American community took on a decidedly more dire and urgent tone. Worried as the capitalist economic structure gave way, defeated as Hoover abysmally failed to shore it up, White remained anxious as Franklin Roosevelt fortified it in a manner beyond the vision of an old-line progressive. With some reservations, the Kansas editor supported most of the president's program; he especially appreciated FDR's ability to lead the nation through a critical passage into yet another new era. Still, White was dismayed by the extension of execu-tive power; and he worried over the strained social structure.

White's conception of a potentially harmonious postwar community had disintegrated as the class structure caved into the Depression. In the flush of the 1920s White's vision of an all-encompassing middle-class soci-ety had held some credibility; despite a host of contradictions, a middle-class cultural consensus clearly was in the making. When the bottom fell out in the thirties, the idealized "Great American Middle Class" cracked and turned upon itself; distinct fissures within the new order no longer could be rosily camouflaged. White saw the middle class, which he now divided into upper and lower sectors, caught between a powerful, disin-terested, and callous wealthy class and an increasingly militant laboring class. He feared the strong president was politicizing class-consciousness; the panicked middle classes could rush into the hands of a reactionary successor to Roosevelt who felt free to exercise the excessive powers granted to the chief executive. That this was a real possibility was, of course, suggested by developments abroad. That White was no alarmist was easily supported by an array of social, political, economic, and cultural signals: Upton Sinclair's EPIC (End Poverty in California) gubernatorial campaign; Milo Reno's Farmers' Holiday Association barricades; William

Randolph Hearst's ominous film *Gabriel over the White House*; Sinclair Lewis's apocalyptic novel *It Can't Happen Here;* and FDR's court-packing imbroglio were but a few of the decade's intimidating guideposts. The nation was in trouble, threatened from within and increasingly, as the decade ground on, from without. White himself was troubled, threatened, ground down, and confused, and he did not hesitate to express his concern to his massive readership.[1]

Throughout the Depression Era White sought to reconfigure for himself and his readers a more workable definition of middle-class America. Ultimately, he found an uneasy peace with the conception of an "upper middle class" as truly representing greater American values and norms. A more sanguine perspective would come, for White as for the nation, with the onslaught of war. The Sage of Emporia regained real peace of mind as a united people prepared to battle what he saw as the foreign incarnation of its own economic, political, and social maladies. Far from his jeremiads of the thirties, White in his last few years hailed the future of America, and the world. He came full circle, foreseeing the dawn of a new age, the morning light which had faded quickly after the First World War. Once again upper class and lower class, and most important, the far reaches of the aspiring middle class, were joined together in a shared vision of American community. Here, in his view, were just people prepared to play a neighborly role in a greater world community, ready to carry forth within a broadened, less divisive middle-class consensus their hopes of a more secure postwar order at home and abroad. Again, White hardly occupied a solitary vantage point: Wendell Willkie's *One World* was a runaway bestseller in 1943; Franklin Roosevelt articulated the Four Freedoms; Henry Wallace rhapsodized over a postwar world linked by international highways and American automobiles; and Henry Luce campaigned for an American Century. Indeed, this was a period of expansive and exhilarating visions. William Allen White was once again most assuredly within his element.

■ ■ ■

Reacting to the current events and the rambunctious rhythms of American life in the 1920s and 1930s, White laid out, within the national press, as he did in the *Emporia Gazette,* a careful, if not always consistent, analysis of the changing meaning of community in the United States. In his singular responses to the campaign of 1928, to the continuing Depression crisis, and to the approach of war lay a clear expression of his biases, hopes, fears, and confusion. Significantly, within these years and in these commentaries, White articulated what he perceived to be a new, emerging national ethos. Focusing upon middle-class concerns, the Kansas editor came to identify ever more closely with what would later be popularly construed as Middle America.

Following World War I, White began to engage with others in what the *Nation* identified as "the new literature of national self-analysis." White recognized new forces were at work in American society; he set out to stake a position as a spokesperson for a growing middle-class constituency less concerned with reform, more concerned with material accumulation, and in his view still at base interested in retaining a neighborly disposition toward other Americans amidst the flux of postwar change. Prior to the 1920 Republican convention, which selected Warren Harding to carry its standard into the New Era, White in the *Saturday Evening Post* reflected upon himself and who he was: he was a good Republican, no "pink-cheeked reformer who is trying to build a world of cream puffs above what he considers the decaying mudsills of a lost humanity." Still, "The gentle reader must not get the impression that my mouth always has been agape to whatever treacle of program the Squeerses of politics might pour in." In step with the times, the program White had in mind for postwar America was practical and ostensibly apolitical. As he explained to *Post* readers a year later in "Why I Am a Progressive," his program was in essence middle class. A new day had dawned. America's laborers, farmers, clerks, teachers, businessmen, and professionals were all marching down a widening socioeconomic middle road. The suburban life, the consumer life, was becoming the American standard. Above all else these Americans demanded self-respect. White explained that as progressives he and his compatriots understood the needs of this population. For years they had argued for a middle-class America where all self-respecting Americans received a fair shake. Now it was within reach. Power was shifting from the politicians to the interest groups. The progressives, White contended, needed to establish their claim to leadership—the middle class was the greatest interest group in the country and by all rights its power belonged to the progressives. Pragmatic and understanding, the progressives always stood for change, for moderation, for the middle way. They could fulfill the needs of America's new "average man"; they could help him pull out of his postwar malaise and shed his money-grabbing instinct; they could help him demand that the politicians institute a new and better order for all Americans. Most important, in a reactionary time they could ensure the permanency of their middle-class status.[2]

In 1923 in a set of articles for *Collier's,* White made another play for progressive leadership and a remarkable claim for his own role as spokesman for Middle America. The editors claimed that in "Blood of the Conquerors," followed by "The Dawn of a Great To-morrow: We Are Making America Over to Give an Equal Chance to Every Man," White presented "a brief epic of the change in American life in the past generation." Americans had become middle class, or, as White proposed, they had become Emporians:

> In America most of us are Emporians in one way or another. Some of us live in towns ranging from five thousand to a quarter of a million, others were born in or around these towns, and still others of us cherish golden dreams of going back to some Emporia, there to see life in the sunset. People say to us Emporia dwellers: "Why do you live in Emporia?" and the answer seems simple: "Everyone does—more or less." But is that an answer? Isn't it a mere reply, an evasion? Does it explain why everyone in reality or in dreams lives in some old home town?

White offered his explanation. America had undergone a social and economic revolution; in the same manner that Emporians in the past quarter century had come to create a network of neighborly, middle-class relations, so the nation was now interlocked by far-flung interests, laws, and social institutions nurturing equal justice and opportunity for all Americans. The successful progressive political program all along had simply been a greater Emporia platform—re-creating the self-respecting environment of Hometown, U.S.A. Americans longed for "Emporia," for here in the Middle Western small town was the epitome of middle-class life; here was the heart and power of progressivism which had brought to millions their just, middle-class desserts. Here, in Emporia, was the ideal hometown environment that all progressive Americans still strived to re-create in their own distant communities.[3]

Progressivism, of course, proved to be a weak drawing card as the years passed by; but the prewar progressive rallying cry of community retained its power. White succeeded in the twenties and thirties in identifying himself, if not always so successfully his political creed, with the appealing concept. What sort of community do we have, and what sort of community do we want?—the rhetorical questioning had permeated White's work since the turn of the century. Now, as a self-proclaimed and widely acknowledged spokesperson for middle-class America, the queries took on a more formidable presence in his thought. The world was changing fast. It was imperative to control the change, to ensure that long-fought-for ideals were not lost in the vortex of progress. Throughout the 1920s White came to feel more and more pressure. Seeking to locate a place for older, purportedly more harmonious values within the new order, the Kansas editor sensed time itself was infringing upon his communal ideal. In 1928, faced with what he considered a radical challenge to his goals, he demarcated the problem; in the process he red-lined who "we" were and what "we" wanted in an American way of life in a manner that seemed a good deal more exclusionary and less harmonious than his usual vision of community.

Nineteen twenty-eight was not the first occasion White chose to gerrymander communal lines to ensure harmony. In 1896 he had cordoned off his own Populist-inflicted state from from what he considered to be a greater, saner, and more prosperous American commonwealth; following the Progressive election debacle of 1914 he had sought refuge in a supposed Middle Western enclave of reform. In 1922, feeling threatened once more by disharmonious forces within the body politic, White had rigidly redrawn community lines. In the lead story for the July 1, 1922, *Collier's*—below an illustration of teeming, swarthy immigrants overshadowing an aged panorama of westward-moving conquistadors and pilgrims, founding fathers, pioneers and yeoman families, antebellum reformers and Civil War statesmen, Gilded Age entrepreneurs and common American folk—White set out to explain, as his article was titled, "What's the Matter with America?" The problem was not so much the immigrants but the cities within which they swarmed. White had launched plenty of volleys in his time against the city, but none carried a greater sense of rancor than this piece. Cities and the states in which urbanites had overwhelmed the farming population and the residents of towns under fifty-thousand—states like Pennsylvania and Massachusetts and Illinois—were like a cancer, poisoning the body politic from top to bottom. Corruption in and out of government was the symptom; a "moron majority" in the proliferating metropolises was the disease. Moral decay threatened to ravage the republic. The better elements, typified by the social, economic, political, and racial purity of rural and small-town America, had to somehow—beyond providing schooling and a decent living environment—inculcate Anglo-Saxon and Teutonic values into these distant communities. Social education—that is, civic morality—had to be instilled.[4]

Collier's had introduced "What's the Matter with America?" with the caveat that White's pen was "sizzling," as it had a quarter century earlier in "What's the Matter with Kansas?": "Perhaps you will disagree violently with some of the things he says. But what he says is important, because William Allen White is American clear through to his backbone, and is spokesman for a very great number of his fellow citizens." New York columnist Heywood Broun in an accompanying piece did disagree, speaking up for another large lot of fellow citizens, for metropolitan Americans.

In "What's the Matter with White," Broun pointed out that the cities were doing well enough and that White's sweeping generalizations regarding rural and small-town morality were severely flawed. He concluded with a stinging rebuke: "As for the 'moron majority' of which Mr. White speaks, nobody will be disposed to deny that intelligence is far too rare in our broad land. But we wonder why the distinguished Kansan should fall into the habit of using 'moron' as a synonym for 'immigrant.' There is ample evidence that we are perfectly capable of rolling our own." Broun surely knew what really was the matter—it was not a question of immigrants, or really of cities, or small towns. It was a matter of conflicting ways of life. White was irritated; Prohibition was a big issue for him, and it was going badly, especially in the cities. It was all a matter of symbols: Prohibition, cities, foreigners—what sort of community was America to be? White succinctly had summed it up: "All our grand national policies, all our pompous parties, all our crucial issues—all the flubdubbery of politics, are subsidiary to this fundamental clash of ideals: the Puritan ideal and its festive foe, that shrugs a gay shoulder, denies our brotherhood, rejects our cold justice, and giggles out of our homely duties." What bothered White so much in 1922 was a growing sense that his neighborly ideal was losing out, and it was being mocked in the process.[5]

"What's the Matter with America?" was an anomaly as had been "What's the Matter with Kansas?" and the 1914 gerrymandering jeremiad "The Ebb Tide: Can the Progressives Come Back?" Feeling for a moment threatened, White could be triggered to engage in hyperbole; he, too, could be temporarily confused by the line distinguishing rhetoric and reality. Generally he was a restrained analyst. Later in 1922 in two additional items for *Collier's*, one dealing with Prohibition and one with a range of social, economic, and cultural issues, White calmly noted regional differences; identifying his constituency as progressive, middle class, and Middle Western, he was dismal over resolving the Prohibition issue, but he did argue that reconciliation was possible over other matters. As long as White had the reassuring sense America was going his way, or ultimately would go his way, his vision was that of a national community which had room for everyone—everyone who in the end, too, would be progressive, middle class, and in his or her own way Middle Western.[6]

Despite his distress over a bevy of concerns in the twenties, White had come to accept that a conservative order, in its own halting manner, was making progress, moving in his middle-class direction. In March 1927 he felt sufficiently buoyed to write a lead article for *Harper's Magazine* entitled "Cheer Up, America!" The editors wrote soothingly, "There is much harsh criticism nowadays of American manners, culture, and morals. . . . We are glad to give an opportunity to 'William Allen White,' . . . wise and liberal observer of the American scene, to set forth the reasons for his fundamental faith." In the article White laid out his view that the nation was on the right track, and he was willing to see things through. He could tolerate a long list of Menckenesque shortcomings, for more importantly America was instituting a self-respecting, middle-class order. America's greatest strength was its democracy—white, Anglo Saxon, and Protestant, the nation had chosen the right course.[7]

■ ■ ■

Within such a commodius view of the union White even had room in 1926 for Al Smith. In "Al Smith—city feller," published in *Collier's,* the Kansas editor confidently showcased his respect for the governor of New York. Smith was a product of his environment; in the same manner generations earlier Jackson and Lincoln had risen out of America's backcountry. The backwoods were fading away today, but the same corruptive, rough environment was extant in the cities. The challenges of the past had given way to new demands, and new men were rising to meet them. Smith represented the incipient, valued leadership of an industrial democracy. He represented, too, the clash of civilizations. If he was to win the presidency, he would bring great changes to American life as urban-bred Europeans turned upon the Anglo and Teutonic heartland. The Democratic Party clearly was evolving into an urban party; fortunately, Al Smith, the archetypal "city feller," had yet to formulate a national program, to comprehend and speak to issues which touched the concerns of those living beyond the East and outside the large cities. Al Smith had a limited constituency. For now, short of a vision which encompassed all of America, he represented no danger to the established order. For now, there remained time to institute a more moderate, progressive course into the new era whereby older America, alongside a newer America, would guide the nation toward a truly national consensus.[8]

All then in 1926 and 1927 seemed well enough; but this was not enough for White. In "Al Smith—city feller" White made it clear that in looking over the political landscape what he sought was a good deal more than a holding action against an urban presidency. Smith, he explained, could not speak to those who stood at the antipodes of his world—to rural America. Calvin Coolidge was no better, unable to address the urban masses. Someone was needed who could speak to both extremes and more explicitly to those caught in the middle, those who clung to older values but lived in a more and more urban and industrialized world, those, for example, living in states like Wisconsin, Indiana, and Ohio. These Americans represented the nation's true needs, its best hope for the future, and they had no spokesperson. The cities were growing, and if a leader did not appear who could usher in a new order amalgamating the best of an older American life with the new, then possibly in 1928, or 1932, an urbanite would lead a formidable and untimely challenge to take hold of the nation's destiny. Time was running short; temperate, progressive leadership was in demand. The pressure was building; action was needed to head off a crisis. Middle America needed command.

Suddenly the political landscape turned ugly; in 1928 Al Smith's vision seemed to have broadened sufficiently enough for him to capture the Democratic nomination for president. Fortuitously, from White's perspective, he faced the ideal opponent. Back in 1920 White had campaigned for Herbert Hoover as the best man to engineer a new order. Now, after eight years of what White considered to be reactionary rule, Hoover stood as the best candidate to speak to the needs of the nation, to lead the way to a more just order. Hoover could speak for America's middle ground. Not a stalwart to hold back change as Harding and Coolidge, nor an urban progressive ready to move too fast as Smith, Hoover according to White's reading could not have arrived at a more opportune moment. The clash had come, a great contest was to unfold, and Herbert Hoover stood ready to carry forward the standard of moderation.[9]

For White the election became a personal crusade. He threw himself onto the Hoover bandwagon and with a fervor unmatched since the Bull Moose campaigns rose up as one of the candidate's most outspoken supporters. In 1927 he worked hard for Hoover in Kansas; when Hoover received the party's nomination in June 1928 White entered the national fray. He overlooked what he had reported in his syndicated coverage of the convention: the ultra-conservative nature of the party and the platform. Instead, he saw Hoover as a progressive, able to represent the people in all their needs. His opponent, meanwhile, standing on a progressive platform more akin to the Kansan's own views, was seen as representing another proposition which received a good deal of White's attention. Kicking off the campaign with a speech in Olathe, Kansas, on July 12, White underscored what the election was all about: Smith was a Tammany man; he was "wet," and in the past as a New York legislator he had supported gambling and prostitution. The Democratic nominee clearly represented a debased, urban order. White was prepared to do battle for a more moral, all-American order.

White's charges created a sensation. Smith backers claimed the legislative votes had been against unconstitutional and unenforceable measures.

It was clear, amidst charges and countercharges, that the issue was not so much a question of the votes but the candidate's credentials to represent all the people. "Smith," declared White, "must be beaten if America remains American." Liberal columnist Heywood Broun again challenged White's assessment of Americanism: "From down in the cornfields there comes a mournful sound," he wrote in the New York *Telegram*. "If America remains American. It never has and should not. The greatness of this country does not lie in living on a leash tied 'round a stump.'" With the controversy surrounding Smith's votes left unresolved and the more potent Americanism issue up in the air, White sailed for Europe in August. When he returned in late September he campaigned again for Hoover, or more pointedly against Smith, speaking in Kansas, Georgia, North Carolina, and Tennessee. Focusing on Prohibition, to the virtual exclusion of confounding distractions such as the tariff, farm relief, the regulation of utilities, and international relations, White returned to his fundamental question: What sort of community did Alfred E. Smith represent?[10]

In the only campaign article White would write in 1928, the disingenuously titled "Battle Hum of the Republic," he contended that there was little at issue in the campaign excepting the candidates themselves. He noted there was little difference between the party platforms; what he did cite generally reduced down to Republican weaknesses and Democratic strengths. Both Hoover and Smith were admirable men and clearly good leaders. There was one difference to the candidacies, and it was most important. Here lay the great question to be resolved in November: "The differences that will roll like dice out of the ballot box will be between Hoover and Smith. They are the issue. They represent the deeply diverse philosophies, that are at the moment and for the first time in a long generation stirring the hearts of the American people." A new order suddenly engulfed the nation, White explained. Both Hoover and Smith represented new leadership for an urban-industrial state. Would this state incorporate its rural-based, Anglo-Puritan heritage, with its commitment to the enforcement of moral order; or would a cosmopolitan mix of alien religious and ethnic groups establish a chaotic order of indeterminate dimensions? The truth was that White never could quite determine what the opposition tendered and what dimensions he feared; it simply was not what America had known in the past. Different ways to express Americanism were at odds; this he knew. This was the great issue of 1928.[11]

On election day Hoover registered a titanic victory. As much as Smith's Catholicism, urbanism, and "wetness" directly contributed to his loss—and they counted heavily against him, not to mention a dynamic economy—less direct contributions as White's had exerted considerable influence on the election. Focusing solely on Smith's Tammany ties and his opposition to Prohibition, White had struck an emotional chord. For him it was indeed an emotion-laden election. Two ways of life battled, and he and a large number of others, feeling the mounting pressure for years, wanted to hold on to the old and simply, but importantly, to retain some influence over the new. During the campaign White received a deluge of hate mail purportedly supporting his position—one pamphlet ranted, "'The Pope of Rome raises on high his bloody baton of ignorant superstition to lead his battalions of death upon the Temple of Liberty.'" White, having never directly raised the religion issue in the campaign, trusted his message had gotten through to a more thoughtful constituency. In January, 1929 he would write to Justice Louis Brandeis that Al Smith "represented a strange, unfamiliar, and to many narrow minds, an abhorrent tendency in our national life. Partly it was religion that symbolized the distrust. But I think it was chiefly an instinctive feeling for the old rural order and old rural ways." White saw the election as a confirmation of his belief that Americans would look ahead, with him, to the creation of a new order which encompassed the best of the old ways. With Hoover's victory came the greatest spoil of all—time to incorporate temperate, progressive change. Middle America was in the saddle again.[12]

■ ■ ■

White was riding high in 1929. In May in the Kansas-based *Public Affairs Magazine,* he pronouced, "We Have Ceased to Mark Time: New Blood and Leadership Enter with Hoover." Hoover, White argued, represented more than a change in the presidency; here practically was a new Republican Party and in likelihood an even newer era. He and Smith were carried to their nominations by a grass-roots political groundswell rejecting not only the corruption and greed of the Harding years but as well the restoration of order with peace and prosperity during the Coolidge "interregnum." The people were ready for change. They did not, however, desire a sharp break with the past; they rejected progressive Smith for progressive Hoover; they opted for new blood enriched by old tradition. Hoover offered restrained, constructive, altruistic leadership within a period of continued stability and prosperity. "Great things will be done in the next eight years," White declared. "After a decade of inaction, the American people again set out on the highroad of high adventure."[13]

The highroad, of course, shortly dropped off into the depths of the Great Depression. White's hopes for timely and prudent progress toward an urban-industrial idyll were swept away with the rest of the social debris;

change, swift in its coming, alarming in its dimensions, and unpredictable in its course, had descended upon the United States. Looking ahead toward a harmonious era of middle-class selflessness amidst plenty, White instead saw a national community fractured along class lines and turning on itself under intense economic pressure. He had long predicted a crash of sorts was in the offing. In 1926, as one of twenty-three prewar radicals considering the new order of the twenties, White had written in the reform journal the *Survey:* "New times will produce new causes, and sooner or later new issues will call out those qualities in heart and mind which made the old idealists popular and forceful in the land. But their time is not now." White, however, was not sure whose time had come in the 1930s. The Depression was a whole new cause, and the issues it raised often seemed a far cry from those which had rallied "hearts and minds" a generation before. Feeling both a part of the unfolding drama and in a manner lost within it, this prewar radical struggled through the Depression years to interpret the meaning of the unexpected changes surrounding him and to argue for his own conception of communal order. The question of community, the quest for order, and the pressure he had felt building throughout the twenties now had reached true crisis proportions.[14]

Early into the Depression White urged Hoover to exert strong, dramatic leadership. He knew it was asking too much. He had long sensed that Hoover, a fine administrator for good times, was incapable of reaching out to the people; he knew Hoover could not rise to the drama of the hour. As Emporia's economy slipped, White chaired an effort to secure jobs for the unemployed and to provide relief for the destitute. In March 1931 he collapsed and retired to the Southwest to recover. In August he joined Hoover's Committee for Unemployment Relief and a similar commission in Kansas. All the while his confidence in the Hoover administration flagged; White wanted more forceful leadership. As early as 1930 he had despaired to a colleague: "There is no hope for the ineptitude of this administration.... For a man who has high intentions and a noble purpose, our beloved President has a greater capacity for doing exactly the wrong thing at a nicely appointed right time than any man who ever polished his pants in the big chair at the White House." White also wanted more progressive leadership. He believed the government should ensure jobs for the nation's workers; decent food, housing, and clothing; education to the age of twenty-one; and security against poverty and old age. In July 1931 he complained to a fellow Bull Mooser, "I have been wishing for some time that the President would find it in his heart to evangelize a little upon the duties of the great industrial leaders and teach them that duties go with rights." "The President," he added, "has stood bravely and effectively for the privileges of the invested dollar. Now is the time for him to stand also for the duties of the invested dollar." The Hoover administration had fallen calamitously short of White's highest expectations.[15]

Within the national press White hardly addressed the Depression crisis throughout the trauma of the Hoover years. Loyal to the president as a friend and early supporter, with little to say in favor of executive policy, and ever mindful of political exigencies, the generally vociferous journalist seemed to consider it best to keep a low profile. Perhaps he was dazed, perhaps shell-shocked. In December 1931, as one of four individuals pondering "If I Were a Dictator" for the *Nation,* White offered a prescription for recovery which, setting aside the journal's provocative title, could have been written anytime over the past quarter century—he never once mentioned the Depression. After Hoover's resounding defeat by Franklin Delano Roosevelt in the 1932 election, in which White had futilely and half-heartedly supported the president, the journalist seemed freed again to come to terms with what was happening to the nation in its fullest scope and to wonder more forthrightly about the future.[16]

In an inaugural essay for the March 4, 1933, issue of the *Saturday Evening Post,* White tried to approach "the devastating years that have changed America more deeply than any decade in her history." He attempted to explain who Hoover was and what he had stood for, something that Hoover had seemed unable to convey, and he endeavored to direct the best course for the new administration. Looking over the "tragic" descent from ultimate triumph to ignominious defeat, White posed a pertinent question in the title of his "Herbert Hoover—The Last of the Old Presidents or the First of the New?" Hoover, he argued, indeed had been a new type of president, and he had represented a righteous cause. He was a progressive who regrettably could not work with his own kind; while no plutocrat, Hoover was more at ease with the wealthy. He was a businessman—the first to rise to the presidency—and significantly, "President Hoover, more than any other President who has occupied the White House since Theodore Roosevelt left it, was a middle-class President, striving to perpetuate middle-class American ideals." Hoover could not "evangelize" as Cleveland, the first Roosevelt, or Wilson, to a people in need of guidance. Yet his philosophy was sound, for at base Herbert Hoover stood for America's past tailored to its future. Despite failures, which White dutifully catalogued, the Hoover administration represented a big step forward, initiating unprecedented and successful programs to restore confidence while maintaining the historic direction of American progress:

> It is middle class, this American civilization. It holds the pious hope that by curbing the cupidity of its plutocrats through taxation and regulation, society may bring more and more justice to its proletariat, holding the one down, boosting the other up to its own middle-class social and economic status. That is the America of the Fathers. It was the composite vision of Washington, Jefferson and Hamilton. It was the ideal of Andrew Jackson and Abraham Lincoln. In modern times, Theodore Roosevelt and Wilson saw this same America from different angles. It was to save this America intact out of the depression that Herbert Hoover set his face against insidious change in governmental attitude, and so made his fight. It was not for the economic status quo that he contended; only for the preservation of American institutions, social, commercial, political. Somewhere in his heart burns a white flame of passion for this ideal.

His leadership had fallen short but his vision was long. It would bode well for the new administration, White warned, to keep his middle-class ideal in mind. Hoover had looked in the right direction. White cautioned against turning this new president by ill-advised, radical programs into an old president. He rhetorically concluded,

> So history stands hesitant, waiting for time to tell whether Herbert Hoover is merely a failure as a politician or a success as a statesman; whether, by pointing the way to social recovery, this President is the first of the new Presidents come to power fifty years before his time, or whether, by battling so valiantly against assaults upon the American spirit of the fathers, he is the last of the old. So much remains for time to tell history that we must wait for the truth.

Fearing too radical a change in direction, White looked with the rest of the country to Washington.[17]

Time passed quickly, the "truth" began to emerge, and history dramatically was in the making as the new administration ventured to control the nation's precarious state of affairs. Whether Hoover represented the old or the new became a moot question as White attempted to discern what exactly the administration was about. Initially doubtful of Franklin Roosevelt's ability to grapple with such a difficult situation—as a good many others he considered the New York governor a charming patrician with a superficial grasp of governance—White was relieved as the New Deal took concrete form in the First Hundred Days. The Kansas editor enthusiastically backed the President. Roosevelt's direction, if not always his method, was sound.[18]

Fundamentally supporting the administration over the next ten years,

White was persistently troubled by three concerns. He feared too much government intervention and bureaucracy would sap private initiative, which he considered to be the great economic bulwark of American democracy. The goal was to provide Americans with the opportunity to raise themselves while guaranteeing for all a decent and secure standard of living. Once a secure base was provided, he favored Hoover's approach: support large economic, social, and civic institutions and trust their initiative to advance the good of the people. White questioned the growing authority of the presidency beyond the bulky government apparatus. Roosevelt was all right, but his quest for expanded control was opening the door for a less trustworthy executive in another desperate hour easily to assume dictatorial power. Most troubling of all for White was the president's willingness to play one class against another, to risk just such a state of affairs. If the "plutocracy" did not wrest control, possibly the "proletariat" would establish a "mobocracy." The American system was under assault, and it was imperative that the president guarantee the middle class its sovereign power. If he did not, threatened from above and below, this great body itself could be stampeded into the hands of a malevolent dictator whose designs would leave little room for a harmonious, equalitarian American ideal.

In 1933, however, the state of the union was perilous. The first order of business was to stave off total collapse; to begin to refortify the great middle class; and then, with time, to let this class fulfill its benevolent destiny, to spread its ethos to all Americans. During the First Hundred Days, White was dazzled by the breadth of government commitment pledged by the New Deal and by the dramatic quality of Roosevelt's leadership. Here was what Hoover should have done all along. The Kansas editor knew firsthand how badly the social, economic, and political order had been rent over the past few years. In reporting "The Farmer Takes His Holiday" in the *Saturday Evening Post* in late November 1932, he had woefully described the revolutionary climate in neighboring Iowa. The epitome of agricultural prosperity and equitable distribution a decade earlier, this heartland state had been brought to its knees; now the farmers were rising up, and if the government did not act to relieve them, "Khaki Shirts" were sure to become a factor in American democracy. The Middle West, the homestead of the middle class, was buckling. How could the rest of the country endure the calamity?[19]

Clearly, as White had argued early in 1931 in "The Republic Totters" for *Capper's Magazine* (the successor to Kansas's *Public Affairs Magazine*), the answer was not trickle-down economics:

> With this school of economic thought we do not hold. Under such a system, the rich men need only to give bigger and bigger parties and the rest of us could live without working by the simple expedient of rushing from garbage pail to garbage pail, digging out from the coffee grounds and eating stray mushrooms, truffles, and half-masticated hearts of palm.

No, the answer was forceful government intervention. In June 1934, he told a University of Kansas audience, "On the whole and by and large, I am for the New Deal. It is neither Communist nor Fascist. Much of it is necessary. All of it is human. And most of it is long past due." Roosevelt had taken the desperate situation in hand, rescuing the nation from the brink of disaster; confidence was restored. In reviewing the president's 1934 book, *On Our Way,* White could only wonder "But Where Are We Going?" America was refortified. Franklin Roosevelt, as his cousin Theodore, was a classic liberal who recognized that the proper role of government was to save society; he was a fine, patrician leader of a middle-class, democratic order. The New Deal, on the other hand, despite the president's claim to a "grand plan," was haphazard to its core and had not restored excitement and optimism as the president contended. Danger still haunted the republic as it breached an unknown realm:

> But exactly what it is all about, where we are headed, when we shall get there, and what we shall be when we arrive, the book does not reveal—deponent sayeth not!
> What it does reveal, however, is that we are groping across some narrow isthmus in the new world between the precipices of fascism and communism, feeling our way, not knowing how far it is safe ahead, realizing that we must not turn back.

As least on such a fraught journey, White concluded, there was a leader the people could trust:

> The thing of which we may be sure at this time, after reading the President's book, is that we are under the leadership of a brave man, sure of himself, but not cocksure, generous, kind-hearted, and morally honest. He reveals no genius of intellectual leadership, his eye apparently does not penetrate the future. No seer is he; only "a gentleman unafraid," leading a people out of the wilderness of the past, parting the waters of the present into a new, strange promised land, of which he knows as little as we do. He is only certain that we are "On Our Way."

William Allen White had taken stock; he was speculatively banking on Franklin Roosevelt's leadership to pull the country through.[20]

White was not exaggerating his admiration for Franklin Roosevelt. Charmed as so many others, he liked the president, and more important he appreciated what he had accomplished. FDR fascinated the Sage of Emporia and befuddled him. He supplied dramatic leadership and action that the country needed; he acquired more and more personal power; and he retained the mandate to forge ahead no matter how skewed his course proved to be. The New Deal was a remarkable success at the executive level and a dubious enterprise at the grass roots. White was sure Roosevelt was heading for a fall; meanwhile, he was content to cheer him on as he had cleared the immediate hurdle of economic and social collapse.

Behind White's hedged vote of confidence in Roosevelt lurked a grave fear. The president had righted the ship of state, but middle-class America was in trouble. White expressed his concern throughout the early thirties; as the "first" New Deal gave way to the "second," and then as the international horizons darkened in the late 1930s, his anxiety grew. Roosevelt had rescued the middle class from the trough of the Depression, but formidable obstacles to full recovery remained. Throughout White's commentaries lay an increasing sense that while the nation had journeyed into yet another new era, its trek was becoming more harrowing rather than more reassuring. Frequent remarks regarding the double-edged threat of fascism and communism and warnings over excessive presidential power dovetailed with his great concern over the well being of the middle class as the Depression dragged on. The middle class was growing again in size, but it was hardly a benevolent body. White was not sure the great body, pressed from within America and without, was up to preserving the American ideal of equal opportunity and plenty for all—or of seeking it. The nation had entered a rocky period in its history, and indeed White was unsure "what we shall be when we arrive."

■ ■ ■

Always preoccupied with the development of the "Great American Middle Class," White had long recognized some of the amorphous entity's less-than-harmonious attributes—especially in the twenties he had noted a crassness, a selfishness, and worst of all a "moronic" affinity for mobocracy—all of which detracted from its more fundamentally altruistic character. At best there seemed to lurk a double identity to this group; at worst White occasionally alluded to a fractured identity—the existence of an upper and a lower middle class. With the deepening depression, with the prosperous facade removed, the middle class with all its flaws and fissures had to be addressed. Back in late 1931, with the Hoover administration facing open revolt, White had spoken to the issue through a review of Henry Pringle's biography of Theodore Roosevelt. White was clearly worried and ready to lay blame for the trouble at the feet of the middle class itself—or rather, the underside of the middle class. "Here was a man," White recalled, but more to the point here was a class. Roosevelt's glorious rise to power paralleled that of the American middle class. His support was from the best element, the upper and middle reaches of this great body. The ignorant lower middle class who would follow any demagogue catering to all they asked of him had to turn elsewhere for leadership. Theodore Roosevelt's "mob" had intelligence and character:

> So Roosevelt's mob was composed of men and women, educated generally through the high school, who read a daily paper and some sort of a weekly or monthly magazine occasionally, who lived at a minimum in a five-room house or apartment and at a maximum of eight or ten, who hated the very rich and feared the very poor—the one as greedy and powerful, the other as greedy and ignorant, both dangerous. This Roosevelt mob ruled the roost in America during the first decade and a half of this [century].

Fifteen years later, looking back with Pringle, White could only have been pondering what had happened: Where had "this middle class group that came into consciousness of power and so into sovereignty in those days" gone awry?[21]

Close to three years later White updated his identification of the better element, now generally tagged the "upper middle class," in an article written, appropriately, for the *Atlantic Monthly*. The editor's topic and title was "Good Newspapers and Bad," in which he expressed his disgust with the low-class ethics of a paper like the *Denver Post* and his admiration for the likes of the high-class *Christian Science Monitor*. The middle class was on the skids, and it could be seen in the newspapers they read. The mob, with its movie and sports idols, with its cheap literature and its booze, rushed to the vulgar *Post*. The sophisticated, those with good judgment, picked up the *Monitor*. And where did one find the *Post* readers? They were urban types; look to cities over two hundred thousand, White declared. Here ruled the mob; here, the lowest common denominator set the standard; here was the breeding ground for the demagogue. "What are we going to do about them—'we' meaning the average citizen, 'them' meaning these literate millions who make the intellectual underworld?" The nation was becoming urbanized, and the middle class was becoming debased—the upper and middle strata were becoming overwhelmed by, of all things, the historically homogeneous character of the class itself:

Now this issue in American life between those of the low intelligence quotient and those with a normal degree of intellectual capacity would seem to point to stratification. But no—they do not stratify. In the blood strain of our national life the genes which carry the thing, whatever it is, called brains, or the lack of it, are liable to occur in any grade, step, or stratum of our social, economic, or intellectual life. We are likely to go from moron to genius in a generation, and from genius to moron in the next generation. The same parents breed children of widely different qualities, so completely have we mixed our social classes here in the last three hundred years. There can be no hereditary ruling class because of this pied blood stream of ours—which fact brings some comfort.

That fact not too long ago, indeed, had brought White great satisfaction. Trusting in the middle class, and especially those living in smaller communities of less than two hundred thousand, he had looked to the development of a benevolent greater middle class which ruled by the sheer weight of its numbers. Now that had devolved into a moronic, majoritarian urban threat (existing to some extent in smaller communties as well), and there seemed little time, if any, for the situation to turn around, for the genius to take over. White concluded his piece wondering what was happening to American ideals. The upper middle class still ruled, but he questioned, for how long?[22]

White always had advocated a leadership of the best element to secure a more intelligent, more benevolent greater populace which ultimately would require little guidance. Whenever times were good, from his perspective, he saw less need of this leadership. When times were bad he would fall back on it. So in 1896 White had allied himself with the best element represented by McKinley Republicanism; in 1914 he had retreated to the Middle West, the true home of enlightened Bull Moose progressivism; in 1922 he had ruminated about inoculating moronic urbanites with civics lessons; and once more, in 1928, he lined up with the representatives of an older America to determine the future of a newer America. Suddenly, that newer America had swept in with a vengeance. Within a chaotic urban-industrial order there seemed fewer with whom he could ally, less room within which he could safely retreat, and no clear spot to draw a line in the sand. The best element itself was in serious trouble. The upper middle class, the leadership, undercut by degenerative urban values and overwhelmed by a depressed economy, now seemed ripe for reaction. As the Depression became institutionalized in the 1930s, White appealed to this leadership group, compromised as it might be, to fight to preserve a middle-class American ideal. His concern increased with the decade's passing as precious time seemed to slip away and events took on more and more a "moronic" character. Middle America had to fight.

The battle line for White had come down to the upper middle class. Increasingly he felt the need to address the group, to arouse it in its hour of need to act in the interests of all Americans; at the same time he felt pressed to warn the government, and the upper and lower classes, not to push those who held in their power all that was dear in America to the point of sacrificing everything out of fear of losing everything. The matter came to a head after the 1936 election. White was not enthusiastic about the candidacy of his old friend and political colleague Kansas governor Alfred M. Landon: the Republican standard bearer was not fully prepared to assume the immense responsibility of the presidency; his campaign had come under the influence of reactionary forces; and significantly, the incumbent was phenomenally popular and competent to continue his leadership in a deeply troubled time. White campaigned for Landon in a lackluster manner; when he penned a *Saturday Evening Post* piece backing the nominee, his former Bull Moose ally, prominent New Dealer Harold Ickes was prompted to write, "I could not for the life of me see, even on the basis of your deft portrayal of him, why anyone should vote for him for President." White had poorly masked his real allegiance. The dilemma was the Depression; the solution lay in rallying the middle class, not in displacing Franklin Roosevelt.[23]

Beginning in 1937 White wrote a number of articles addressing the middle class and its unique problem. In "The Challenge to the Middle Class" published in the *Atlantic Monthly* in August 1937, he raised the alarm—the long established American way of life was being put to a severe test. "The old middle class," or "the upper middle class," housed in communities with population of up to two hundred thousand, was being squeezed from the top and the bottom. Alien elements to middle-class American life lived in the cities, the epicenters of the new order. White was reviewing three books focusing on community: Robert and Helen Lynd's *Middletown in Transition,* Charles Rumford Walker's *American City: A Rank-and-File History,* and Gilbert Seldes's *Mainland.* The authors, in his opinion, pinpointed the problem: America had built a vast middle-class society which over the years had expanded to incorporate more and more of the citizenry into the security of its ranks. A new urban, industrial order under severe economic stress had set up barriers to reaching this harmonious state. The proletariat, living in the cities, had become "class-conscious" and were susceptible to the machinations of bosses, who in their turn could be controlled by plutocrats (the urban middle class as well could be corrupted by bosses and capitalists). The "public-be-damned" attitude of the spoiled plutocrats had long been tolerated; the attitude of industrial unionist John Lewis and the likes of the Congress of Industrial Organizations (CIO) was not acceptable. The hope of society always had rested in the ability of the laboring class to work its way into the middle class: "A middle-class complacency has been the ideal American life" offering "a salving sense of security." In espousing its own agenda, labor had become dangerously alienated from the historic mainstream of American society. Somehow the old middle class had to assume its leadership post and work out a compromise; somehow the upper middle class had to bring, immediately, the urban dispossessed into the security of its own ranks. Somehow "middletown" had to work within the new urban order to revivify its dominant ethos, to defend America from the extremes of plutocratic reaction and labor radicalism.[24]

The solution was not hard to discern. It was necessary to combat the growing conservatism of a fearful middle class. Labor's agenda was legitimate; the middle class simply had to lay aside its fear of losing its property and status and respectfully welcome the workers into its own fold. There really was little to compromise; the middle class had only to adopt a more benevolent posture and convince the workers that its agenda was their own agenda—it was the American ideal. It was the old Bull Moose attitude. It was the attitude of the New Deal. But here, indeed, was the rub. While indicting the conservatism of the middle class, White also worried that the New Deal was pushing the middle class further toward reaction. The administration was going too far, too fast. In December 1937 in a piece for the *New Republic,* the Kansas editor issued "A Yip from the Doghouse":

> These lines are written because they have been lying heavily on my chest for a long time, say five or six years. . . . I seem to represent, or at least feel I speak for, a group of neolithic liberals who once inhabited these lands and had a place of some power and prestige before the coming of the great Ice Age, and now all that we stood for, our whole ideology and dialectic, is rejected and we are in the doghouse and we know it.

White argued that in working for better housing, wages, education, and, most of all, for self-respect, the old-line progressives sought to bridge more than class differences: "The thing we were trying to do from the days of the first Roosevelt and during the dark years that followed Wilson, through Harding, to Hoover, was to brace up the human spirit in those social and economic areas where class differences were cruelly marked and wickedly depressed." This goal of boosting the human spirit while expanding the middle class had been lost amidst the prosperity of the twenties: "We forgot our objective. . . . We began to think that the whole trick could be done by distributing toothpaste, automobiles, radios, bathtubs, parks, playgrounds, high schools, libraries, extension courses and canned soups to those who hitherto had been denied these sweet boons." The Bull Moosers, and the middle class, had fallen short. They had forgotten to emphasize the development of a benevolent spirit as well as the distribution of goods—when the crunch came in 1929 Americans turned upon one another. The old progressives were in disrepute, but their aim in raising human sights should not be:

> We still believe that it is the spirit we are seeking to benefit and enlarge. We still believe that the quest for justice cannot be achieved by force. We are confused, bedeviled, bewildered, at strong-arm methods. We are shocked at the sit-down strike; we are sick at heart at the [employer violence] revelations of the LaFollette [sic] committee; we hate the tyrannies of fascism and the Nazis; we are nauseated at the Soviet executions. At home we loathe ["Little Steel" corporate leader] Tom Girdler and distrust the class-conscious appeal of the one big union. We know theoretically that the principle of the CIO is right. It must come to that in the end. But we are a bit white-livered and don't like to see it come to that by coercion and the labor racketeer.

The administration, White believed, was making a grave error. Too much government intervention, too much bureaucracy, and too much presidential power, especially exercised in behalf of labor, was threatening the middle class. Nurture benevolence, he argued; do not pressure the middle class to resort to force. The government, and particularly labor could no longer wait, given the chronic economic condition, for a gradual evolution as the Bull Moosers had tried to do. But in pressing for change, it was imperative to promote middle-class liberalism and court middle-class public opinion. To not do so, to not allow the middle class to determine the order of change was to court the greatest of calamities. For the middle class still represented the greatest interest group in the country. Push it too far, White warned, and you "will turn it fascist overnight—and dirty."[25]

White was desperate that the middle class somehow open up to labor, win its backing, and, as a result, reassert its voice as the dominant representative of all Americans. At all cost force in American society had to be avoided. He was angry that the administration had politicized the class issue by courting labor votes in 1936. He believed Franklin Roosevelt had assumed the powers of a dictator; his aims were good but he had established an unsavory precedent for a plutocrat or communist demagogue to seize power. Force, within American society and abroad, had become an all-too-easy alternative. In an address printed in *Vital Speeches* in

November 1938 he pleaded for all Americans—capitalists, consumers, and laborers—"to give a little," and not encourage the government to resort to further intrusive measures into American life. He claimed he was speaking for the middle class, and he asked that, in a time of increasing domestic and international tension, calm prevail. The Depression continued unabated; tyranny stalked abroad:

> We must all give a little. This hour has no time for the man who refuses to compromise even to his own hurt. Half of the civilized world today beyond our borders has surrendered the rights, privileges and blessings which democracy accords to free men. Should not the roaring waters of disaster flooding ever nearer the feet of those who follow the tyrants, warn us to turn to the ways of peace with justice which are the only guarantees of freedom?

After a decade of strain White feared for the worse: middle-class America could easily turn to totalitarianism to solve its dilemma. The just solution rested in its hands; it alone could restore equanimity to the land; it alone could resurrect a greater, harmonious, American order.[26]

Throughout the 1930s White publicly was asking questions. Which way to turn? Where are we going? What is the answer? These queries had seldom appeared in his earlier work. The answers he provided were often muddled. But he was honest. He was confused over the state of the American union, and he did not hesitate to say so. He had doubts about the New Deal but knew it was necessary; he admired Franklin Roosevelt but feared his power; he placed his faith in the middle class but was no longer quite certain who belonged to that august body; and while he despaired over the quagmire of seemingly insurmountable domestic problems, he could not ignore developments in Europe and Asia. In "The Challenge to Democracy: It Is a Glib Shibboleth," the Sage of Emporia in 1938 tried to come to terms with the confusion on all fronts; in the end, he fell back upon the one answer within which he always could find solace. In the face of mounting rather than diminishing problems, Americans had to look to their past and trust in the security of the middle-class ideal:

> Let us therefore assume that the anchor of our liberties lies in the security of our people. Today that security is the bone and sinew of the middle class. . . . This security of the middle class is our salvation. This saving security is founded somewhat upon law but not much, somewhat upon commercial customs and credits, and largely upon the ethics, the common decencies of the common life of the common people—there are, indeed, the brakes of democracy. If we would hold the cart from slipping as a nation, we must widen the base of privilege. . . . when the American people really care to widen the avenues of privilege, when they

are ashamed to see outside of their middle class walls people who are underfed, illclad, and underhoused, the vast majority of the American people will find a way to admit their less acquisitive brethren to the ranks of the privileged.

The challenge to democracy, as always, was a challenge to benevolence. The privileged had to find it within themselves to allow the others their just middle-class due:

> If the brakes of democracy hold as we go through this world of collapse and cataclysm, it will be because we have broadened the brakes, widened the wheels of our chariot, let more people ride. In short and in conclusion we will be just as safe as we are wise and kind. For after all, quite apart from its pietistic association, the old wisdom still holds:
> 'Righteousness exalteth a nation and sin is a reproach to any people.'

The people needed to right their ways and to do so quickly. A decade into the Depression the republic continued to totter.[27]

■ ■ ■

In calling forth chariots full of decent common folk, and in speaking of a righteous nation opposed to sin, White was beginning to hoist a familiar flag. The crusader's pitch was strongly reminiscent of the chauvinistic tone he had struck in 1917. Here were the old watchwords; here was the progressive banner under which so many could gather as one community working for the common good. Here, indeed, was the answer. White, as a troubled Bull Mooser, had hoped for domestic renewal through foreign adversity; now in the late 1930s, as a troubled national spokesperson, he sensed that the danger of totalitarianism could regenerate the American ideal. White was hardly a warmonger; rather, the perennial optimist saw the possibility that the people, faced with the antithesis of all they professed to believe, could find unity and harmony, a greater sense of community based upon the elusive qualities of selflessness and benevolence, to ward off their undoing.

The danger had loomed on the horizon for years, and White had taken close note of it. Since the First World War he had kept abreast of foreign affairs. The Fascists, Nazis, and Communists increasingly concerned him. In a talk to the graduates of Northwestern University in 1937 he had contrasted the inherent unity and virtue of democratic, middle-class America to the disorder and "spiritual pestilence" festering in Europe, particularly fostered by nationalistic Italy, Germany, and the Soviet Union. America had its divisive problems, but it also had the means to achieve social harmony. "Social faith" was the answer; the practice of neighborliness would lead to the development of social equity and self respect. Here was the means to grow strong and to immunize the nation against the alien danger. Middle-class virtue was the antidote to stave off collapse.[28]

As the danger increased White alluded to it more in his work. In a remarkable article, "Moscow and Emporia," in the *New Republic* in 1938, he drew the ideological contrast in detail. Comparing the two communities, White demonstrated the depth of his commitment to the ideal of middle-class harmony, to the point of obfuscating the facts. The editor of the *Gazette*, "as a competent middle-class witness ... , as an average American," began by presenting his credentials as an old sympathizer to the Soviet cause even though he doubted Communism would succeed. He could not understand, however, the fanatical extremes of injustice occurring in the purge-ridden Soviet Union. The mass madness generated abroad by the proletarian Russians, as well as the plutocratic Nazis, stood in stark contrast to the social harmony prevailing in democratic America. Despite the Depression the United States was a just, tolerant society, respectful of individual rights, at peace with itself and the world. The reason was its middle-class foundation. To demonstrate his point White offered up his own town "as a fair sample":

> These lines are written of a summer afternoon on the front porch of a middle-class country-town home in the Middle West. An avenue of elm trees, one of a dozen or so such avenues in town, arches across the bluegrass lawns. And in the town twelve thousand people are at work making what is commonly termed a good living. In one of the larger houses in town, I had about the same breakfast and lunch that my average neighbor has. Every one of my 12,000 neighbors will have meat for dinner. Five or six hundred people here, in addition to this 12,000, are living either on relief and out of work or in the dread of loss of employment. Of course until these five or six hundred people are given an opportunity to live according to their ability, our democratic experiment in social and industrial justice has failed. But these five or six hundred people can and do send their children to school up to and including high school. Their economic misfortunes are not marked by their clothes. Their houses do not brand them with poverty. Organized social sympathy feeds, houses and clothes the two or three hundred out of work and in actual need, not well, but decently.

Here in Emporia were middle-class people, taking care of themselves, learning to take care of the needs of others, looking toward that day when all their neighbors would have the chance to be middle class as well. Emporia was on the right track; White went on to present national figures to demonstrate the fact that so too was America: "Our American experiment has succeeded in bringing comfort, some luxuries, to probably 85, certainly 80 percent of the American people." The nation was still short of utopia, but it was heading in the right direction driven by its middle-class ethos.[29]

Two and a half months later, in response to this reassuring report, novelist, social activist, and erstwhile politician Upton Sinclair wrote an open letter to White in the *New Republic*. Sinclair challenged the *Gazette* editor's "amazing" figures and his naïve vision of America. Where, he wondered, had White been the past decade? "I am not going to try to discuss Russia with you. You have been there, and I have not. I wish to talk about the United States of America, and the picture you draw 'of a summer afternoon on the front porch of a middle-class country-town home in the Middle West.'" Sinclair proceeded to hurl a barrage of statistics at White. The United States was far from middle class by any measure, and Emporia's small percentage—probably 25 percent as elsewhere—was living off the failing credits of the New Deal. The American people, fearful, impoverished, and more and more dependent on one form of dole or another were ready to turn to demagoguery for relief. If White could not see that hate was spreading at home as well as abroad, Sinclair charged, he should take a closer account of Kansas's Gerald Winrod who had just secured fifty thousand votes in a demagogic campaign for the Republican gubernatorial nomination. White, Sinclair surmised, could not face the truth: "Haven't you heard about all this? Perhaps you won't know about it—until the Winrod black shirts storm into your house and take a mild and benevolent liberal to a concentration camp. Even then you won't know what it means; because you simply cannot bring yourself to face the fact that the capitalist system is collapsing." White, in Sinclair's estimation, could not face up to the true extent of the national calamity.[30]

Sinclair accurately had dispelled White's harmonious imagery. He had missed the mark, however, in charging that White could not face up to reality. The editor surely knew, as another correspondent to the *New Republic* pointed out, that Emporia's statistics were "strangely disproportionate" to the rest of the country. He also certainly was aware, as a former Emporian noted in another letter to the journal, of "a much more serious 'seamy side' to the city" than he had indicated in the article. Delineating a precise portrait of Emporia had not been White's purpose. He had sought to create an "impression" of the community, and in so doing to draw out another truth. As he replied to Sinclair (after pulling together a feeble statistical defense of his position and an oddly hypocritical discounting of the danger of Winrod), "And finally mine 'is a truth that never can be proved' and so alas is yours, Upton. But let's both thank God for our fighting faith." White's truth was grounded in his faith in the middle-class ideal. No one needed to point out to him that the country was in deep trouble. He had been raising the alarm for years and in 1938 publicly despaired over the latest relapse of the economy. He did trust in capitalism, but he had lodged plenty of criticisms of the economic order. More than capitalism, he had feared all along for the collapse of the middle class, which he considered to be the benevolent, saving grace of the system. In "Moscow and Emporia" he was a good deal more concerned with reviving the domestic middle-class ideal, through a distorted contrast with its perceived foreign antithesis, than he was in making a foolproof defense of capitalism. Sinclair did not care to talk of Russia but White did, for in looking to Russia and the rest of troubled Europe he believed Americans could once again get hold of their ideal, join together, and save themselves. He did not consciously endeavor to hide the truth, nor hide from the truth; rather, in his view, it was more important to revivify a more elusive truth: in the regeneration of the middle class, in an ethos of selflessness and harmony, lay a viable solution to the threatening calamity he feared as much as did Upton Sinclair.[31]

In glossing over statistics White was hardly ingenuous and hardly the fool. He was committed to an ideal; to a great extent he had built his life around the ideal. For years he had sought a more harmonious American community. In 1896 he had made a fevered defense of his stalwart vision of community; through the Progressive Era he had sought to expand and better define his reformed ideal; in the 1920s he had become preoccupied with the meaning of community and rose as a preeminent spokesperson for a communal ideal which he now clearly identified at base as middle class; and throughout the 1930s he sought to come to terms with the rapidly changing nature of American society. Having long addressed problems of community, it was easy for White to see the problem of community —the need to maintain a semblance of community life within an urban, industrial society—thrown into bold relief during the Depression decade, as soluble within the confines of a vague, expansive middle-class ethos. White had come to develop and to stand by a rhetoric of community. He never really was much concerned with the numbers, for he believed that in the quest for the ideal the numbers ultimately would meet the promise. Believing that Americans trusted in the ideal as he did—that all could live harmoniously in an affluent, just society, White never seemed to mind, in time of need, imposing his illustrative fancy over discouraging facts. Most important of all was the need to believe the ideal remained viable; this was the most fundamental truth, both for the greater good and for his own peace of mind.

As the hard decade, thus, came to a close, with all that was clearly good in American life seemingly challenged by all that was patently bad, at home as well as abroad, White once more began to see light. As the threat loomed larger and larger from abroad, it seemed possible that within it salvation could be found at home. In recognition of the threat and in defense against it, Americans would once again join hands. The time had arrived to wave the flag and to gather together under a banner of community. February 12, 1940, addressing the Abraham Lincoln Association, White recalled another decade of grave crisis and placed his faith in a democratic, middle-class majority to see its way through "a dark day in the world's history." An election was coming amidst the crisis; a leader must be chosen who could represent the just cause of the people. Most important, the hour had arrived for the people to recognize their common fellowship:

> I believe with all my heart that the democratic process with its slow progress but sure, is the one hope of this hate-riddled world. But we need more than one leader. We need an army to follow him, an army of brave, wise, self-respecting followers! I am sure that under the stress of these times that deeply kind and soundly wise leader shall rise. Some gentle, brave and honest man, wise with the love of the people. Him we shall choose and having chosen, we shall trust his leadership. Then shall we cry out again: "We are coming, Father Abraham, ten hundred thousand strong!"

For William Allen White the nation truly seemed, once again, within reach of its communal home. It only needed to raise up its banner, to rise up to its virtuous standard, to crusade once more for an enlightened, middle-class world.[32]

Forging a Middle American Ethos

WILLIAM ALLEN WHITE WAS, as Upton Sinclair had charged, "a mild and benevolent liberal." To the California activist the Kansas editor's faith in a middle-class ideal of equitably distributed justice seemed inexcusably foolhardy and ultimately self-defeating. Yet confronted with the hard realities of the day White remained a national spokesperson of considerable influence. He believed that through portraying the ideal Americans would continue to reach for it. Middle class, benevolent, and liberal—in a time of crisis at home and abroad it was all the more important to present the soundness of the ideal. The restoration of faith was key. White's liberal vision by some measures may have been short on substance, but it was, far and away beyond the criticism of the Upton Sinclairs of America, a most popular twentieth-century fancy; in the end, past the challenges of the 1930s and 1940s, middle-class America would emerge a formidable postwar victor, resting evermore secure upon a greater factual as well as a fanciful base.[1]

In 1939 in a series of lectures delivered at Harvard University, the Kansas journalist attempted to draw together his thoughts on the substance of a middle-class ideal. With the international crisis pressing from without and the economy continuing to lumber within, it seemed of utmost importance to get a grip on the nation's greatest resource—its sense of community. The talks, later published as *The Changing West: An Economic Theory about Our Golden Age,* were weak on historical fact and economic expertise but powerful on idealism. Asked to speak about his region, the Sage chose to focus upon the West and to establish it as a metaphor for the changing notion of community in America. William Allen White often interchanged West and Middle West as regional metaphors—gerrymandering always came easy. The West was not a clearly delineated region, nor was it inhabited by a specific group of people within a precise time frame; more to the point the West represented a way of life founded upon security and plenty. Now, after 150 years of progress, the great communal heritage of America was threatened with dissolution. In addressing the issue White recognized both his academic limitations and his strength as a revered overseer of the "passing show." He prefaced his remarks:

> Alas, I have no statistics with which to back up this thesis. I am a country editor not a trained economist. Economists may come along and shatter the hypothesis. But here it is, the story of America's golden age as I have seen it through at least seven decades of the fifteen in which the West was unfolding: the vast magic carpet of prairie and plain and mountain, of lakes and rivers, deserts and forests, all yielding their wealth which was bent more or less consciously to the purposes of free and aspiring men.... a first and shining example of a free people, morally and intellectually literate, using their own devices, their own sense of justice, to develop the wealth of a region and to distribute it as a common wealth. I may be wrong about the spiritual secret of the mainsprings of this unfolding of wealth controlled and directed by the democratic ideal of justice; but as a reporter I have tried to tell a straight story about the outward and visible way the mainspring worked which moved men westward in a widening, deepening stream of social and economic justice.

Duly qualifying his credentials, White ventured forth to reset the main-spring of American progress—to make his case for an ethos of community built upon the rock-solid virtue of middle-class responsibility.[2]

Within *The Changing West* White tracked the evolution of what later commentators loosely designate a Middle American ethos. In the far reaches of the West—"the territory west of Buffalo and Pittsburgh, north of the Ohio River, onward to the Pacific Coast from Los Angeles to Seattle"—settled since the adoption of the Constitution, there developed a unique, communal way of life. A "Golden Age" had transpired as "an agrarian rural civilization ... merged into the American industrial empire." Machines of "iron and steel, stone and copper" led to the development of "still newer and stranger devices of a stuff not made with hands ... I mean legal machines, social machines, economic machines all whirring in unison—the steel levers, the wheels, and the cogs clicking in the meshes made by the new political, financial, social gadgets and inventions that set up a new way of life." Gradually, in epochal fashion, "The new way of life spread into the valleys of the Ohio, the Mississippi, the Missouri, the Snake, the Columbia, the Sacramento, and down the little dry streams that in the rainy season go rushing through the sands of southern California to the sea." "Why," asked White, "have the machines, material and intangible, established themselves as the very basis of this western civilization of ours?" The answer was clear: "For the first time pioneers had stood upon the mountaintops overlooking rich, noble lands and had brought with them to enlarge their vision a philosophy which was to establish a way of life that never before had risen above the plow of other pioneers." That philosophy, unique to the United States, was a profound faith in middle-class justice.[3]

White went on to explain that America, represented by the West, had been and remained a nation of socially progressive white, Anglo-Saxon Protestants—from the "good middle-class Puritans" who first settled the eastern coast to the natives of the great western expanse dominated today by "the farming areas and the small cities and towns." There were, of course, some large western cities—"Cincinnati, Cleveland, Detroit, Chicago, the Twin Cities, St. Louis, Kansas City, Denver, Seattle, Portland, San Francisco, and Los Angeles"—but they were of little political or social consequence. These urban conglomerations, "outside of the small tenement area," fortunately were inhabited by those "largely American-born of American-born parents." As most agrarian-rooted westerners, they sprang "from what is called the old American stock, English, Scotch, Irish, German, and Scandinavian citizens who have been in the country for half a century or more." The American civilization these archetypal immigrants had been creating in hamlet, town, or metropolis was at bottom middle class. One need only look to a country town located in the Mississippi Valley, ranging in population from fifteen hundred to a hundred thousand, to find the essence of the modern American middle class:

> This American middle class runs the same across the land. The one thing that marks the West is that there the middle class is larger than elsewhere. It dominates the scene. Its stores on Main Street, its tall office buildings, the doctors' and the lawyers' offices and business places of realtors and the traders, are built on one model, the urban model that prevails all over the country. In the residences radios prattle by the hour, mechanical babblers pouring out their idiocy unchecked and often unheeded. For the radio and the automobile are two modern machines that have transcended class lines. They tend to equalize the privileges of the plutocrat and the proletarian. The car, the telephone, and the radio are no longer marks of the middle class anywhere—except in great urban areas. The county-seat town of the Mississippi Valley goes to the farthest salient of democratic civilization in its comfort and in the distribution of its luxuries. Life is probably easier there for the common man, and opportunity probably more wide-open for his children than it is anywhere else on earth.

These townsfolk had built a resplendent "semi-urban" civilization in the heartland. Luxuries had become conveniences, opportunity abounded for all, and a bustling main street showed no trace of blight or division. Here rested the great middling mass of America, materially and spiritually comforted within a philosophy of justice for all.[4]

Having built a technologically and socially superior civilization, middle-class America was now in danger. Security and plenty had given way to fear and scarcity; economic decay threatened the American ideal. The problem, White argued, was not so evident in the West. There life remained vibrant, and the tool of progress—a democratic sense of justice based upon a faith in one's fellow citizen—was still in hand. The West, however, had become intricately linked to the rest of the country and to the world. It could not escape their problems. Short of "utopia" itself in the depressed thirties, the West, middle-class America, still offered the best hope for salvation. The highest calling was that of duty to society; in a troubled era America at its heart needed to act, to serve the greatest good:

> Speaking broadly, even now out West democracy is anchored in the hearts of the people. The anchors are barnacled a little in the industrial centers. Agriculture has a real problem which in too many marginal cases is becoming acute. The dissatisfied industrial worker in Ohio, Michigan, Illinois, to a certain extent in Indiana, Minnesota, and California, and the discontented farmer all over the West, have set red danger signals blinking. It is not critical, this danger, but it is there. We find it easy to say, "Well, given good times, the trouble will all be over." But what are good times? Where are good times? Why are good times delayed? How long can these danger signals blink at us and not mean real danger. The number of marginal farmers is probably increasing. Unemployment even in the West is not perceptibly falling. For a catastrophic decade, western middle-class democracy founded upon the Christian ethic and grounded in capitalism has stood like a rock. But like a rock our democratic capitalism has forces beneath it which slowly are eating into a place where the rock may shift and veer if it does not tumble.

At its middle-class core America remained strong. To avoid total catastrophe it was essential for the people to act on their best middling instincts; it was essential to ensure that all citizens prosper, to save the greater community.[5]

The Changing West represented White's communal ideal; it was tempered with a more realistic assessment of the nation's problems than the editor had cared to note earlier in "Moscow and Emporia." (Still, statements and figures boggle the mind: WASP Chicago with few tenements? What would Upton Sinclair say? Cities like Chicago and Cleveland with no political clout? What would FDR say?) As with "Moscow and Emporia," however, White's primary concern was to rally the American people. To avoid catastrophe, he looked to the ideal; he looked to the West, and in particular to the "Valley of the Mississippi" as the wellspring of a vague Middle American ethos promulgated by all-American folks—like Kansans—residing primarily in smaller cities and towns—like Emporia. Here in the heartland older-stock Americans, imbued with tested values, represented the best the nation had to offer for a new urban-industrial era. In the West "altruistic yearnings" and "acquisitive instincts" as elsewhere did battle, but in the West the "yearning to be neighborly" had beaten back, as nowhere else, the "instinct to grab and to hold." Here was a model for the rest of the nation to emulate. Goodwill and neighborly kindness could be seen in the material quality of Western life. Under a banner of community, in a time of travail, the American people needed to come together once more. The ideal had to be transformed into reality; all Americans potentially were neighbors: "In democracy all men, strong or weak, wise or dumb, have the precious right to be neighborly to rich or poor, to Jew or Gentile, black or white, to Catholic, to Protestant or athe-ist, to fellow patriot or foreigner." In troubled times, more than a right, it was a duty to come to the service of one's community: "Concluding, let me reiterate that what man did . . . with the settlement of the West, man can do now as he plunges into the new era. But he must carry in his heart the two things that made the wilderness blossom as the rose: first, a neighborly faith in the decency of man; second, a never faltering vision of a better world." Reckoning on that vision, White professed his own profound faith in "the survival of the West" and in the resiliency of middle-class America.[6]

■ ■ ■

White was a rhetorical master. He was approaching the end of his life; he was speaking at Harvard University. *The Changing West* at first glimpse, replete with paeans to the Middle West, to Kansas, and to Emporia, might seem an appropriate peroration to a career long concerned with commu-nity. But White's rhetoric always carried a substantive message. In estab-lishing his faith in "the survival of the West," in hoisting the banner of community, he was as intent upon defending an American way of life as he was interested in defining it. White's vision of a better world was threatened by decisions being made overseas as well as at home. *The Changing West* called for immediate action; indeed, it was an appropriate peroration for White as a man of deed as well as word. *The Changing West* raised the alarm as other White pieces had in the late 1930s. The issue was not simply the West, or the Middle West, or Emporia: the issue was the defense of community. Work was in order: middle-class work. White toward the end of his years, as he had throughout his life, beckoned Americans to come to the aid of their neighbors, whatever the communal exigency. Now, the global danger loomed large.

As he had striven for a better community in Emporia, as he had called forth Americans to work with him for a more formidable national community, White was prepared to do more than write in the late 1930s to aid the world community. A call came directly from the White House. To the Sage of Emporia, a liberal Republican from the isolationist Middle West and a molder of national public opinion, Franklin Delano Roosevelt sent an invitation asking the Whites to stay a night at the executive mansion: "I need a few helpful thoughts from the philosopher of Emporia," charmed Roosevelt:

> Things move with such terrific speed, these days, that it really is essential to us to think in broader terms and, in effect, to warn the American people that they, too, should think of possible ultimate results in Europe and the Far East. . . . Therefore, my sage old friend, my problem is to get the American people to think of conceivable consequences without scaring the American people into thinking that they are going to be dragged into this war.

The President was fairly sage himself. In turning to White he knew he was aligning himself with a spokesperson for Middle America, a friend with whom he could work congenially, an ideological ally on most domestic matters, and an active internationalist. Roosevelt needed help, and White could provide the aid because the Kansan spoke "truths" Americans could understand.[7]

Roosevelt wrote White in mid-December 1939; White responded December 22, appreciative of the invitation, stating the trip depended upon Sally White's health. White had known Roosevelt before his rise to the presidency. Through the thirties and into the forties he developed a great respect for the president and grew closer to him. Their personal and professional relationship was well summarized as White expressed his thoughts regarding his later, closest contact with FDR as head of the Committee to Defend America by Aiding the Allies:

> I knew I had his private support. . . . I never did anything the President didn't ask for, and I always conferred with him on our program. . . . He never failed us. We could go to him—any members of our executive committee, any member of our policy committee. He was frank, cordial, and wise in his counsel. We supported him in his foreign policy, many of us who voted against him in the election. . . . He was broad-

gauged, absolutely unpartisan, a patriot in this matter if ever there was one.

And Roosevelt well recognized White's greatest attribute, his powerful folk stature. The Sage of Emporia received many honors crediting his influence upon public opinion. In 1934 the Roosevelt Memorial Association awarded him a Theodore Roosevelt Medal "as an outstanding interpreter of the American mind." The awards committee explained:

> A keen observer, a genial student of his fellow-men, a writer of gracious and effective prose, his influence in two generations has been largely due to his ability to keep in the company of millions, the neighborly point of view, the kindliness, the realism and the tolerance of a man who knows the best and the worst about every man in town, and is neither deceived nor embittered.

These two astute charmers had a lot in common.[8]

White had become increasingly aware of the need to arouse public opinion to the danger abroad. He knew the best and the worst about human nature, and he was petrified by the dictators. Never a virulent isolationist, the Kansas editor had succumbed in the mid-1930s to the drive for neutrality legislation. By the late-1930s he had regained his internationalist bearings. He opposed war; he recognized interventionism could lead to conflict; but he believed a non-interventionist stance would only assure a final call to arms. With the outbreak of European hostilities in September 1939 a more cautious regard for Franklin Roosevelt's drift toward intervention gave way to full scale support for the president's foreign policy. In September White was asked to chair the Non-Partisan Committee for Peace through Revision of the Neutrality Law. At seventy-one years old he was reluctant to take on the task. The battle, however, was heating up over the president's call for "cash-and-carry" legislation to assist the nation's allies; close friends pressed him, and duty called. As one member of the newly organized committee later explained to him: "For many years your name has stood for the highest ideals of honor and integrity in American politics. . . . We knew that around your name would rally a large number of people who, anxious to promote the best interests of our country . . . would recognize in your leadership the answer to their difficulties." White agreed to take on the chairmanship, to serve the cause of the global community. Somehow, the conflict had to be restricted to Europe.[9]

The committee had turned to White for the same reasons that Roosevelt would a few months later. The Kansan was a spokesperson of considerable influence and position: his Middle Western base and Republican ties were valuable; his role as a representative of Middle America was incalculable. When Roosevelt contacted White in December "cash-and-carry" had been passed by Congress. The Non-Partisan Committee had played a significant role; and White, actively speaking for and organizing internationalist forces, had proudly held aloft the standard of the cause. Back in Emporia after the vote, the editor modestly, and disingenuously, chronicled in the *Gazette*, "This was the first time I had ever had hold of a lever that controlled a national current."

> It was interesting—but scary! I had turned the juice off and on in Kansas many times for forty years and knew this switchboard fairly well. But I was so jittery, sitting before the big national switchboard that my mouth was dry and I kept licking my lips most of the time and batting my eyes. It was "Dorothy" before the Scarecrow, and when the old Scarecrow, Major John Q. Public, if you must know his real name, came to life and began to walk, I was tickled pink—again like "Dorothy."

The Sage of Emporia decidedly was back on comfortable ground.[10]

White's perceived leverage over John Q. Public weighed in once more in the harrowing spring of 1940. With Hitler's armies storming across Western Europe, he rushed to New York to remobilize internationalist forces. The goal was to aid the threatened democracies, to buy time to build up neglected American defenses, and principally to consolidate and formulate public opinion to encourage Congress to act. On May 20, 1940, the Committee to Defend America by Aiding the Allies formally declared its organization. William Allen White was chairman of the committee; the Emporia editor set out with the assistance of a powerful, New York-based executive board to save the democratic ship of state at home and abroad.

The "White Committee" quickly became embroiled in the battle over the direction of United States foreign policy. The organization, owing in large part to White's prestige, rapidly expanded; within six weeks over three hundred chapters had been established across the country. As Hitler scored successive victories in Europe White's work became more fevered. When Mussolini in June 1940 joined the attack on France, the chairman wired Roosevelt: "My correspondence is heaping up unanimously behind the plan to aid the Allies by anything other than war. As an old friend, let me warn you that maybe you will not be able to lead the American people unless you catch up with them." Mobilizing letter-writing campaigns, organizing public rallies, running newspaper advertisements, and funding radio addresses, the committee's goal was clear: aid to the Allies, short of war. In June, as France buckled, White spoke at the University of Kansas. He outlined what exactly, from his own perspective, was at stake:

> The two philosophies—the philosophy of force and tyranny, and the philosophy of neighborly kindness that we call democracy—cannot meet and mingle on the same planet! The world has shrunken. Our great

round earth with its vast ocean and high land has been drawn together with machinery until it is a little place, a veritable neighborhood that cannot live half slave and half free. I don't know in what form the dictator philosophy in the totalitarian state will meet you in your lives, dearly beloved. But it is out of bounds today. It stands just beyond our borders waiting. What your sacrifices will be, what hardships you may meet, what anguish you may know, I cannot prophesy. I only know unless that beast is chained upon the fields of France your lives will be maimed and mangled by its claws.

The world had grown frighteningly small; as any endangered people Americans needed to band together and reach out to their more far-flung neighbors.[11]

The danger was clear. The White Committee, running in tandem with the president on the fast track of current events, grew in power and prestige. The organization, with 750 local chapters, struggled with its most pronounced isolationist opposition, the America First Committee, for the nation's support. The Axis forces advanced, legislative successes mounted, and public opinion aligned with the interventionists; but the pace seemed to get away from Chairman White. The nation was heading toward war, and he began to lag. Age and poor health, increasing isolationist attacks upon the committee and himself, and policy differences within the executive board of the organization amidst increasing pressure to meet the foreign policy crisis head-on led to a break. White was not prepared in late 1940 to advocate the convoying of aid to Britain; in December, amidst great controversy, he resigned his chairmanship. He believed the United States would soon have to enter the conflict; no longer could he stop the progression toward war, nor could he bring himself to promote it. It was a bittersweet moment. In a sense, White's leadership of the Committee to Defend America by Aiding the Allies represented his last great hurrah. An old man, he spearheaded a drive for national unity in the face of a philosophy alien to all he had stood by for half a century. Now, with the nation mobilizing for action, he found it necessary to step aside, to let an increasingly united people gird themselves for a war he had hoped to avoid. His work was honored and his dilemma recognized, as the *New York Times* editorialized on January 4, 1941:

> Like the rest of us he has no doubt been pulled two ways—toward doing everything possible to beat Hitler and toward doing nothing that will get us into war. In this conscientious facing of a difficult problem, as in his hatred of stupidity, tyranny and injustice, we would like to think that he is a representative American. We do know that this would be a poorer, more cynical, less generous country without Will White of Emporia.[12]

■ ■ ■

Feeling that in true progressive fashion he had given his best to address the nation, to educate the people, and to rally Americans under a banner of justice, William Allen White returned to the sidelines to monitor what had become the increasingly hostile show. He supported the president's actions and excoriated those isolationists he saw hindering the nation's defense. With the December 1941 declaration of war, he concerned himself with war-drive activities in Emporia, with political affairs in Kansas and Washington, and as always with running the *Gazette*. He began writing his autobiography, and despite his declining health, he continued to write articles for the national press. His primary concern expressed in these pieces was the character of the postwar world. The United States would be an enormous power; he was intent that the country act as a force for righteousness, not greed. The old progressive still feared the hegemony of big business; and he distrusted the counteracting strength of big government. He campaigned for a compromise, where government would restrain overly aggressive corporate executives but not unnecessarily intervene in the daily affairs of entrepreneurial middle-class Americans. A harmonious people, White contended, could best lead a collective effort to secure world peace. The United States, still short of a middle-class idyll, must do all in its power to advance just precepts at home and abroad. In the *Yale Review* in September 1942 White noted that the United States and the democracies of the world had edged to the brink of catastrophe in the 1930s; now they were fighting back. A great international neighborhood would be established, based upon the United States' endeavor to create middle-class values of community. A struggle lay ahead beyond the peace; it could be a century-long battle. The United States must lead the way:

> Democracy's rebirth will be hard, most ungodly hard. But enslavement would be harder. We have no other alternative. We must conquer by heroic self-denial or be conquered by ruthless force. World democracy, rich and proud and pharisaical, is a camel before the gate of the needle's eye. He must go through. He must bend low, even to the dust. He must slip off his load and his proud trappings of purse and power. To be saved, for "a new Heaven and a new Earth," the diverse peoples of democratic civilization must think in new terms—new terms as citizens, new terms as nations, new terms as a modern, remade world, in a new day and time.[13]

A "new Heaven and a new Earth"—White rarely had used the phrase since the disappointing peace at Versailles. In a sense the world since World War I seemed, in 1942, to have come full circle for the old Bull Mooser.

Seeing progressivism ebb in the 1920s and then desperately and uncertainly surge forward again amidst the vicissitudes of the 1930s, White, approaching the end of his life, perceived that his vision of spiritual regeneration at home and abroad once again was within reach. He hedged his bet more than he had in 1919 as he looked to the establishment of a United Nations and a more just postwar order at home. The world, with its mass men and technologies, was more complex than ever before; and he was less naïve regarding its altruistic nature. But renewal was no less necessary; and community was no less the solution. The United States was no paragon of virtue, but it had the right idea. In the *Yale Review* White pointed out that diverse peoples, races, and creeds, divided amongst far-flung regions and rural and urban ways of life in the United States were working to achieve a more harmonious order. One need only look, he hastened to point out, to the Middle West, and particularly to his own plains region, for an exemplar of American community. Here people had come closest to achieving the ideal and preserving "the dignity of the human spirit" and the value of self-respect. All the world should observe:

> Until the world has learned the lesson which the United States has learned, at least in part—the lesson of unity under compromise—the lesson which democratic Switzerland learned so long ago—the lesson of neighborly conduct which is the basis of our Christian philosophy—the hopes for the permanence of the United Nations and for international peace upheld by justice are fantastic. When that neighborliness and justice come, there can be world peace. It is worth a century of struggle and sacrifice.

It was, in the end, the middle-class ideal—White had been fighting for it for fifty years.[14]

Struggle and sacrifice, American leadership, a Middle Western model of excellence—from White's perspective the world indeed seemed to have travelled a circular, or circuitous, route, right back to his own philosophical front porch. All along he had advocated a communal resolution to the world's problems; and now another moment of truth had arrived. Four months after the outbreak of war White penned an article for the *New Republic* entitled "Emporia in Wartime." Not surprisingly, the piece was a mix of fact and fancy as the town editor, sitting back on that front porch, determined where lay Emporia's past and the nation's future. White was a realist. In these early days, he was not optimistic that Emporians were prepared to embrace "some kind of a world association, union, alliance or treaty-making organization to promote economic justice on a world scale." While neighborly, democratic, and just, Emporia, after all, was located in the isolationist Middle West. It may be, he feared, too much to hope for an international commitment. Still, in that same Middle Western heritage White more fancifully located that hope, for Emporia was so obviously middle class. Drawing upon a recent survey of Emporia's youth, he compiled a promising array of facts and figures. These kids, about to go off to war, for the most part white, Anglo Saxon, and Protestant, were educated, hard-working, and church-attending citizens living comfortably amidst a plenitude of houses, cars, radios, and the various amenities provided by a prospering civilization. They intended to carry on their postwar lives living in similarly solid, middle-sized towns like Emporia, ranging from fifteen thousand to one hundred thousand in population. The future to them looked bright: "Only a negligible percent of these Emporia youth were embittered, which would seem an accurate barometer of middle-class attitude. They are living on easy street. Ninety-two percent of the youth were either enthusiastic or hopeful about the future." Here, hence, lay a special promise. In the middle class, especially in their offspring, in the prosperous heartland—for "Emporia is just another name for the Middle West"—resided America's destiny:

> I have made every check I can on this, and find it accurate. What does it mean? Read for the word Emporia any middle-class town north of the Ohio, west of the Alleghenies, from Michigan to California, omitting New Mexico and Arizona, in which large sections of the population are Mexican. Let us say it means that in these towns, towns of from 1,500 to 100,000 population, we have a homogeneous middle-class population with wealth pretty generally centered in the middle class, with few rich and few poor, with a high living standard. They were not keen about going to war before the Japanese attacked Pearl Harbor. Since then enlistments have rapidly increased and the daily sale of defense stamps and bonds tripled in a week.

"What does it mean?" Having finally been chilled by the shadow of the Axis challenge, having committed themselves to war, perhaps middle-class Americans, led by these enlightened young citizen-soldiers of "Emporia," would find the means within themselves to ensure a lasting peace. Expanding "easy street," or Main Street—spreading the middle-class way of life, through the just auspices of world community—provided an answer. "In any case," the Sage concluded, "we must make the chief objective of this war an educational one, second only to victory."[15]

The lesson was obvious. White's figures testifying to Emporia's middle-class standard of living, typically, were questionable; at the same time his intent in writing "Emporia in Wartime" was absolutely clear. Americans, as he had long declared, had to be educated. Going off to war, "Emporians" held aloft a banner. A "new Heaven and a new Earth" was within reach. Americans had to recognize the immense responsibility they carried into battle. Two decades earlier, in his First World War odyssey, *The Martial Adventures of Henry and Me,* White had fantasized that a similar opportunity awaited mobilized Emporians to carry forth to the world the same standard. "Now of course Emporia was only . . . a symbol—a symbol of all America—all middle class, with no particular beginnings . . . and with no pride of ancestry, but a vast hope of posterity." Americans in 1918 and once more in 1942 had a progressive, enveloping message to convey. Indeed for White, sitting in Emporia, watching the passing show, the circle closed. "What's the Matter with Kansas?" "What's the Matter with America?" The world? He sounded one last time from the perspective of main street that nothing was the matter that could not be resolved within the promise of middle-class community.[16]

■ ■ ■

In looking back in *The Changing West,* White had observed, "The morals of the community grew out of a yearning for justice, the striving of men toward an ideal of human rights." He recognized that the West had fallen short of the ideal, but most importantly it had continued to strive. With the coming of war, with avoidance no longer the issue, another opportunity arose to secure a more ideal national and world order. "Emporia" in wartime offered hope. Whether that hope was real or fanciful almost seemed beyond the point; the nation, in White's perspective, had properly realigned its sights. It never was easy to draw the line between fact and fancy in White's work; particularly so when that work directly focused upon the question of community. Myth and reality became a muddle of fact and metaphor. But in the final analysis the exact parameters and measures of any one geographic entity—be it Emporia, the Middle West, the West, or the Alliance—was of little consequence to the Kansas editor. What mattered, "what was the matter," was locating a way of life and something to work for as a community. It was the very lack of distinguishing physical characteristics that gave vitality to White's language of community. Caught up with the problem of community in the twentieth century, White recognized that a small-town rhetoric, tailored to an evolving urban-industrial order, offered a freely flowing standard under which diverse groups of Americans could find solace and direction, if not always solutions for a wide range of problems. For close to half a century, William Allen White, priding himself on his role as an educator, got caught up in the building of an ethos that spoke of human rights, of justice and decency, and of improvement and service; he proclaimed an American destiny, a national goal of creating a middle-class civilization devoid of material and spiritual want. Who could argue? Who would argue with such a vision? More than a small-town journalist, a novelist, or a backroom politician, William Allen White rose to fame as a spokesperson for an amorphous group of twentieth-century Americans, a minority growing in number who ultimately would stamp the nation with a majoritarian middle-class ideology. William Allen White spoke their language; he was intimately involved in the forging of an all-embracing Middle American ethos.[17]

There was a certain lack of depth to White's views but an attractiveness to their consensual sweep. In both his personae and his vision of a harmonious American community, he seemed to catch what a good number of citizens wanted out of life. As Norman Rockwell graced the covers of the metropolitan-based *Saturday Evening Post* with representations of idyllic small-town values and norms, so White added to that journal and others, and to the national discourse, his comforting small-town rhetoric of community. February 10, 1938, the Sage of Emporia marked his seventieth birthday, and millions of Americans joined in the celebration. Emporia, the *Gazette* office, and the editor were photographed by *Life* and *Look* magazines and filmed by Fox Movietone News; newspapers across the country ran stories and editorials. It was the editor himself who possibly best summed up what the celebration was all about. Writing an autobiographical piece for *Collier's*, White recalled that he and his town had lived through a magnificent epoch in which individualistic Americans were welded through scientific technology and socialized through political progressivism into "a communal life." Prior to "the collapse of the boom," and despite depression, he could see that a new way of life had been forged:

> It was not an equitable distribution, of course. Human justice is always approximate. It was still the highest approximation of economic justice that a complex civilization has ever achieved. The eighty per cent privileged became the ninety per cent. There was indeed some relation, even if hazy and inexact, between a man's service to his fellows and the size and value of his reward. The rich rapidly grew richer but the poor did not grow poorer. The differences between the food and housing and clothing, between the amusements and diversions and between the general takings of the rich and of the poor from our commonwealth were more obvious than real. For Americans wore about the same kind of clothes. We all lived in fairly comfortable houses in which were installed something like the same kind of plumbing. We all ate the same packages of prepared foods. And the rich could not eat any more than the poor.

Connected by an impressive array of cars, radios, trains, planes, and silver screens, it all added up to a comforting if skewed vision of the American show. It was almost as if all Americans lived "nearer and nearer" to one another, in one middle-class community just like Emporia. "What a show I have seen, what a grand show!" White concluded. "I am so proud to have seen it and so happy that I don't care if pretty soon I shall have to slip out quietly to catch the five-fifteen!"[18]

The celebration, then, seemed to be in honor of a triumphant ethos as much as in honor of the congenial man who so well expounded upon it. Emporia was the nation's "hometown," and William Allen White was an American folk hero. The nineteenth-century yeoman had been, in the editor's own long-ago view, transformed into the townsman, into the Middle American. White was fond of linking individuals to great causes, to movements, to the tides of history. Throughout his career he was fascinated with biography. At first there were sketches—Cleveland, Bryan, McKinley, Platt, Roosevelt—for the magazines. White covered them all, and always there were the campaign pieces focusing on the men as much as the programs. Since the twenties White wrote biographies: one of Wilson, two of Coolidge, and one started of Theodore Roosevelt, which he never somehow could complete. Beginning in the thirties there were the reviews, especially for the *Saturday Review of Literature,* of the biographies and autobiographies of the aging and dead of the Progressive Movement. From the heated electoral frays of the late 1890s to the Second World War, from Thunder Mountain, Idaho, to Beaume, France, to Hickville on the Hudson, and finally back to Emporia, White had covered the news. And interpreting the news—the importance of the men, the causes and the movements of his time—was for him, at base, a matter of community. White took the complexities of his age and tried to sort them out and to simplify them. He saw the national pageant in his own lifetime as having passed through "two acts": the first ran up to the First World War; the second followed the peace at Versailles. It was during the second that twentieth-century community came to full, if not yet satisfactory, fruition. This development, the product of a progressive renaissance in political and social relations, he hailed as the greatest of all time. He surely must have taken great comfort in being identified as a spokesperson for Middle America, as the epitome of the American townsman. The tide of history had washed right up to his front porch.[19]

Despite his birthday denial White was anxious to catch the "third act" of the progressive show. In December 1940 he wrote to Nicholas Murray Butler, president of Columbia University:

> I wonder if in any fifty years on this planet the human spirit has produced such changes in man's environment and brought humanity to

such a level of literacy and information about the universe and in wisdom about his conduct as that decade in which you and I have lived as young men, as citizens, and now as puzzled, somewhat saddened but I believe unshaken disciples of a great faith in man's essential long-run intelligence, integrity, purpose and courage. I hate to go out here at the end of the second act of this fast drama of the changing spirit of man for I know that the third act will have a happy ending. God knows how!

William Allen White died of cancer, at his home in Emporia, January 29, 1944. Tributes poured forth. From Harold Laski in London came possibly the most pointed, and most poignant tribute:

> White seemed to me to be part of that America of which the supreme representatives were Jefferson and Lincoln; the America which is concerned first of all with the ordinary people and their lot in life; the America which is simple, kindly and proud to think that an humble man can there become a significant man . . . White was a noble representative of the average American at his best.

It was a tribute which surely would have pleased the chronicler of men, causes, movements, and community. The consummate commoner—it was an honor he himself had bestowed once, long ago in the heyday of progressivism, upon Theodore Roosevelt. It was a fitting eulogy to America's preeminent townsman.[20]

Provincial and cosmopolitan, mixing the essence of *Gemeinschaft* and *Gesellschaft* within his thought and his personae, White seemed to embody the twentieth-century search for community. This perhaps was his most enduring contribution to the nation: he helped to forge a Middle American ethos; he helped to give character to a quest for an identity and to find a resolution of the evasive problem of community. His answer, "the town," was as malleable as the ethos itself, as indistinct as Middle America. In the end what mattered most, what the ethos was all about, was the search for a satisfactory communal experience. As White told Upton Sinclair, "And finally mine 'is a truth that never can be proved.' . . . But let's both thank God for our fighting faith." White had faith in the middle-class ideal. The search was right; in the final analysis, it was all that counted. He recalled on his birthday in 1938, "The battle for social and economic justice is not won. It never will be won. The fight gaunts us down, keens our edge, measures our progress." This is what community was all about; this is what, in White's view, appealed to the folks, summed up what they wanted out of American life. This in the end was what ought to matter to Middle America.[21]

Utopia, White often remarked, was an illusion—but progress toward it was key. It is impossible to say what William Allen White would have thought of postwar America, or "the third act." To "a mild and benevolent liberal" from Republican Kansas, one would think Dwight Eisenhower's middle-class, consensual reign would appeal. One could see White at home within the developments of bucolic, suburban America; the "semi-urban" extension of Main Street through the sprawling malls would mark familiar ground. The vast expansion of educational opportunity; the growth of labor, capital, and the public interest, and the government as "boss on this continent"; and membership in an American-dominated community of nations would fit his progressive bill. White, it would seem, from past experience would have been prepared for the tension of the Cold War, and for the political, social, economic, and cultural disruptions of the 1960s and 1970s. The end of the Cold War and the visions of a victorious America on the edge of the twenty-first century hardly would have caught him up short. Nor would he be overwhelmed by urban sprawl, gutted central cores, environmental blight, the possibilities of a permanent under class, multiculturalism, computerization, agribusiness, and decaying heartland main streets. The latest turn in suburban subdivisions—small-town neighborly recreations—probably would elicit a chuckle; and the demographic movement back to the towns would surely be taken as a confirmation of his philosophy. Progress, he frequently declared, was a cyclical affair consisting of reform and then retrenchment. Progress toward a middle-class ideal would be ever more evident to White. Most important, the quest would appear in order.

In the end, White might have drawn a good deal of pleasure from the style, if not necessarily the substance, of the Reagan presidency. The president was a polished communicator, able to formulate elusive national goals and to express the overarching aspirations of the American people. White, always the "pol" as well as the rhetorician, would have appreciated the remarkable strategy of the 1984 campaign. *Newsweek* highlighted the imagery:

> He was . . . America as it imagined itself to be—the bearer of the traditional Main Street values of family and neighborhood, of thrift, industry and charity. . . . Reagan had never lost that quality of next-door neighborliness. . . . He was still playing best friend, a citizen cast up among politicians; the American heartland saw his communion with the past and his cocky, can-do grin into the future and recognized itself.

If the citizenry had any trouble seeing itself mirrored, a slick advertising package projected the message home—it was "Morning Again in America," a land of good health and abundant wealth: "a tug leaving a harbor, a tractor tilling a field, a family hauling a rug into a new home and a black man white-washing a fence." A voice-over amplified the theme: "Just about every place you look things are looking up. Life is better—America's back—and people have a sense of pride they never thought they'd feel again. And so it's not surprising that just about everyone in town is thinking the same thing—now that our country is turning around, why would we ever turn back?" The rhetoric was familiar; progressive small-town imagery was pervasive in the campaign as it had been throughout Reagan's first term. Hard core urban dilemmas disappeared into the morning mist. The quest for community was being fulfilled: "Everyone in town" understood. The 1984 victory provided striking testimony that small-town rhetoric tailored to a Middle American ethos remained a highly marketable commodity in the late-twentieth century. And four years later, Reagan's studied successor was not about to be left out in the cold. Inaugurating his administration of a "kindlier and gentler" nation, George Bush in January 1989 broadcast his own warming brand of "front porch democracy" to reach out to his fellow denizens, and everyone understood.[22]

Perhaps they understood a bit too well. The message did not wash. Few considered George Bush a fellow townsman; fewer in fact were considering themselves townspeople. Four years later Bush would be replaced by William Jefferson Clinton and his hollow tiding of a town called Hope. Six years later, amidst rampant prosperity, government scandal, and rabid tabloid news stories, small town imagery is just one more gimmick. Certainly at the end of the century it appears the old dominant saw, the small town myth, has run its course. Ronald Reagan may well have been the last president capable of representing small-town values. Reagan, as he himself summarily noted, has now ridden off into the West. But surely the West, the frontier, and a new myth will assist the people, as Reagan urged in 1984, in "staying the course," in generating, and in regenerating the American dream.

Grappling and designing for half a century, William Allen White liked to see America as Reagan pictured it, as a land of health and wealth, where color lines blurred, ethnicity faded, class lines disappeared to a virtual nonentity, and Americans as a whole, as a singular community, took pride in past values with an eye toward the future. It was a highly exclusive vision, which only left room for those citizens, whatever their ethnic or racial heritage might be, who adhered to what White proudly identified as white, Anglo-Saxon Protestant values. And it was popular. It is a vision which remains paramount to this day: America as a just and decent land of equal opportunity and middle-class harmony. Albeit, now as an increasingly sensitive multicultural view of the matter emerges, one might guess William Allen White, too, would have grown to understand—few ever criticized the Sage of Emporia for not keeping abreast of current affairs.

In 1983 *Newsweek* celebrated its fiftieth anniversary. The editors compiled a special issue to focus upon "The American Dream." To analyze "the true story of America" the magazine traced the "extraordinary saga of five heartland families, of ordinary Americans whose names seldom appear in print, but whose lives testify to what our country has been and is becoming." To locate these individuals, to connect the past to the present, reporters journeyed to Middle America:

> The setting is Springfield, a city of 73,000 on the banks of Buck Creek in central Ohio. It has been a town of tinkerers and inventors, of farmers and their ties to the land, of immigrants and black Americans with their visions of a better life, of entrepreneurs and executives and union men from the big International Harvester plant. It is its own place, different from every other. But at another level it is every American town, and the people who come to life in this narrative are connected by circumstance and character to all of us. Their joys and pains, their fears and victories are ours.

Newsweek found in Springfield the elusive truth White had located in Emporia: "a symbol—a symbol of all America—all middle class, with no particular beginnings . . . and with no pride of ancestry, but a vast hope of posterity." Springfield was an ordinary city, standing tall at the demographic, and more squarely the cultural, crossroads of twentieth-century America. Rhetorically, Springfield, as Emporia, was Middle America writ small.[23]

Newsweek surely had unearthed an apt symbol to commemorate its half-century chronicle of the American saga. Springfield indeed did appear in the midst of the Reagan era to represent America demographically and culturally. But the story had gotten too small; it made for a good capstone but not a harbinger of times to come. Perhaps Springfield epitomized what the country had been but surely, just a decade and a half later, it seems a far cry from what it rapidly is becoming. It is difficult to imagine the newsweekly profiling a similar community in a similar manner today. The nation is too fissured, too aware of its differences for better and for worse, too cynical, and perhaps too savvy to buy the imagery of a bunch of folks living along the banks of Buck Creek in central Ohio, the descendents of "tinkerers and inventors, of farmers and their ties to the land, of immigrants and black Americans with their visions of a better life, of entrepreneurs and executives and union men. . . ." It's too simple. The packaging is wrong. David Shi argues in the end of his study *The Simple Life,* looking ahead, not back:

> Simplicity in its essence demands neither a vow of poverty nor a life of rural homesteading. As an ethic of self-conscious material moderation, it can be practiced in cities and suburbs, townhouses and condominiums. It requires neither a log cabin nor a hairshirt but a deliberate ordering of priorities so as to distinguish between the necessary and superfluous, useful and wasteful, beautiful and vulgar.

This is a twenty-first century society; everyone knows the simple life, however one may want to define it, no longer is satisfactorily epitomized by the small-town idyll. Moderation comes in lots of shapes and sizes, just like frontiers.[24]

At the end of the twentieth century the United States, indeed, is leaving behind the old shibboleths. My hunch is that in catching the end of the third act, William Allen White would have understood, and he would have been busy prepping for the next act. Long ago, in an earlier part of the century, one of his journalist colleagues caught the editor in the act. Lewis Gannett offered this backstage view:

> One long evening on the lawn behind his house in Emporia, Will White lay, as usual, in the hammock, looking rather like a watermelon with legs attached, talking about his newspaper. I accused him of having invented himself, of creating his own character as the shrewd, kindly, country editor. He was really, I said, a sophisticated city guy. He tried to tell me that his paper was no better than a dozen other Kansas county-seat papers, and the next morning he took me over to the office, and showed me the exchanges to prove it. They were good country papers, often good imitations of "The Emporia Gazette." But nobody read them in New York, or even in St. Louis; and everybody knew "The Emporia Gazette." Partly that was because Will White must have been born with more salt in him than most babies; also, partly because he was the New Yorker in Emporia as well as the Emporian when he came to New York. New York is full of small-town boys trying their best to forget that they are small-town boys. Will White made a career out of remembering it, but he remembered it with a city perspective.

William Allen White knew exactly what was being staged. He preached a simple life for a complex time. White epitomizes David Shi's argument that a vast majority of Americans have long and consistently held to a progressive view of the possibilities ahead of, not behind the country. He believed in moderation, but the message, as beguiling as it always has been, was a good deal more sophisticated than it appeared.[25]

Notes

Introduction
Simple Points

1. Ida M. Tarbell, *All in the Day's Work: An Autobiography* (1939; reprint, Boston: G. K. Hall, 1985); George H. Douglas, *H. L. Mencken: Critic of American Life* (Hamden: Archon, 1978); Lincoln Steffens, *The Autobiography of Lincoln Steffens* (New York: Grosset and Dunlap, 1931); Peter Kurth, *American Cassandra: The Life of Dorothy Thompson* (Boston: Little, Brown and Company, 1990); Robert E. Herzstein, *Henry R. Luce: A Political Portrait of the Man Who Created the American Century* (New York: Charles Scribner's Sons, 1994); Ronald Steel, *Walter Lippmann and the American Century* (Boston: Little, Brown and Company, 1980); Gore Vidal, *Palimpsest: A Memoir* (New York: Random House, 1995).

2. Tom Wicker, *One of Us: Richard Nixon and the American Dream* (New York: Random House, 1991). For a prescient view of the Reagans, see Gore Vidal, "Ronnie and Nancy: A Life in Pictures" in Gore Vidal, ed., *At Home: Essays, 1982–1988* (New York: Random House, 1988), 76–91. James Oliver Robertson, *American Myth, American Reality* (New York: Hill and Wang, 1980).

3. Slotkin's study offers a seminal analysis of myth along with a superb bibliography. Richard Slotkin, *The Fatal Environment: The Myth of the Frontier in the Age of Industrialism, 1800–1890* (New York: MacMillan, 1985; New York: Harper Perennial, 1994), 11, 12, 16; see especially chapters 1 and 2. Daniel T. Rodgers in *Contested Truths: Keywords in American Politics since Independence* (New York: Basic Books, 1987) splendidly surveys key words such as utility, the people, government, interests, and freedom. For a succinct summary, see the prologue, pp. 3–16.

4. Slotkin, *Fatal Environment*, 19–20. Slotkin assiduously places his work within the continuing scholarly debate over myth: see note four, p. 536. For more on historical memory, see the exhaustive treatment in the *Journal of*

American History 75 (March 1989): David Thelen, "Memory and American History," 1117–29; Michael Frisch, "American History and the Structures of Collective Memory: A Modest Exercise in Empirical Iconography," 1130–1155; David W. Blight, "'For Something beyond the Battlefield': Frederick Douglass and the Memory of the Civil War," 1156–1178; Robert E. McGlone, "Rescripting a Troubled Past: John Brown's Family and the Harpers Ferry Conspiracy," 1179–1200; and John Bodnar, "Power and Memory in Oral History: Workers and Managers at Studebaker," 1201–21. See also Mike Wallace, *Mickey Mouse History and Other Essays on American Memory* (Philadelphia: Temple University Press, 1996). This well-written, challenging collection is more accessible to the general reader.

5. Slotkin, *Fatal Environment*, 24.

6. Ibid., 25–26. A large body of work addresses the complexities of hegemony. I found particularly helpful the analysis of T. J. Jackson Lears in his *No Place of Grace: Antimodernism and the Transformation of American Culture, 1880–1920* (New York: Pantheon, 1981; Chicago: University of Chicago Press, 1983); see especially pp. xvii–xviii and 10. For a considerably greater treatment see T. J. Jackson Lears, "The Concept of Cultural Hegemony: Problems and Possibilities," *American Historical Review* 90 (June 1985): 567–93.

7. Slotkin, *Fatal Environment*, 26 and 30. For an extended discussion of the placement of popular culture see the "AHR Forum": Lawrence W. Levine, "The Folklore of Industrial Society: Popular Culture and Its Audiences," 1369–99; Robin D. G. Kelley, "Notes on Deconstructing 'The Folk,'" 1400–08; Natalie Zemon Davis, "Toward Mixtures and Margins," 1409–16; T. J. Jackson Lears, "Making Fun of Popular Culture," 1417–26; and Lawrence W. Levine, "Levine Responds," 1427–30, *American Historical Review* 97 (December 1992), 1369–1430.

8. Slotkin, *Fatal Environment*, 31.

9. William Allen White, "It's Been a Great Show," *Collier's*, 12 February, 1938, 65.

10. Frederick Jackson Turner, "The Significance of the Frontier in American History" in Frederick Jackson Turner, ed., *The Frontier in American History* (New York: Henry Holt and Company, 1921), 1–38; Patricia Nelson Limerick, "Turnerians All: The Dream of a Helpful History in an Intelligible World," *American Historical Review* 100 (June 1995), 697–716. For another recent work exemplifying the continued interest in Turner's frontier, see David M. Wrobel, *The End of American Exceptionalism: Frontier Anxiety from the Old West to the New Deal* (Lawrence: University Press of Kansas, 1993). Wrobel's bibliographical research is strong.

11. Henry Nash Smith, *Virgin Land: The American West as Symbol and Myth* (Cambridge: Harvard University Press, 1970), ix, 11, and 37. For a complimentary reassessment of Smith's pathbreaking study, see Ann Fabian, "Back to *Virgin Land*," *Reviews in American History* 24 (September 1996): 542–53.

12. William Allen White, *The Changing West: An Economic Theory About Our Golden Age* (New York: Macmillan Company, 1939), vi–vii.

13. Henry F. May, *The End of American Innocence: A Study of the First Years of Our Own Time, 1912–1917* (1959; reprint, Oxford: Oxford University Press,

1979), xii–xiii. May's classic still reads well. For a retrospective consideration of the pioneering study, both qualifying and highly complimentary, see Joan Shelley Rubin, "In Retrospect: Henry F. May's 'The End of American Innocence,'" *Reviews in American History* 18 (March 1990): 142–49.

14. May, *End of American Innocence*, 6–9, quoted p. 7.

15. Ibid., 18; Steel, *Walter Lippmann*, 114.

16. May, *End of American Innocence*, 155.

17. Jean B. Quandt, *From the Small Town to the Great Community: The Social Thought of Progressive Intellectuals* (New Brunswick: Rutgers University Press, 1970), 24. This well-written, well-documented study remains interesting despite occasional, dated lapses. I disagree with Quandt's view that the "communitarians" were out of touch with "the issue of basic structural change in America," and hence despite their great strengths they failed to develop a viable "social philosophy" that would survive beyond their reform era. See pp. 1–2.

18. Ibid., 8 and 10.

19. Ibid., 25, 26, and 30.

20. Daniel T. Rodgers, "In Search of Progressivism," *Reviews in American History* 10 (December 1982): 113–32. This remains an excellent resource for a selective bibliography. Strong bibliographical guides are offered in three reviews of recent Progressive Era studies. See Robert M. Crunden, "Thick Description in the Progressive Era," *Reviews in American History* 19 (December 1991): 463–67; Bryant Simon, "One Side of Main Street," *Reviews in American History* 22 (September 1994): 461–67; and James Livingston, "Why Is There Still Socialism in the United States?" *Reviews in American History* 22 (December 1994): 577–83. Amongst studies of progressivism, a helpful cross-section would include Nell Irvin Painter, *Standing at Armageddon: The United States, 1877–1919* (New York: W. W. Norton and Company, 1987); John Whiteclay Chambers II, *The Tyranny of Change: America in the Progressive Era, 1890–1920*, 2d ed. (New York: St. Martin's Press, 1992); Arthur S. Link and Richard L. McCormick, *Progressivism* (Arlington Heights: Harlan Davidson, 1983); Robert M. Crunden, *Ministers of Reform: The Progressives' Achievements in American Civilization, 1889–1920* (New York: Basic Books, 1982; Urbana: University of Illinois Press, 1984); Otis L. Graham Jr., *An Encore for Reform: The Old Progressives and the New Deal* (New York: Oxford University Press, 1967); and David P. Thelen, *Robert M. La Follette and the Insurgent Spirit* (Boston: Little, Brown and Company, 1976; Madison: University of Wisconsin Press, 1985).

21. Chambers, *Tyranny*, 133.

22. Lawrence W. Levine, *The Unpredictable Past: Explorations in American Cultural History* (New York: Oxford University Press, 1993), 304, 312–13, 318, and 319. For a masterful treatment of the role of "the people," see Rodgers, *Contested Truths*, especially chapters four and six, 112–43 and 176–211, and the epilogue, 212–17.

23. Levine, *Unpredictable Past*, 115, 319, and 205.

24. Warren I. Sussman, *Culture as History: The Transformation of American Society in the Twentieth Century* (New York: Pantheon Books, 1984), xxi–xxiii.

25. Ibid., 213.

26. Joan Shelley Rubin, *The Making of Middlebrow Culture* (Chapel Hill: University of North Carolina Press, 1992), 98 and 109.

27. David Glassberg, *American Historical Pageantry: The Uses of Tradition in the Early Twentieth Century* (Chapel Hill: University of North Carolina Press, 1990), 150 and 267; Roland Marchand, *Advertising the American Dream: Making Way for Modernity, 1920–1940* (Berkeley: University of California Press, 1985), xix and xxi. For works on the role of film, see Robert Sklar, *Movie-Made America: A Cultural History of American Movies* (New York: Random House, 1975); Lary May, *Screening Out the Past: The Birth of Mass Culture and the Motion Picture Industry* (New York: Oxford University Press, 1980; Chicago: University of Chicago Press, 1983); Andrew Bergman, *We're in the Money: Depression America and Its Films* (New York: New York University Press, 1971; Chicago: Ivan R. Dee, 1992); and Emanuel Levy, *Small-Town America in Film: The Decline and Fall of Community,* (New York: Continuum Publishing Company, 1991). For radio see Erik Barnouw, *A Tower in Babel: A History of Broadcasting in the United States,* vol. 1—to 1933 (New York: Oxford University Press, 1966).

28. Robert L. Dorman, *Revolt of the Provinces: The Regionalist Movement in America, 1920–1945* (Chapel Hill: University of North Carolina Press, 1993), 23.

29. Lears, *No Place of Grace,* xvi and xxviii.

30. May, *End of American Innocence,* 77–78. May makes the observation regarding William Lyon Phelps's "nervous crisis" in 1891, "it is surprising how often such an episode figures in the lives of the period's distinguished optimists."

31. Dorman, *Revolt,* 50.

32. D. W. Meinig, "Symbolic Landscapes: Some Idealizations of American Communities," in *The Interpretation of Ordinary Landscapes,* ed. D. W. Meinig (New York: Oxford University Press, 1979), 164–92, quoted p. 165. Other pieces in this collection are of interest. James R. Shortridge, *The Middle West: Its Meaning in American Culture* (Lawrence: University Press of Kansas, 1989), 7 and 33. This geography study, while rich in spots in content and argument, suffers from a weak understanding of both history and literature. For Shortridge's extended treatment of pastoralism, see chapter three. Three additional works, focusing more on place but still preoccupied with idea, offer important complementary perspectives: George E. Mowry, *The Urban Nation, 1920–1960* (New York: Hill and Wang, 1965); Kenneth T. Jackson, *Crabgrass Frontier: The Suburbanization of the United States* (New York: Oxford University Press, 1985); and John S. Gilkeson Jr., *Middle-Class Providence, 1820–1940* (Princeton: Princeton University Press, 1986). See also the provocative collection Edward L. Ayers, et al., *All Over the Map: Rethinking American Regions* (Baltimore: Johns Hopkins University Press, 1996).

33. Carl L. Becker, "Kansas," in *Everyman His Own Historian: Essays on History and Politics,* ed. Carl L. Becker (1935; reprint, Chicago: Quadrangle Books, 1966), 27–28. For a testimony to the continuing appeal of Becker's piece, see Dudley T. Cornish, "Carl Becker's Kansas: The Power of Endurance," *Kansas Historical Quarterly* 41 (spring 1975): 1–13. For two works catching the high and

low spots of the popular Kansas profile, see Robert Smith Bader, *Hayseeds, Moralizers, and Methodists: The Twentieth-Century Image of Kansas* (Lawrence: University Press of Kansas, 1988); and C. Robert Haywood, *Tough Daisies: Kansas Humor from "The Lane County Bachelor" to Bob Dole* (Lawrence: University Press of Kansas, 1995).

34. David E. Shi, *The Simple Life: Plain Living and High Thinking in American Culture* (New York: Oxford University Press, 1985), 7.

35. Ibid.

36. Ibid., 170 and 173.

37. Ibid., 231–32. For an excellent analysis of the acute tension between individualism and cooperation during this era, see Robert S. McElvaine, *The Great Depression: America, 1929–1941,* rev. ed. (New York: Times Books, 1993).

38. Shi, *Simple Life,* 232.

39. Ibid., 278; Levine, *Unpredictable Past,* 205.

40. Shi, *Simple Life,* 280; Quandt, *From the Small Town to the Great Community,* 46; Steel, *Walter Lippmann,* 199.

41. Quandt, *From the Small Town to the Great Community,* 46 and 58.

42. Chambers, *Tyranny,* 133; Rodgers, *Contested Truths,* 4, 11, and 179. Rodgers' entire treatment of the Progressive Era is impressive. See in particular chapters four and six.

43. Rodgers, *Contested Truths,* 178.

44. William Allen White, "Blood of the Conquerors," *Collier's,* 10 March 1923, 5–6, and 30, quoted p. 6.

45. Shi, *Simple Life,* 7.

Chapter One
"Too Good a Town": White, Community, and Rhetoric

1. The most famous twentieth-century abuser of small-town values and norms is, of course, Henry L. Mencken. In 1984 Senator John Glenn of Ohio, in a run for the Democratic presidential nomination, took on Reagan and his rhetoric. In a hometown speech launching his campaign in archetypal New Concord, Ohio, Glenn delineated the difference between the president's supposedly nostalgic understanding of town values and his own progressive conception: "all Americans share the simple values we learned in this small town—the values of excellence, honesty, fairness, compassion for those who have less, and confidence in the future." He drew the line, explaining that the administration "likes to talk about those values. Unfortunately, its deeds have fallen far short of its words. . . . instead of a confident advance into the world of the future, we see a nostalgic retreat into the myths of the past." See "Remarks of Senator John Glenn. Declaration of Candidacy for the Office of President of the United States, Thursday, April 21, 1983, New Concord, Ohio," courtesy of the senator's Senate

office. Social commentator Nicholas von Hoffman in an acerbic indictment of Reagan as a dangerous ideologue referred to the transition from nineteenth- to twentieth-century myth: "The American ideologue would come as Lincoln had come before, dressed in the raiment of our culture, a cartoon exaggeration of ourselves. He would be the boy next door grown old, the kid who got through college on an athletic scholarship, a Hollywood media hero, modest and patient, the early twentieth-century small-town equivalent of Father Abraham in his log cabin. Abe split rails and Ron broadcast for the Chicago Cubs," "Contra Reaganum," *Harper's,* May 1982, 29–36. The rhetoric was effective. Washington commentator Elizabeth Drew concluded: "Of course he oversimplified . . . but his oversimplification allowed him to send powerful messages. . . ." ("Letter from Washington," *New Yorker,* 4 July 1988, 70–80, quoted p. 80). For a lengthy assessment of the Reagan style see Paul Boyer, ed., *Reagan as President: Contemporary Views of the Man, His Politics, and His Policies* (Chicago: Ivan R. Dee, 1990). In particular see the "Cultural Icon," pp. 74–85. See also Mike Wallace, *Mickey Mouse History and Other Essays on American Memory* (Philadelphia: Temple University Press, 1996), especially "Ronald Reagan and the Politics of History," pp. 249–68, for an enlightening analysis of Reagan's conscious use of myth.

2. The best bibliography for White's articles and books is Walter Johnson and Alberta Pantle, "A Bibliography of the Published Works of William Allen White," *Kansas Historical Quarterly* 15 (February 1947): 22–41. For White's speeches, Robert Lee Wilholt's "The Rhetoric of the Folk Hero: William Allen White" (Ph.D. diss., University of Illinois, 1962), 167–81, offers an extensive bibliography. Complete collections of the *Emporia Gazette* are easily obtained. For selected editorials see Helen Ogden Mahin, comp., *The Editor and His People: Editorials by William Allen White* (New York: Macmillan Company, 1924), and Russell H. Fitzgibbon, comp., *Forty Years on Main Street* (New York: Farrar and Rinehart, 1937). For the best bibliography of books and articles about White see Wilholt, "Rhetoric," 202–13. A more accessible listing of books (but much less comprehensive for articles) is Donald S. Pady, "GLR Bibliography: William Allen White," *Great Lakes Review* 5 (summer 1978): 49–66. Pady additionally cites reviews of White's books and his obituaries. White's extensive papers principally are housed in the Library of Congress. Based upon a selective review of the collection, I share the view of other scholars that, as White claimed, he told the truth as he saw it; there are no surprises in the collection, no hint that White's public record in any substantial way conflicted with his personal beliefs. This in part may well account for the revered nature of his "genuine" popularity. *Washington Post* quoted in Wilholt, "Rhetoric," 95–96. White's preeminent national stature took form in the 1920s. Walter Johnson, *William Allen White's America* (New York: Henry Holt and Company, 1947), convincingly argues this point, and my readings support his view; White came to represent, as Johnson argues, the "consummate American," a folk hero; Josephus Daniels was to recall, "I always thought about him and Will Rogers as typical Uncle Sams of our generation," quoted ibid., 477. I have depended heavily upon Johnson for biographical information on White. His account is objective, accurate, and comprehensive.

Other biographers are helpful but Johnson's is the authoritative voice. Everett Rich, *William Allen White: The Man from Emporia* (New York: Farrar and Rinehart, 1941), is not quite as accurate nor as comprehensive but advantageously departs from Johnson's predominantly political perspective to give a rounder view of White. Taken together, Johnson and Rich offer the best introduction to White.

3. Quoted in Johnson, *William Allen White's America*, 477. The *New York Times* reflected upon White's death that his "neighbors lived all along the great American Street that runs from sea to sea," ibid., 3. Commentators often noted White's combination of small-town provincialism, a concomitant frontier, democratic vitality reminiscent of the past century, and a refined twentieth-century cosmopolitan perspective and lifestyle. See for example author Dorothy Canfield Fisher's remembrance of her old friend and editorial colleague, "Country Editor . . . and Cosmopolite," in *William Allen White: In Memoriam* (n.p.: Book of the Month Club, n.d.). For complementary perspectives upon this transition see Samuel P. Hays, *The Response to Industrialism: 1885–1914* (Chicago: University of Chicago Press, 1957); Robert H. Wiebe, *The Search for Order, 1877–1920* (New York: Hill and Wang, 1967); Alan Trachtenberg, *The Incorporation of America: Culture and Society in the Gilded Age* (New York: Hill and Wang, 1982); Lawrence Goodwyn, *The Populist Moment: A Short History of the Agrarian Revolt in America* (Oxford: Oxford University Press, 1978); Daniel T. Rodgers, *The Work Ethic in Industrial America, 1850–1920* (Chicago: University of Chicago Press, 1979); and Joan Shelley Rubin, *The Making of Middlebrow Culture.* (Chapel Hill: University of North Carolina Press, 1992).

4. Long-time employee Frank C. Clough well summarizes White's lifestyle and general character in his laudatory biography of "the boss," *William Allen White of Emporia* (1941; reprint, Westport: Greenwood Press, 1970). See also Johnson, *William Allen White's America*, 243–44. Regarding White's political activities, the best published source is Johnson. Friend and political colleague David Hinshaw offers good insights in his work *A Man From Kansas: The Story of William Allen White* (New York: G. P. Putnam's Sons, 1945). Both Johnson and Everett Rich analyze White's role as a social and cultural critic.

5. Most students of White recognize his philosophy as addressing the present with little thought given to "old times." An exception is argued weakly in Patrick Alan Brooks, "William Allen White: A Study of Values" (Ph.D. diss., University of Minnesota, 1969).

6. Elizabeth S. Sargeant, writing in *Century Magazine*, January 1927, quoted in Johnson, *William Allen White's America*, 477; Finley quoted ibid., 493.

7. Lippmann and Winchell are quoted in ibid., 475. White's explanation is quoted in Richard W. Resh, "A Vision in Emporia: William Allen White's Search for Community," *Midcontinent American Studies Journal* 10 (fall 1969): 26. Resh discusses White's preoccupation with the middle-class nature of the crusade and his use of Emporia as a symbolic community.

8. Rodgers, "In Search of Progressivism," 113–32, quoted p. 113. Rodgers selectively surveys the literature of the 1970s and early 1980s.

9. Ibid., 123.

10. Ibid., 117.

11. White met Roosevelt in 1897 and was overwhelmed by the future president's personality and philosophy. Years later White recalled the occasion: "I was a young, arrogant protagonist of the divine rule of plutocracy. I think I called it 'brains.' He shattered the foundations of my political ideals. As they crumbled then and there, politically, I put his heel on my neck and I became his man. In the handclasp that followed and the gesture of good-bye he became my life long liege and I a yeoman in his service." Quoted in Hinshaw, *A Man From Kansas*, 114. White hardly exaggerated the effect of Roosevelt upon him. For a quarter of a century he devotedly followed Roosevelt, occasionally disagreeing with him, but never disavowing his total and unabashed loyalty.

12. Rodgers, "In Search of Progressivism," 124. White never entirely abandoned the rhetoric of anti-monopolyism. The "plutocrats" would remain a handy target throughout his career.

13. White was a formidable Republican insurgent, a founder in 1912 of the Progressive Party, and one of its leaders to its virtual demise in 1916. As the head of the powerful progressive wing of the Kansas Republican Party during the Progressive Era, White successfully campaigned for a number of state reforms.

14. Rodgers implies that the idea and rhetoric of social harmony did not survive into the twenties. For White it clearly did, as it did for many progressives. Social harmony, anti-monopolyism, and social efficiency no longer so heavily dominate social and political discourse, but each has demonstrated ideological currency well into the late-twentieth century. Rodgers does say social efficiency, the last progressive cluster of ideas, continued as a viable social language. See Rodgers, "In Search of Progressivism," 127. White never picked up on social efficiency. As Rodgers notes, the techniques and vocabulary of the social efficiency experts, who sought a rational and controlled environment, often crossed those of the social harmonizers. Social efficiency probably seemed too abrasive for White.

15. Thomas Bender, *Community and Social Change in America* (Baltimore: Johns Hopkins University Press, 1982), 3–4. While addressing himself to sociologists as well as historians Bender's primary aim is to redirect the work of historians. For a sociological survey see Roland L. Warren, *The Community in America*, 2d ed. (Chicago: Rand McNally, 1972). See 14–20 for a brief analysis of "the community 'problem.'"

16. Bender, *Community and Social Change*, 108 and 117. Warren, *Community in America*, labels this fundamental social transformation "the great change." He defines it as "the increasing orientation of local community units toward extracommunity systems of which they are a part, with a corresponding decline in community cohesion and autonomy." The effect on individuals is marked. Warren lists seven contributing factors: division of labor; differentiation of interests and association; increasing systemic relationships to the larger society; bureaucratization and impersonalization; transfer of functions to profit enterprise and government; urbanization and suburbanization; and changing

values. See pp. 53–54. Warren summarizes five classic community studies demonstrating the differing rate, manner, and time in which communities have undergone the great change. These are Olen Leonard and C. P. Loomis's study, *Culture of a Contemporary Rural Community: El Cerrito, New Mexico* (Washington, D.C.: U.S. Department of Agriculture, 1941); Arthur J. Vidich and Joseph Bensman's work on the pseudonymous community of Springdale, New York, *Small Town in Mass Society: Class, Power and Religion in a Rural Community* (Princeton: Princeton University Press, 1958); Robert S. Lynd and Helen Merrell Lynd's two studies of Muncie, Indiana *Middletown: A Study in American Culture* (New York: Harcourt Brace Jovanovich, 1956) and *Middletown in Transition: A Study in Cultural Conflicts* (New York: Harcourt, Brace, 1937); and John R. Seeley, R. Alexander Sim, and Elizabeth W. Looseley's *Crestwood Heights: A Study of the Culture of Suburban Life* (New York: Basic Books, 1956).

17. Bender, *Community and Social Change,* 58 and 12. Throughout his study Bender offers a succinct indictment of the movement of sociologists and historians well beyond Tönnies' original typological "theory" to such misconstrued typological "realities" of urban and folk, modern and primitive societies.

18. Ibid., 55.

19. Ibid., 42–43; sociologist Robert Redfield quoted.

20. Ibid., 6.

21. "Too good a town" appeared in a *Gazette* editorial condemning factionalism in the wake of the KKK mayoral victory. See "Yesterday's Election," *Emporia Gazette,* 4 April 1923. White was traveling in the Middle East; it is unclear whether in readiness he had written the editorial before leaving the country or wired it from abroad. White's staff occasionally wrote editorials, but while the style varied, the sentiments seldom crossed his own. In this case the style appears to be White's; the sentiment, without question, is his own.

22. James Oliver Robertson, *American Myth, American Reality* (New York: Hill and Wang, 1980), 346 and 21. *American Myth, American Reality* is refreshingly broad in scope. Unfortunately, poor organization, some inaccurate historical analysis, and clumsy writing detract from a generally powerful argument. Robertson's views regarding myth differ in important aspects from those of Richard Slotkin discussed in the introduction.

23. Ibid., 218 and 222. Of course the small town has long projected, particularly since the 1920s, the opposing image of stultification: "For Americans who are bewildered, bruised, or defeated by the freedom and competition and loneliness of the modern world, the images of static rural community still offer refuge. At the same time, these images make the rural community a place of stagnation, hypocrisy, and mindless conservatism." Ibid., 218. Robertson's interest is in demonstrating what he considers to be the small town's more dynamic progressive image.

24. Ibid., 260, 218, and 261.

25. Ibid., 227 and 228. Schrag made the observation in his book *The End of the American Future.*

26. As Rodgers makes clear and as the work of Jean B. Quandt, *From the*

Small Town to the Great Community: The Social Thought of Progressive Intellectuals (New Brunswick: Rutgers University Press, 1970) and Morton White and Lucia White, *The Intellectual versus the City: From Thomas Jefferson to Frank Lloyd Wright* (Cambridge, Harvard University Press and M.I.T. Press, 1962) demonstrate, many progressives were concerned with community and spoke to the issue. White, however, held a more popular and influential national position as a spokesperson for community than most progressives. See introduction.

Chapter Two
The Progressive Promise I: Portraying the Idyllic Community

1. "The Downhill Pull" is the last chapter White wrote in his unfinished autobiography (his son William Lindsay White briefly concluded the work). White ended his story with the beginning of the "deflating" postwar era. This final word is melancholy as White wonders, looking back upon the intra-war decades, "Where were our hopes and dreams of yesteryear?" He recalls his fiftieth birthday in 1918 as a sad milestone when he, as the nation, had entered another era: "I had crossed the meridian, and I did not like the new country." See William Allen White, *The Autobiography of William Allen White* (New York: Macmillan Company, 1946), 625–27. White posthumously received the Pulitzer Prize for his autobiography. Not as polished as much of his writing (certainly owing to his inability to revise the work), it remains a delight to read, a moving, jocular, and analytical account of his life and times. An abbreviated, extensively annotated edition is available. See Sally Foreman Griffith, ed., *The Autobiography of William Allen White*, 2d ed., rev. and abr. (Lawrence: University Press of Kansas, 1990). William Lindsay White's own illustrious, if shadowed, life as a journalist and novelist is sensitively presented in E. Jay Jernigan, *William Lindsay White, 1900–1973: In the Shadow of His Father* (Norman: University of Oklahoma Press, 1997).

2. It is important to recognize that White's mellow, conciliatory postwar image was a new development. Over the years the Kansan threw sharp barbs at many a political opponent and ideological foe. He was highly ambitious, often taking on more work than he could handle. Throughout his life he was plagued with nervous breakdowns: In 1901 he collapsed in Emporia; recovering out West, for two months he could not read newspapers or correspondence; it took until 1909 to recover fully. In 1920 he was about to break again and had to stop work for a month. Eleven years later, in the midst of chairing efforts to relieve depression-wracked Emporia, White collapsed once more; it took six months to regain his health. See Walter Johnson, *William Allen White's America* (New York: Henry Holt and Company, 1947), 136, 326, and 429; and Everett Rich, *William Allen White: The Man from Emporia* (New York: Farrar and Rinehart, 1941), 114. White refers to his first collapse in his autobiography. See White, *Autobiography*,

346–48. Regarding his finances, he recalls: "Between my late forties and my early fifties came the period during which I began to feel a sense of security, the sense that I was 'well fixed,' though of course I had, even at the valuation of an inflated dollar, no more than a quarter or a third of a million." See ibid., 542. Jernigan, *William Lindsay White*, discusses in-depth the emotional problems of father, mother, and son.

3. For material relating to the history of Kansas I have depended upon William Frank Zornow, *Kansas: A History of the Jayhawk State* (Norman: University of Oklahoma Press, 1957). Robert W. Richmond, *Kansas: A Land of Contrasts*, 3rd ed. (Arlington Heights: Forum Press, 1989) offers a readable but more dated general overview. Richmond often cites White: "William Allen White is quoted frequently because no other Kansas commentator had so much to say about what went on for a half century nor did anyone say it quite as well." See p. viii. Homer E. Socolofsky and Virgil W. Dean, comps., *Kansas History: An Annotated Bibliography* (New York: Greenwood Press, 1992) is an important resource.

4. White's parents, by his own reckoning, were an odd couple. Mary Ann Hatton White was the daughter of Irish immigrants. Orphaned at sixteen and taken in by Congregationalists in New York, she moved west to Illinois where she was drawn into the Abolitionist Movement and then on to Kansas. She was a strong-willed, humorless woman, well-educated and cultured, never fully at home in frontier Kansas. Allen White was considerably better natured and more comfortable on the open frontier. An ambitious itinerant of Puritan stock (removed to New York and then to Ohio), he trekked about the new region practicing medicine and dispensing drugs from a general store, running a farm, a hotel, investing in land, participating in town-building and civic affairs—all the while making good money. William Allen White was the couple's only child to survive infancy. He seemed to have inherited the sociability and good business sense of his father and the interest in religion, learning, and culture of his mother. For an interesting if overdrawn analysis of the reformist influence of White's parents and nineteenth-century Kansans upon the twentieth-century progressive see Lynda F. Worley, "William Allen White: Kansan Extraordinary," *Social Science* 41 (April 1966): 91–98.

5. White remained grateful his entire life to Nelson for his apprenticeship. He considered Nelson one of the great publishers of his day. David Hinshaw argues that Nelson was one of the five most influential people in White's life, the other four being his parents, his wife, and Theodore Roosevelt. My readings confirm Hinshaw's view. See Hinshaw, *A Man From Kansas: the Story of William Allen White* (New York: G. P. Putnam's Sons, 1945), 22–23.

6. Quoted in Frank C. Clough, *William Allen White of Emporia* (1941; reprint, Westport: Greenwood Press, Publishers, 1970), 72–74.

7. Johnson, in *William Allen White's America*, contends White carefully plotted the base for his career: "White was aware that constant references to him as a simple country editor would attract more attention than the publicity he might secure if he became a city newspaperman. It was unique to be a famous country editor and refuse offers to leave for the big city. 'From Emporia' gave him a

vantage point of influence with the American people that never could be secured in New York City or Chicago. Distinguished men 'from New York' and 'from Chicago' were plentiful but not 'from Emporia.'" See pp. 78–79. Chester Rowell, a California editor, Progressive Republican, and White's close friend, backed Johnson: "White used the small-town angle for all that it was worth." See ibid.

8. Sally Foreman Griffith, in *Home Town News: William Allen White and the "Emporia Gazette"* (New York: Oxford University Press, 1989), well argues the importance of local and personal factors, political and economic in nature as well as moral, in contributing to White's change of view toward reform. See chapter four. In her work Griffith insightfully focuses upon the journalist's evolving "booster" relationship with his home community and the impression the "booster ethos" makes upon his national perspective. Progressive historiography makes clear the murkiness of the motives energizing the reformers. For White's similarity in background and motives to so many, see Robert M. Crunden, *Ministers of Reform: The Progressives' Achievements in American Civilization, 1889–1920* (New York: Basic Books, 1982; Urbana: University of Illinois Press, 1984). See also Jean B. Quandt, *From the Small Town to the Great Community: The Social Thought of Progressive Intellectuals* (New Brunswick: Rutgers University Press, 1970).

9. For a study of White's voluminous relationship with Roosevelt see Thaddeus Seymour Jr., "A Progressive Partnership: Theodore Roosevelt and the Reform Press—Riis, Steffens, Baker, and White," (Ph.D. diss., University of Wisconsin, Madison, 1985). For White's role within the context of early-twentieth-century Kansas politics see Robert Sherman La Forte, *Leaders of Reform: Progressive Republicans in Kansas, 1900–1916* (Lawrence: University Press of Kansas, 1974). See also Donn Charles Riley, "William Allen White: The Critical Years. An Analysis of the Changing Political Philosophy of William Allen White during the Progressive Period, 1896–1908" (Ph.D. diss., Saint Louis University, 1960); and Jean Lange Kennedy, "William Allen White: A Study of the Interrelationship of Press, Power and Party Politics" (Ph.D. diss., University of Kansas, 1981). National magazines and large metropolitan dailies began their futile courtship of White during this period, trying to lure him out of Emporia. He refused lucrative offers from the likes of the *Saturday Evening Post, McClure's, Cosmopolitan,* and the *Chicago Tribune.* Twice he accepted national posts, wiring his material to New York, but he disliked meeting others' deadlines and the prohibitive distance from his editors. From December 1921 to August 1922 he wrote a weekly commentary for the humor magazine *Judge;* and for about a year beginning in May 1922, he wrote a syndicated weekly editorial column for the Sunday *New York Tribune.* Over the years White served on a small number of journal editorial boards. In 1906 he joined a group of dissidents from the *McClure's* staff to revamp the *American Magazine* into a formidable progressive organ. For magazine and journal background information I have depended upon Frank Luther Mott, *A History of American Magazines, 1885–1905* (Cambridge: Harvard University Press, Belknap Press, 1957) and Thomas Peterson, *Magazines in the Twentieth Century* (Urbana: University of Illinois

Press, 1956). For a strong analysis of the journals, see Matthew Schneirov, *The Dream of a New Social Order: Popular Magazines in America, 1893–1914* (New York: Columbia University Press, 1994).

10. White's muddled progressive perspective is noted by John Milton Cooper Jr., *The Warrior and the Priest: Woodrow Wilson and Theodore Roosevelt* (Cambridge: Harvard University Press, Belknap Press, 1983). Arguing that real differences existed between the New Nationalism and the New Freedom, Cooper points to White as representative of a mistaken perception at the time that few differences existed. He quotes White's remark from his 1924 biography of Wilson: "Between the New Nationalism and the New Freedom was that fantastic imaginary gulf that always has existed between tweedle-dum and tweedle-dee." See pp. 206–27, quoted p. 208. While the debate over the differences between Rooseveltian and Wilsonian progressive policy in all likelihood will never be resolved, White's observation seems most reflective of his own blurred ideology, especially considering his zealous loyalty to Roosevelt and the Progressive Party.

11. The reference to Alice Roosevelt is related by White, *Autobiography*, 369. A good deal of White's irregularity was a matter of power brokerage; a fair measure of it, as well as the outspokenness, could be attributed to ideological flexibility and White's avowed commitment to speak the truth as he currently saw it. White's political inconsistency at times cost him dearly. His irregularity naturally galled party regulars, and when possible they made him pay. On the other hand, his generally consistent support for the straight Republican ticket, once chosen, evoked criticism from fraternal ideologues and tarnished his reputation as a political commentator. Johnson, in *William Allen White's America*, records this 1920 comment of national Democrat George Creel: "The case of William Allen White is a sad one. Here was a natural-born reporter, keen in his observation, photographic as to impression, a master in winnowing chaff from the wheat, and with an unerring instinct for facts. Inherited Republicanism was his trouble. White lives in Kansas, a Republican State; his friends are Republicans, and all of them have office, want to stay in office, or else are running for office. Even today William Allen White is a good reporter between campaigns, but where a Republican candidate has been decided upon he heaves a weary sigh, puts reporting by and takes up the burden of propaganda." See p. 330. Franklin Roosevelt made a similar observation. At a whistle-stop in Emporia during the 1936 campaign the president spotted White hanging back at the edge of the crowd, hailed him to his platform, and regaled the people with the remark, "Bill White is with me three and a half years out of every four." Ibid., 331.

12. "Realists or Idealists?" *Emporia Gazette*, 1 February 1919.

13. For the most comprehensive analysis of White's wartime activities, see Richard W. Resh, "A Vision in Emporia: William Allen White's Search for Community," *Midcontinent American Studies Journal* 10 (fall 1969): 19–35. Resh draws upon his doctoral research into the changing war views of five individuals from the First World War to the Second. His analysis of White's progressive philosophy as intensely chauvinistic and compromising is distorted by this telescopic, martial view of his thought.

14. William Allen White, *A Certain Rich Man* (1909; reprint, Lexington: University Press of Kentucky, 1970). For late-nineteenth-century literary analysis I have relied upon Jay Martin, *Harvests of Change: American Literature, 1865–1914* (Englewood Cliffs: Prentice-Hall, 1967). Martin offers a good overview of the period and pointed analyses of a variety of works. See too the more recent studies by Amy Kaplan, *The Social Construction of American Realism* (Chicago: University of Chicago Press, 1992), and David E. Shi, *Facing Facts: Realism in American Thought and Culture, 1850–1920* (New York: Oxford University Press, 1995).

15. By the 1920s, of course, a Middle Western identity had become so pervasive that it served as the primary device for raining criticism upon American culture. Frederick J. Hoffman in his fine study *The Twenties: American Writing in the Postwar Decade* (New York: Viking Press, 1955) writes, "The Middle West had become a metaphor of abuse; it was on the one hand a rural metaphor, of farms, villages, and small towns; on the other, a middle-class metaphor, of conventions, piety and hypocrisy, tastelessness and spiritual poverty." See p. 328. The entire chapter "Critiques of the Middle Class" is of great interest.

16. For assessments of Howe and Garland see Martin, *Harvests of Change*, 116–20 and 124–32. See also E. W. Howe, *The Story of a Country Town* (1882; reprint, New York City: Blue Ribbon Books, n.d.), and Hamlin Garland, *Back-Trailers from the Middle Border* (New York: Macmillan Company, 1928).

17. For the Middle Western historical novel see John T. Flanagan, "The Middle Western Historical Novel," *Journal of the Illinois State Historical Society* 37 (March 1944): 7–47. For the broader context see Ernest E. Leisy, *The American Historical Novel* (Norman: University of Oklahoma Press, 1950). For the political novel see Joseph Blotner, *The Modern American Political Novel, 1900–1960* (Austin: University of Texas Press, 1966).

18. For the small town see Ima Honaker Herron, *The Small Town in American Literature* (1939; reprint, New York: Pageant Books, 1959). For Howe, Garland, Kirkland, and Riley's extensive influence on a host of writers see ibid. and Martin, *Harvests of Change*. White pays particular homage to Howe, Garland, and Riley in White, *Autobiography*, 147–48, 211–12, 217, 271–72, and 292–93.

19. Anthony Channell Hilfer, *The Revolt from the Village, 1915–1930* (Chapel Hill: University of North Carolina Press, 1969), 4.

20. Herron, *Small Town*, 334; William Allen White, *In Our Town* (1906; reprint, New York: Double Day, Page and Company, 1909); Twain, referring to William Dean Howells, quoted in Johnson, *William Allen White's America*, 152; Hilfer, *Revolt from the Village*, 17.

21. William Allen White, *The Real Issue: A Book of Kansas Stories* (1896; reprint, New York: Doubleday and McClure Company, 1899). Some of *The Real Issue* stories first appeared in the *Kansas City Star*. White in his early years also wrote poetry. With Albert Bigelow Paine he published his mediocre work in *Rhymes By Two Friends* (Fort Scott, Kans.: M. L. Izor and Sons, 1893).

22. White, *The Real Issue*, 22. "A Story of The Highlands" carries a similar message as an optimistic pioneering couple faces tragedy when a high plains drought drives the woman to madness and death. White again distinguishes between the trauma of this section of Kansas and the good life of central and

eastern Kansas: "Crops are as bountiful in Kansas as elsewhere on the globe. It is the constant cry for aid, coming from this plateau—only a small part of the state—which reaches the world's ears, and the world blames Kansas. The fair springs on these highlands lure home-seekers to their ruin." See p. 77.

23. Ibid., 122 and 145. Sherwood Anderson, *Winesburg, Ohio* (1919; reprint, New York: Viking Compass, 1958); Frank Norris, *McTeague: A Story of San Francisco* (1899; reprint, New York: Rinehart and Company, 1950).

24. For a striking indictment of town gossip and cruel respectability see *The Real Issue*'s "The Prodigal Daughter" and its sequel "The Record on the Blotter." For an attack on the provincial mentality of nineteenth-century inland business-men preoccupied with commerce, and double standards of morality, see "'The Fraud of Men.'" Counterfeit boosterism in a town on the commercial skids is portrayed in "The Undertaker's Trust." Hucks also appears in the most famous story of the collection: "The Regeneration of Colonel Hucks." In this melodra-matic but still evocative tale White depicts the colonel's return to the bosom of the Republican Party and his family after dallying with the Populist insurgency. For further analysis of *The Real Issue*, see Patrick Alan Brooks, "William Allen White: A Study of Values" (Ph.D. diss., University of Minnesota, 1969), 218–24; George L. Groman, "W. A. White's Political Fiction: A Study in Emerging Progressivism," *Midwest Quarterly* 8 (October 1966): 79–93; E. Jay Jernigan, *William Allen White* (Boston: Twayne Publishers, 1983), 9, 11–12, 14, 75, 77–80, 83 (Jernigan offers a comprehensive analysis of White's fiction and non-fiction); Johnson, *William Allen White's America*, 21–22, 96–100; John DeWitt McKee, *William Allen White: Maverick on Main Street* (Westport: Greenwood Press, 1975), 28–30, 41–43; and Rich, *William Allen White: The Man from Emporia*, 57–58, 60, 65. Joe W. Kraus in "The Publication of William Allen White's 'The Real Issue,'" *Kansas Historical Quarterly* 43 (summer 1977): 193–202, details White's intense and ambitious interest in the promotion of the book. Chicago's literary journal, *Dial*, praised *The Real Issue* as a collection of "truthful studies of Kansas life, with occasional touches of humor and a heavy burden of pathos. The general effect is almost as sombre as that produced by Mr. Howe's 'Story of a Country Town.'" Quoted in Johnson, *William Allen White's America*, 98.

25. William Allen White, *The Court of Boyville* (New York: Doubleday and McClure Company, 1899) was a critical as well as a commercial success. For further analysis see Brooks, "William Allen White," 24–31; Joseph Lynn Dubbert, "The Puritan in Babylon: William Allen White" (Ph.D. diss., University of Minnesota, 1967), 23–24; Herron, *Small Town*, 184–86; Jernigan, *William Allen White*, 2, 11, 75, 80–82; Johnson, *William Allen White's America*, 22–23, 115–16; and Rich, *William Allen White: The Man from Emporia*, 98. Hilfer, ever-critical of small-town writers, deprecates the connection between the charm of childhood and the town and farm myths: "it was an appeal the adult had to resist." See Hilfer, *Revolt from the Village*, 25. White recalls his own boyhood in a pristine western landscape, an Eden for child and adult, long since scourged by the advance of industrialized civilization. See White, *Autobiography*, 23–28, especially 28.

26. Critic quoted in Johnson, *William Allen White's America,* 153; White, *In Our Town,* 3. For town character see *In Our Town's* "Scribes and Pharisees" and "By the Rod of His Wrath." For class biases see "The Coming of the Leisure Class," "A Bundle of Myrrh," and "The Passing of Priscilla Winthrop." Good citizenry is depicted in "A Question of Climate." The case against liquor is made in "'And Yet a Fool.'" For corruption see "A Kansas 'Childe Roland.'" The wages of sin are paid in "Sown in Our Weakness." *In Our Town* was a commercial and a critical success. For further analysis see Griffith, *Home Town News,* 151–53, 155, 172, 233; Herron, *Small Town,* 337–39; Jernigan, *William Allen White,* 19, 75, 87–90, 97; Johnson, *William Allen White's America,* 152–53; McKee, *William Allen White: Maverick,* 76; and Rich, *William Allen White: The Man from Emporia,* 101–03.

27. William Allen White, *Stratagems and Spoils: Stories of Love and Politics* (New York: Charles Scribner's Sons, 1901). Howells is quoted in Johnson, *William Allen White's America,* 131. Theodore Roosevelt appreciated the work by his fraternal ideologue; for years he gave copies of *Stratagems and Spoils* to foreign diplomats. The stories first appeared in *Scribner's.* For despotic community control see "The Man on Horseback." For the cynical disregard of public opinion see "A Victory for the People." Corruption parades in "'A Triumph's Evidence'" and is eradicated in "The Mercy of Death." Populism and demagoguery are indicted in "A Most Lamentable Comedy"; the protagonist is modeled in part on Kansas's infamous Sockless Jerry Simpson. For further analysis see Brooks, "William Allen White," 218–24; Dubbert, "Puritan in Babylon," 42–44, 67–69; Groman, "W. A. White's Political Fiction," 82–85; Jernigan, *William Allen White,* 12, 75, 79, 83–87, 97; Johnson, *William Allen White's America,* 53–54, 59, 116, 131, 152–53; McKee, *William Allen White: Maverick,* 63–64; Resh, "A Vision in Emporia," 20; and Rich, *William Allen White: The Man from Emporia,* 60, 85, 97–100.

28. William Allen White, *In the Heart of a Fool* (New York: Macmillan Company, 1918). William Allen White's *God's Puppets* (New York: Macmillan Company, 1916), a collection of stories first appearing in the *Saturday Evening Post* and *Collier's,* touched on what were becoming a number of familiar White themes: enslaving materialism; the need for faith in and mercy towards fellow beings; the rise of a progressive order within a small-town milieu; and the reclaiming of the small-town, classless idyll. For further analysis see Groman, "W. A. White's Political Fiction," 88–89; Jernigan, *William Allen White,* 26, 75, 96–98; Johnson, *William Allen White's America,* 258; McKee, *William Allen White: Maverick,* 129–31; and Resh, "A Vision in Emporia," 20.

29. For further analysis see Dubbert, "Puritan in Babylon," 100–04; Griffith, *Home Town News,* 155–56, 182, 185; Groman, "W. A. White's Political Fiction," 85–88; Herron, *Small Town,* 339–41; Hinshaw, *A Man from Kansas,* 156; Jernigan, *William Allen White,* 20–21, 68, 75, 83, 90–96, 101; Johnson, *William Allen White's America,* 144–47; McKee, *William Allen White: Maverick,* 76–78; and Rich, *William Allen White: The Man from Emporia,* 140–49.

30. "Saturday Review of Books," *New York Times,* 31 July 1909, 462; the *Craftsman* article is quoted in Johnson, *William Allen White's America,* 175; *Nation* 89 (19 August 1909): 163; The *Graphic* article is quoted in Johnson, *William Allen White's America,* 174; *Outlook* 71 (21 August 1909): 921–23; Roosevelt is quoted in Johnson, *William Allen White's America,* 176.

31. *In the Heart of a Fool,* 124–25 and 614. For further analysis see Brooks, "William Allen White," 268–69; Joe L. Dubbert, "William Allen White's American Adam," *Western American Literature* 7 (winter 1973): 271–78; Groman, "W. A. White's Political Fiction," 90–92; Herron, *Small Town,* 339–41; Jernigan, *William Allen White,* 24, 27, 75, 101–4, 126; Johnson, *William Allen White's America* , 283–86; McKee, *William Allen White: Maverick,* 147–49; Resh, "A Vision in Emporia," 20–22; and Rich, *William Allen White: The Man from Emporia,* 200.

32. William Allen White, *The Martial Adventures of Henry and Me* (New York: Macmillan Company, 1918), 5–6. An additional, more down-to-earth reason for publication was to boost Henry Allen's ultimately successful gubernatorial candidacy. For further analysis see Jernigan, *William Allen White,* 28, 75, 98–100; Johnson, *William Allen White's America,* 278–79, 282–83, and 286; Resh, "A Vision in Emporia," 25–27; and Rich, *William Allen White: Man from Emporia,* 183–88.

33. F. H., "The Voice of Kansas," review of *The Martial Adventures of Henry and Me,* by William Allen White, *New Republic,* (17 August 1918): 81–82. Hackett was not alone in his praise. In the headline review of the *New York Times Review of Books,* 7 April 1918, sec. 6, 145, White's brand of an all-American, tolerant, and provincial nationalism, was arrayed against Germany's reactionary, vicious, and catastrophic offering. It was no contest as Henry and me, Wichita and Emporia ("which means America") prevailed, expressing "the American spirit in this war as simply and as poignantly as it could be expressed."

34. F. H., "In the Heart of a Fool," review of *In the Heart of a Fool,* by William Allen White, *New Republic* (15 February 1919), 91–92.

35. Ibid., 92. White responded to Hackett three months later from the Versailles Conference, arguing America's puritan mission was as valid in 1919 as ever before. Hackett answered with a severe indictment of "American Puritanism." See W. A. White, "William Allen White to F. H.," *New Republic,* (17 May 1919): 88; and F. H., "The Lilies of the Field," *New Republic,* (17 May 1919): 84–85. The *Chicago News* critic is quoted in Johnson, *William Allen White's America,* 286. Randolph Bourne, "Morals and Art from the West," *Dial* 65 (14 December 1918): 556–57. The reviews were not all bad. See *Publishers' Weekly* 94 (28 December 1918): 2033; *Outlook* 120 (18 December 1918): 640; *New York Times,* 10 November 1918, sec. 3, p. 4.

36. The shift in literary and political currents towards "realism" and "disillusionment" at this time was profound. Resources are abundant. For histories, see, for example, Henry E. May, *End of American Innocence: A Study of the First Years of Our Own Time, 1912–1917* (1959; Reprint, Oxford: Oxford University Press,

1929); William E. Leuchtenberg, *The Perils of Prosperity, 1914–32,* 2nd ed. (Chicago: University of Chicago Press, 1993); Ellis W. Hawley, *The Great War and the Search for a Modern Order: A History of the American People and Their Institutions, 1917–1933,* 2nd ed. (New York: St. Martin's Press, 1992); Paul A. Carter, *The Twenties in America,* 2nd ed. (Arlington Heights: Harlan Davidson, 1975) and *Another Part of the Twenties* (New York: Columbia University Press, 1977); Roderick Nash, *The Nervous Generation: American Thought, 1917–1930* (Chicago: Rand McNally, 1970; Chicago: Ivan R. Dee Publisher, 1990); and Lynn Dumenil, *The Modern Temper: American Culture and Society in the 1920s* (New York: Hill and Wang, 1995), which offers a superb, exhaustive bibliographical essay.

Chapter Three
The Progressive Promise II: Politicking for the Ideal

1. William Allen White, "What's the Matter with Kansas?" in Helen Ogden Mahin, comp., *The Editor and His People: Editorials by William Allen White* (New York: Macmillan Company, 1924), 244–49. White referred to his flowering conservatism as an addendum to Mahin's work. In regard to his sensitivity to popular concerns and his ability to pin down the issues, Walter Johnson notes, "There was nothing original in 'What's the Matter with Kansas?' except the clever phrases and White's unique manner of expressing ideas already held by millions of others." See Walter Johnson, *William Allen White's America* (New York: Henry Holt and Company, 1947), 94.

2. William Allen White, "Kansas: Its Present and Its Future," *Forum,* March 1897, 75–83, quoted 75 and 83. Just prior to the publication of this article White had traveled to a Republican victory celebration in Ohio. Everett Rich writes: "The immediate result of the Ohio trip was to confirm White still further in his opinions. He wrote [in the *Gazette*] of it as 'a wonderful discovery.' For the first time in his life he saw men 'regularly at work.' The industrial development 'was wonderful.' In his twenty odd years in Kansas he had 'never actually seen a factory in operation,' and he concluded that the reason Kansas was laughed at was that it would rather vote for government aid than develop its natural resources.'" See Everett Rich, *William Allen White: The Man from Emporia* (New York: Farrar and Rinehart, 1941), 96.

3. William Allen White, "The Business of a Wheat Farm," *Scribner's Magazine,* November 1897, 531–48. In "Kansas: Its Present and Its Future," Social Darwinist White had raised the alarm against the "new socialism": "Wherever this American is found battling against the natural order,—the order which makes every man responsible for his own success and blamable for his own failure; wherever a man is found seeking aid, other than that of his own two hands and the devices of his own brain, to escape destruction in the industrial mill; wherever a man is found asking his fellow-men to make him, by legislation, the mental or the financial equal of another man,—there is the exponent of the new socialism. The

contention with the new socialism is the chief political affair before the American people to-day. And it is a question as vital in Massachusetts as it is in Kansas." See White, "Kansas: Its Present and Its Future," 78. Later White would eulogize Herbert Spencer in "The Natural History of a Gentleman: Being the Autobiography of Mr. Herbert Spencer," *Saturday Evening Post*, 30 July 1904, 13–15.

4. William Allen White: "A Tenderfoot on Thunder Mountain: I—The Trail," *Saturday Evening Post*, 8 November 1902, 1–2 and 14–15; "II—The Foot of the Rainbow," *Saturday Evening Post*, 15 November 1902, 3–5; "[The Foot of the Rainbow]: Continued," *Saturday Evening Post*, 22 November 1902, 15–16; and "The Pot of Gold," *Saturday Evening Post*, 29 November 1902, 3–5 and 18–19.

5. William Allen White, "The Boom in the Northwest: Opening Up a Country That Must Be Developed by Capital," *Saturday Evening Post*, 21 May 1904, 1–2; "The Boom in the Northwest: With Pick and Shovel in the Mining Camps of Montana, Wyoming and Idaho," *Saturday Evening Post*, 28 May 1904, 1–2.

6. William Allen White, "Ready-Made Homes Out West," *Saturday Evening Post*, 26 April 1902, 12; and "Uncommercial Traveling," *Saturday Evening Post*, 3 May 1902, 12. In a *Collier's* article published two weeks after "Ready-Made Homes Out West," White again drummed away at the theme that homes and communities similar to the rest of the nation had rooted into a West ready for industrial development. See William Allen White, "The Building Up of the Prairie West," *Collier's*, 10 May 1902, 10. Even in the epic land rush to Oklahoma, White had found signs that the Old West was a matter of the past, and a homo-geneous national culture was in the making. Having visited riotously settled Lawton, he noted that Americans had come from all over the nation, had blended together, and had set about to establish Eastern-like institutions in their new community. See William Allen White, "Lawton—The Metropolis of the Wilderness," *Saturday Evening Post*, 7 September 1901, 3–5 and 14–15.

7. In his argument for a study of progressive rhetoric, Daniel T. Rodgers notes that the "progressives shared an inordinate faith in the word . . . and they preached and wrote with consuming zeal." He explains: "Like all partisans, the progressive publicists used words less to clarify a political philosophy than to build a political constituency. What their slogans meant lay not only in what they said but in what these slogans were designed to accomplish." See "In Search of Progressivism," *Reviews in American History* 10 (December 1982): 113–32, quoted 122. For a good analysis of the provincial roots and reactionary nature of White's earlier outlook see Rich, *William Allen White: The Man from Emporia*, 119–29. Sally Foreman Griffith, in *Home Town News: William Allen White and the "Emporia Gazette"* (New York: Oxford University Press, 1959), points out that White retained a booster's speculative business interest in the development of the West, particularly in the aforementioned "boom in the Northwest." See pp. 107–08.

8. Russel B. Nye in his classic work *Midwestern Progressive Politics: A Historical Study of Its Origins and Development, 1870–1958* (East Lansing: Michigan State University Press, 1959), picks up on the shuffling and fusing of

representative national figures in the late-nineteenth century. He writes of the debate over the meaning of Bryan's 1896 tally of over six million votes: "The 'Atlantic Monthly' thought most of Bryan's vote came from the farmer; that 'sturdy yeoman' had somehow turned into a 'hayseed,' lacking 'habits of thrift and commercial morality,' and was an easy mark for 'demagogic witchery.'" Nye quotes Frederick Jackson Turner's election analysis appearing in the *Forum:* "This . . . is the real situation: a people composed of heterogeneous materials, with divers and conflicting ideals and social interests, having passed from the task of filling up the vacant spaces of the continent, is now thrown back upon itself and is seeking an equilibrium. The diverse elements are now being fused into national unity." See pp. 119–20.

9. Arthur Link and Richard L. McCormick in their bibliographical synthesis, *Progressivism* (Arlington Heights: Harlan Davidson, 1983), argue the important role public opinion played in this era and its unique national character: "Progressivism was the only reform movement ever experienced by the whole American nation." Its "national appeal and mass base produced an unprecedented public influence upon policy-making." The "dynamics of progressivism were crucially generated by ordinary people—by the sometimes frenzied mass supporters of progressive leaders, by rank-and-file voters willing to trust a reform candidate. The chronology of progressivism can be traced by events which aroused large numbers of people—a sensational muckraking article, an outrageous political scandal, an eye-opening legislative investigation, or a tragic social calamity. Events such as these gave reform its rhythm and its power." As to who constituted the "ordinary people," Link and McCormick conclude they were a fusion of "businessmen, lawyers, doctors, ministers, and other professionals," as well as "skilled workers, merchants, farmers who were not tenants or sharecroppers, and myriad others." In short, just about everyone, except "the very rich and the very poor" flowed into the progressive majority—shorter still, the historians have identified the makings of the era's "common man." Link and McCormick take stock of Theodore Roosevelt's astuteness in exploiting the phenomenon: they see him as a shrewd self-advertiser, a manipulator of his public image; he was a celebrity who made good magazine and newspaper copy. Roosevelt courted public opinion, inspired it, and in so doing nurtured its growth as an important, independent political force. This, along with the creation of administrative government, "mark[s] Roosevelt as the most creative politician of the early twentieth century." See pp. 7–9 and 37. For additional material on Roosevelt and the political environment see the comparative view offered by John Milton Cooper Jr., *The Warrior and the Priest: Woodrow Wilson and Theodore Roosevelt* (Cambridge: Harvard University Press, Belknap Press, 1983).

10. Link and McCormick's analysis of the complexities of the political environment during the Progressive Era helps explain Roosevelt's successful presentation of himself as a spokesperson for "all the people." They note the growing popular conception that strong government was better than weak; an increased opportunity to work beyond the two-party system; the slow popular acceptance that class and economic interests were not necessarily harmonious and accom-

modation was necessary. Roosevelt, with the help of White and other publicists, skillfully portrayed himself as the strong leader, above partisanship, who could arbitrate the conflicting interests of an incorporating order. The strength of this appeal within the altered political environment was most dramatically evinced by outsider Roosevelt's strong primary challenge to William Howard Taft in 1912 and his remarkably large third-party share of the November vote.

11. Herbert David Croly, *The Promise of American* Life, ed. Arthur M. Schlesinger Jr. (1909; reprint, Cambridge: Harvard University Press, Belknap Press, 1965), 149.

12. Eventually White drew six sketches for Sam McClure's magazine and one more for William Randolph Hearst's *Cosmopolitan.* A recent convert to progressivism, White sympathetically treated established figures while he eagerly anticipated a new political era. Taken together the sketches represent a last admiring glance back by White at the nineteenth-century order with which he had enthusiastically identified; his sights now were fixed on the twentieth century. See William Allen White's, "Bryan," *McClure's Magazine,* July 1900, 232–37; "Hanna," *McClure's Magazine,* November 1900, 56–64; "Croker," *McClure's Magazine,* February 1901, 317–26; "Theodore Roosevelt," *McClure's Magazine,* November 1901, 40–47; "Platt," *McClure's Magazine,* December 1901, 145–53; "Cleveland," *McClure's Magazine,* February 1902, 322–30; and "Harrison," *Cosmopolitan,* March 1902, 489–96. White's swift switch in ideological allegiance is thrown into relief in his 1904 eulogy to Mark Hanna, whom he always had personally liked and owed much to professionally. Ensconced in the new era, White no longer could consider Hanna "a representative American" nor ultimately very important—as he had portrayed him in 1900. He had great potential, he argued, but had squandered it on old dreams. See William Allen White, "McKinley and Hanna: A Study of Hanna the Man, and the Ruling Passion of His Life," *Saturday Evening Post,* 12 March 1904, 1–2.

13. William Allen White, "The New Congress," *Saturday Evening Post,* 28 December 1901, 5–6. White in the article is particularly concerned with Roosevelt's patronage battles with Congress. He would occasionally step down from his lofty rhetorical perch and do battle for Roosevelt on grittier political turf. Roosevelt fought plenty with Congress. For a sense of White's political posturing for the president relative to the House of Representatives and the Senate see a series of articles he wrote for the *Post:* William Allen White, "The Politicians: Our 'Hired Men' at Washington," *Saturday Evening Post,* 14 March 1903, 1–3; "The Brain Trust: The Oligarchy that Rules the Country," *Saturday Evening Post,* 21 March 1903, 1–3; "The Balance-Sheet of the Session: A Survey of Things Done and Left Undone by the Most Important Peace Congress the Country Has Yet Known," *Saturday Evening Post,* 28 March 1903, 8–9 and 22–23; "The President: The Friends and the Enemies He Has Made—The Curious Spectacle of a Smiling Support Ready with the Knife in the Hand behind the Back," *Saturday Evening Post,* 4 April 1903, 4–5 and 14. In the first two articles White is full of praise for first the House, then the Senate. In the third he is more critical. In the final piece about the president he turns with fury upon the

Congress, seeing it as representative of the most abusive elements of the incorporating order. He sees the president as the people's only true representative within the government.

14. William Allen White, "One Year of Roosevelt," *Saturday Evening Post,* 4 October 1902, 3–4.

15. William Allen White, "Swinging Round the Circle with Roosevelt," *Saturday Evening Post,* 27 June 1903, 1–2.

16. Cooper, *The Warrior and the Priest,* 151. For a general summary of Roosevelt's administrative goals, and particularly for his substantive educational use of public rhetoric, see chapters six and eight. As Daniel T. Rodgers notes in "In Search of Progressivism," anti-monopolyism gave way amongst reformists, sometime during the first decade of the twentieth century, to a more dominant rhetoric of social harmony. Roosevelt and White continued to lash out at the malevolency of the plutocrats, but harmony was their most prominent theme.

17. Link and McCormick, *Progressivism,* draw a helpful tripartite distinction between "social progressives," "reforming progressives" who applied their expertise to relieving social disorders, and "coercive progressives," those nativists intent on imposing their way of life upon racial and ethnic minorities. Their basis for distinguishing the three groups is the different emphasis placed upon social justice as opposed to social control. They do note the social progressives had control, though more benign, in mind, as did the others; ultimately, increased control is the result of all three movements. For the analysis see chapter three. The blurred distinction between justice and control, along with the breadth of the progressive agenda, would naturally result in an overlapping of "group" memberships. While clearly a social progressive, White supported the efforts of the professional "reforming progressives," and at times he advocated coercion, most consistently in regard to his intense interest in prohibition. For an early piece condoning force in the name of temperance see William Allen White, "Carrie Nation and Kansas," *Saturday Evening Post,* 6 April 1901, 2–3.

18. The legislative analysis is drawn from Cooper, *The Warrior and the Priest.* In "Political Signs of Promise," *Outlook,* 15 July 1905, 667–70, White rebukes the overly critical press and government reformers who were portraying a far from harmonious state of the union. He, of course, shared this antipathy toward the "muckrakers" with Roosevelt. Still, White had highly praised reform sleuth Lincoln Steffens's *The Shame of the Cities* (1902; reprint, New York: Hill and Wang, 1957) in a review for *McClure's.* Steffens, according to *McClure's* insider Ida Tarbell, had recommended to *McClure's* that White undertake a similar expose of government corruption in the states. White, if ever offered the opportunity, would not have been philosophically inclined to leave his high middle ground to rake about too much in society's muck. For the review see William Allen White, "William Allen White on Mr. Steffens's Book, 'The Shame of the Cities,'" *McClure's Magazine,* June 1904, 220–21.

19. William Allen White, "The Reorganization of the Republican Party: The Great Problems before the Nation," *Saturday Evening Post,* 3 December 1904, 1–2. White wrote a number of articles underscoring the meaning of the upcom-

ing 1904 election. Contests over the tariff, the currency, even the all-encompassing issue for White of equitable distribution—all were overwhelmed by the question of "morality." Theodore Roosevelt was the great leader of an aroused national citizenry, battling with corruption in the Congress and within his own party. The corruption reflected the decayed spiritual state of a people awash in decades of material prosperity; the campaign reflected a great movement to cleanse the national soul. Even the Democracy had rejected Bryan's madness and socialism. The only real question for the people to decide was one of leadership—the impulsive Roosevelt, ready quickly to move the nation, or the circumspect Parker, waiting to deliberate the course of change. The only real issue was whether the people had the moral courage to launch an ordered, conservative change in the conduct of American life. Elect Theodore Roosevelt president, White argued, and the answer would be yes. For a pre-election indictment of Congress see William Allen White, "Grafting and Things," *Saturday Evening Post,* 7 May 1904, 4; for intra-party strife see "The Dollar in Politics: Some Modern Methods in Popular Misgovernment," *Saturday Evening Post* 2 July 1904, 8–9. In "Seconding the Motion: How a Great National Convention Became a Manikin," *Saturday Evening Post,* 23 July 1904, 4–5, White hailed the Roosevelt nomination as a moral victory of the people over dishonest government and party, signaling the forthcoming progressive crusade. Roosevelt stood as a symbol to concerned people at all community levels, as a guiding light toward a renaissance in government decency. White regularly covered the conventions of both parties. The Democratic conclave was reported in "The Democratic Revival: A Near View of the Building of a Safe and Sane Platform at St. Louis," *Saturday Evening Post,* 13 August 1904, 6–7.

20. William Allen White's "Why the Nation Will Endure," *Saturday Evening Post,* 4 March 1905, 12 (White's piece headed the editorial page of the "Roosevelt Number"); "Political Signs of Promise," *Outlook,* 15 July 1905, 667–70; and "The Golden Rule," *Atlantic Monthly,* October 1905, 433–41, quoted 441.

21. William Allen White, "The Kansas Conscience: Its Revolt against the Iniquities of an Unrestrained Competitive System—The Deeper Meaning of the Oil Fight and the Wider Significance of the Struggle for Industrial Independence," *Reader Magazine,* October 1905, 488–93, quoted 489–90. Robert Sherman La Forte's *Leaders of Reform: Progressive Republicans in Kansas, 1900–1916* (Lawrence: University Press of Kansas, 1974) offers a good summary of Kansas's battle with Standard Oil. See pp. 46–50. In William Allen White, "Folk: The Story of a Little Leaven in a Great Commonwealth," *McClure's,* December 1905, 115–32, White offered another example, in the more cosmopolitan state of Missouri, of spiritual victory over materialism. Progressive governor Joseph W. Folk is praised for turning a corrupted, machine-ridden state into a model commonwealth of equitable distribution. In White's view Folk had led Missourians to uphold the greater community interest, the well-being of all citizens, over meaner, local, individualized interests. It was a victory of the decent majority over the unsavory minority. White's frequent references to the battle between spiritualism and materialism were not uncommon for the period. While White often used religious references

in his writing, they were more a matter of malleable rhetoric than theological conviction. White's primary interests were earthly, not heavenly. For a different view of the place of religion in his work see Joseph Lynn Dubbert, *The Puritan in Babylon: William Allen White* (Ph.D. diss., University of Minnesota, 1967). Dubbert argues that "divine destiny" underlies all of White's thought. Another perspective is found in Jack Wayne Traylor, "William Allen White and His Democracy, 1919–1944" (Ph.D. diss., University of Oklahoma, 1978). Traylor discusses the strong influence of modernism upon White.

22. William Allen White, "Emporia and New York," *American Magazine,* January 1907, 258–64. Generally White qualified his definition of "all the United States." In "Emporia and New York" he did not include the South in his vision of a socially harmonious American commonwealth based upon social sympathy. He noted the similarity between Kansans and westerners and easterners, but as so often in his life's work he considered the South a caste-ridden land alien to the America envisioned by the founding fathers and close to resurrection in his own time. A year later White spoke at Chicago's City Club. According to the introduction to his published remarks, most of the members "were treated to a surprise when Mr. White in his address forsook Emporia and what is generally conceived to be her point of view, to take up the industrial problems which seem most sharply focused in the larger cities." In White's perspective, however, Chicago's problems were Emporia's—and within its point of view lay Chicago's salvation. In his address White called for government legislation to insure old-age security for workers. He argued that those who earned the wealth for the country deserved a bigger share. He asked the "well-off" members to help, to join Theodore Roosevelt and reformers of both parties in the battle between the rich and the workers, to secure justice and righteousness through equitable distribution. See William Allen White, "A National Responsibility," *City Club Bulletin,* 20 March 1908, 48–50.

23. William Allen White, "The Partnership of Society," *American Magazine,* October 1906, 576–85, quoted 581, 582, and 579–80. White was a contributor and editorial associate, along with Peter Finley Dunne, to the reorganized magazine. Ida M. Tarbell, John S. Phillips, Albert Boyden, Lincoln Steffens, and Ray Stannard Baker left *McClure's* and took control of the *American Magazine* with the aim of establishing it as a prominent progressive organ. White was welcomed as a popular and representative spokesperson from America's heartland who could add levity as well as ideas to the cause. The introduction to the staff quoted Norman Hapgood of *Collier's* as he spoke about his magazine's frequent contributor: "Among American writers of our day we know none characterized more surely by rightness and health of spirit than William Allen White of Emporia, Kansas. None sees the world more justly in its true proportions, as it is. None, therefore, is more kind, more charitable, with gentler humor, or in more every-day fashion entirely wise. He can, with this wisdom, amiability and amusement that are his, do things that stiffer spirits find impossible. He can criticize with no suggestion of hostility. He can praise with no hint of partiality.

In his freshness, in the openness of his manner and the breeziness of his words, there is much that we are proud to call American." See ibid., 573. According to the editor in his preface to the article, this all-American type spoke for moderation in a period of crisis: "We need such discourses from sane minds always and we need them at this period, more than ever before, when Conservatism is a wallow of selfishness and radicalism a riot of hate." See ibid., 576. Theodore Roosevelt concurred. He wrote White: "That is an A-1 article and I am delighted with it. . . . I feel as if I could have written it myself—perhaps I should be more accurate in saying that I feel as I ought to have written it myself. By George, I would like to have that article circulated as a tract!" Quoted in Johnson, *William Allen White's America,* 160. The importance to White of the national community over the local again is emphasized in his "What's the Matter with America: I The County," *Collier's,* 20 October 1906, 18–19 and 28; "What's the Matter with America: The State," 10 November 1906, 16–17 and 30; and "What's the Matter with America: III The Nation," 1 December 1906, 16–17. White argued that the solution to the nation's political ills lay with the people. Through social sympathy, clearly understood at the local level but most effectively expressed nationally, the nation's problems would be solved. Work must be done, at all community levels, but the ultimate aim was the perfection of the greater national community.

24. William Allen White, "Taft, A Hewer of Wood," *American Magazine,* May 1908, 19–32. Reporting the Republican convention, White saw the gathering as a battleground between Rooseveltian spiritualism and conservative materialism, with Theodore Roosevelt at least temporarily victorious over his powerful opponents. See William Allen White, "A Brief for the Defendant: Being a View of the Chicago Republican Convention through Friendly Eyes," *Collier's,* 4 July 1908, 9–10. In William Allen White, "Twelve Years of Mr. Bryan: 1896–1908, A Period of Political Progress in Which New Doctrines Have Become Familiar and Radicalism Has Stepped Faster Than Its Prophet," *Collier's,* 17 October 1908, 12–13, White praised third-time candidate Bryan as an influential spokesperson whose time had passed to lead the nation. The people now needed a judge between the strong and the weak, not an agitator. Theodore Roosevelt had carried out Bryan's work, White claimed, and Taft was right to complete the job. White partially credited the Populists for their contribution to the progressive cause in William Allen White, "Certain Voices in the Wilderness," *Kansas Magazine,* January 1909, 1–5. With the passing years White would give increased due to the defunct Populists as well as to the diminished Bryan.

25. William Allen White, "Roosevelt: A Force for Righteousness," *McClure's Magazine,* February 1907, 386–94, quoted 392.

26. William Allen White's articles in *American Magazine:* "'The Old Order Changeth,'" January 1909, 219–25; "The Old Order Changeth: II—The Beginnings of the Change," February 1909, 407–14; "The Old Order Changeth: III Certain Definite Tendencies," March 1909, 506–13; "The Old Order Changeth: IV—Progress in American Cities," April 1909, 603–10; "The Old Order Changeth: V. The Leaven in the National Lump," May 1909, 63–70; "'The

Old Order Changeth': VI The Schools—The Main Spring of Democracy," August 1909, 376–83; and "'The Old Order Changeth': What About Our Courts?" February 1910, 499–505. In the first article White spread out his grand vision of a twentieth-century nation abandoning materialism and embracing spiritualism. In the second he offered his view of progress in democratizing the political system; in the third he covered corporate regulation. In the fourth article White portrayed the urban renaissance, and in the fifth he described the national nature of the reform movement. In the sixth article he argued education was the key to progress, and government intervention was necessary to ensure its quality. In the final piece he cautioned patience with the reactionary federal courts, believing they would eventually reflect public sentiment. The articles were gathered together and published as a book in 1910 by Macmillan, entitled *The Old Order Changeth: A View of American Democracy.* For a similarly optimistic and important analysis of the changing order see W. A. White, "A Theory of Spiritual Progress," *Columbia University Quarterly* 12 (September 1910): 408–20. The article is excerpted from White's honorary master of arts address. White's chauvinism regarding America's mission to the world always permeated his work. For an early example, steeped in ethnocentrism and jingoism, see William Allen White, "An Appreciation of the West: Apropos of the Omaha Exposition," *McClure's Magazine,* October 1898, 575–80.

27. William Allen White's, "The Insurgence of Insurgency: What the Radical Wing of the Republican Party Stands For, and What It Has Accomplished," *American Magazine,* December 1910, 170–74; "The Progressive Hen and the Insurgent Ducklings," *American Magazine,* January 1911, 394–99; "The Old Problem of the Dog and the Engine," *American Magazine,* February 1911, 517–20; and "'When the World Busts Through,'" *American Magazine,* April 1911, 746–47. The progressive hen is a sedentary Theodore Roosevelt, and Robert La Follette is one of the obstreperous ducklings; in the piece White sized up the two leaders' political personalities and positions as he sensed their impending clash. An early supporter of La Follette's presidential candidacy, White would abandon the Wisconsin senator at the eleventh hour to support Roosevelt. In William Allen White, "Storming the Citadel: Capture of the Outworks of the Senate by the Insurgents Significant of Greater Changes," *American Magazine,* September 1911, 570–75, White surveyed in detail the political landscape, spoke of the permanency of the Progressive Movement, third-party rumblings, and La Follette as the leader of the movement. In William Allen White, "Three Years of Progress: The Ground Covered during Three Years of Political Skirmishing," *Saturday Evening Post,* 24 February 1912, 3–5 and 38–40, White offered additional detailed political analysis.

28. William Allen White, "Should Old Acquaintance Be Forgot? A Statement of the Relations between President Taft and His Friend Colonel Roosevelt," *American Magazine,* May 1912, 13–18. The editor noted the article appeared to be biased and possibly short-changed the contribution to the reform movement of La Follette. White's remembrance appears in the final paragraphs of his por-

tion of *The Autobiography of William Allen White* (New York: Mamillan Company, 1946), 627. White was hardly alone in sensing this was an epochal moment—countless accounts attest to the power of the meeting.

29. The 1912 election analysis is drawn in large part from Cooper, *The Warrior and the Priest,* particularly chapter thirteen.

30. William Allen White, "The Ebb Tide: Can the Progressives Come Back?" *Saturday Evening Post,* 19 December 1914, 3–4 and 37. This lead article for the *Post* was White's first political commentary to appear in a national journal since May 1912. He analyzed the election, diagnosed the party and its program, and ventured his thoughts as to its future. His discounting of candidates and elections was a telling turnabout as he assumed an unaccustomed minority status. He wrote a lot more about the matter in the article. In his autobiography White recalled those who had stood with Roosevelt at the Bull Moose Convention: "Here were the successful middle-class country-town citizens, the farmer whose barn was painted, the well paid railroad engineer, and the country editor. It was a well dressed crowd. We were, of course, for woman suffrage, and we invited women delegates and had plenty of them. They were our own kind, too— women doctors, women lawyers, women teachers, college professors, middle-aged leaders of civic movements, or rich young girls who had gone in for settlement work. Looking over the crowd, judging the delegates by their clothes, I figured that there was not a man or woman on the floor who was making less than two thousand a year, and not one, on the other hand, who was topping ten thousand. Proletarian and plutocrat were absent. . . ." White concluded, "the movement which Theodore Roosevelt led in 1912 was in the main and in its heart of hearts 'petit bourgeois.'" See White, *Autobiography,* 483–84. White once previously had noted a "crass" element within the emergent middle-class majority, as he called for the inculcation of higher social aims through education in William Allen White, "A Democratic View of Education," in the avant-garde *Craftsman,* November 1911, 119–30.

31. William Allen White, "The Republican Party," *Metropolitan,* July 1915, 14–15 and 63–64, quoted 63. In William Allen White, "Government of the People, by the People, for the People," *Independent,* 7 February 1916, 187–90, in the first of a series on the expectations and hopes of a number of individuals, White argued that the altruism of the middle class for the past quarter century had created a new social, economic, and political order, saving the capitalist system from a greedy self-destruction that would have led to a socialist reaction. In this piece, as well as in William Allen White, "The Glory of the States: Kansas," *American Magazine,* January 1916, 41 and 65, White foresaw a great deal of work ahead for his more constricted middle class. In William Allen White, "Who Killed Cock Robin? A Post-Mortem Inquiry into Recent Republican Calamities," *Collier's,* 16 December 1916, 5–6 and 26–27, White saw the defeated Republican Party as reactionary and plutocratic, bankrupt in its leadership and agenda. He argued that the Democrats, as a states-rights party of protest and criticism, could go just so far with its progressive measures towards constructive, national

reform. Only the vibrant, forward-looking Progressives offered a powerful voice, albeit as a minority, to speak for necessary economic and social change. White warned that the Republicans would have to reform or remain forever divided from the Progressives. Ultimately he and most other Progressive Party holdouts would unhappily return to the triumphant conservative fold by 1920; White returned, grousing, in 1916.

32. The 1911 war reference was made in White, "Storming the Citadel," 575. Droves of progressive reformers took up the war cry, including the likes of John Dewey, Walter Lippmann, W. E. B. DuBois, and Ida Tarbell.

33. William Allen White, "The Odds against the U-Boat," *Collier's,* 8 December 1917, 5–7; "The Doughboy on Top of the World," *Red Cross Magazine,* June 1919, 45–51; and "The Highbrow Doughboy," *Red Cross Magazine,* August 1919, 19–24, quoted 24. For additional articles dealing with the purity and righteousness of the A.E.F., see William Allen White, "The Y.M.C.A. Huts: 'Safety Valves' for Our Boys in France," *Touchstone,* January 1918, 344–50; and "In Germany with William Allen White," *Literary Digest,* 26 April 1919, 64 and 66.

34. "We Give Thanks," *Emporia Gazette,* 28 November 1918.

35. Nye, *Midwestern Progressive Politics,* 219–22 and 224–36.

Chapter Four
Fashioning the Model American Community

1. David Hinshaw offers this abbreviated list of organizations for which White served as a trustee over the years: The Rockefeller Foundation, the [Theodore] Roosevelt Memorial Association, the Woodrow Wilson Foundation, the Walter Hines Page Foundation, the Pacific Relations Committee, the National Illiteracy Association, and the League to Enforce Peace. He also served on the Pulitzer Award Committee, as president of the American Society of Newspaper Editors, and as chairman of the Committee to Defend America by Aiding the Allies. See David Hinshaw, *A Man From Kansas: The Story of William Allen White* (New York: G. P. Putnam's Sons, 1945), 199. Walter Johnson notes White's internationalist work with the League of Nations Association, the American Association for International Cooperation, the Education Committee in the Interest of World Peace, and the Jury of Award of the Bok Peace Prize. See Walter Johnson, *William Allen White's America* (New York: Henry Holt and Company, 1947), 505.

2. Johnson argues with merit that by the 1920s White really had come to be more at home in such distant locales: "Although the citizens of Emporia greatly respected William Allen White, few of them were on intimate terms with him during the last two decades of his life. There were very few people left in the town who called him Bill or Will. There were more people who called him by his first name in New York City than in Emporia." See Ibid, 493.

3. Ferber quoted in Everett Rich, *William Allen White: The Man from Emporia* (New York: Farrar and Rinehart, 1941), 275.

4. For a strong analysis of the 1920s focus upon the small town, see Paul A. Carter, *The Twenties in America*, 2nd ed. (Arlington Heights: Harlan Davidson, 1975), in particular chapter three, "Of Town and Country," especially pp. 92–105. Carter offers an excellent and provocative review of the rural-urban conflict in "Country Bumpkin vs. City Slicker in the Halls of Congress: or How're You Gonna Keep 'Em Down on the Farm after They've Seen Paree?" *Reviews in American History* 19 (June 1991): 232–37.

5. Robert S. Lynd and Helen Merrell Lynd, *Middletown: A Study in American Culture* (New York: Harcourt Brace Jovanovich, 1956), 80–81. The following interpretation of the Lynds' work is based in large part upon the research of Richard Wightman Fox, "Epitaph for Middletown: Robert S. Lynd and the Analysis of Consumer Culture," in the valuable collection *The Culture of Consumption: Critical Essays in American History, 1880–1980*, ed. Richard Wightman Fox and T. J. Jackson Lears (New York: Pantheon Books, 1983), 101–41.

6. Lynd and Lynd, *Middletown*, 80–81.

7. My analysis of the *Gazette's* changing news and advertising format has been aided by Sally F. Griffith, "Mass Media Come to the Small Town: The 'Emporia Gazette' in the 1920s," in *Mass Media between the Wars: Perceptions of Cultural Tension, 1918–1941*, ed. Catherine L. Covert and John D. Stevens (Syracuse: Syracuse University Press, 1984).

8. William Allen White, "Andy Armstead," *Emporia Gazette*, 23 January 1925. The following analysis of White's editorial commentary is based upon the reading of the *Emporia Gazette* for the period 1 October 1918 to 2 January 1927. From 1927 to 1934 White's son, William Lindsay White, took over a good portion of the newspaper's operation and wrote many of the editorials. With the exception of this seven-year hiatus, William Allen White wrote almost every editorial in the *Gazette* for the forty-seven years he owned the paper. Occasional pieces written by his staff generally represented his opinions, if they lacked his style. While out of Emporia, White would remain in daily contact with the staff, overseeing the general operation of the newspaper. He would leave behind editorials to run, and he would wire in pieces.

9. William Allen White, "'The Old Order Changeth': VI The Schools—The Main Springs of Democracy," *American Magazine*, August 1909, 382.

10. "The Second Coming of Wilson," *Emporia Gazette*, 19 April 1919.

11. "The Republican Party," *Emporia Gazette*, 6 November 1918. Hailing Roosevelt's postwar return to the arena of "social and industrial justice," White detailed the former president's aggressive domestic agenda in "T. R. Hunting Trouble," *Emporia Gazette*, 18 November 1918. In another commentary, "The Republican Party," *Emporia Gazette*, 24 July 1919, White advocated a program encompassing a wide array of progressive measures ranging from strict railroad regulation to a seat for the worker in the councils of management; from government licensing and control over the manufacture and sale of food stuffs to nationalization of resources such as coal, oil, minerals, water, and the fisheries;

and from massive land reclamation for the veterans to membership in the League of Nations.

12. "The Republican Party," *Emporia Gazette,* 24 July 1919; "A Hard Boiled World," *Emporia Gazette,* 11 November 1920.

13. "Carry On," *Emporia Gazette,* 3 August 1923. As his health was breaking, Harding confided to White his famous plaint, "I have no trouble with my enemies. I can take care of them. It is my friends. My friends, that are giving me my trouble." See William Allen White, *The Autobiography of William Allen White* (New York: Macmillan Company, 1946), 623; the entire fascinating account is in chapter eighty–six, "An American Tragedy," 615–24.

14. "The New Crowd Rules," *Emporia Gazette,* 10 June 1924. White was not pleased with the Republicans; it being an election year he was even unhappier with the Democrats. Virtually relabeling the Democracy the party of "rum, Romanism, and rebellion," he came to the aid of his country in a series of editorials covering the Democratic convention; see in particular "Why the Dark Horse Wins," *Emporia Gazette,* 2 July 1924. Intent on Republican victory, White turned on La Follette's Progressive Party candidacy as well as that of Democrat John W. Davis; for a good example of his contorted search for a reason to support Coolidge, see "Coolidge or Bryan," *Emporia Gazette,* 19 August 1924. White argues that a vote for Davis or La Follette could result in a deadlock and a return to power of William Jennings Bryan through the elevation of his brother (Charles Bryan, Davis's running mate) to the presidency. Scapegoating Bryan seemed a particularly tawdry concession to the powers that be or a shameful display of unnecessary animosity toward La Follette. White believed in the cyclical nature of reform: reform followed by reaction leading in turn to a more progressive period of reform. See for example "The Cycle," *Emporia Gazette,* 2 February 1925, where he concluded with a good-natured shrug, "So here's to reaction. Let 'er come. It is a part of the necessary process of nature. Every dog has his day— some of us two days. It's a good world, and the best we know—so far." Still, it is important to note that White's jovial bow to reaction had its limits—generally bounded by economics. In terms of civil rights White was not amused; he had just run a highly applauded independent Kansas campaign for governor premised upon his opposition to the Ku Klux Klan. This campaign may help to explain further White's opposition to La Follette; amongst numerous possibilities, surely ingratiating himself to the national Republican Party during his Kansas bolt ranked high.

15. "For Which All Thanks," *Emporia Gazette,* 27 November 1924. The bibliography on the twenties is rich. Amongst a vast array of studies previously referred to, an old chestnut remains colorful, fairly accurate, and highly evocative of the "feel" of the decade. See Frederick Lewis Allen, *Only Yesterday: An Informal History of the Nineteen Twenties* (New York: Harper & Row, Publishers, 1964).

16. "When People Legislate," *Emporia Gazette,* 21 February 1925; "The Cock-Eyed World," *Emporia Gazette,* 23 September 1925. Perhaps White had been talking a good deal with his friend Walter Lippmann or reading Lippmann's recently published, fundamental questioning of the people, public

opinion, and democracy. See Ronald Steel, *Walter Lippmann and the American Century* (Boston: Little, Brown and Company, 1980), especially chapter seventeen, "Tyranny of the Masses," 211–19.

17. "Light in the Darkness," *Emporia Gazette*, 9 December 1925; "Seven Years," *Emporia Gazette* 6 January 1926; "Them As Has Gits," *Emporia Gazette*, 7 December 1926.

18. "The President's Message," *Emporia Gazette*, 7 December 1926.

19. "The Decline of Jazz Joy," *Emporia Gazette*, 10 November 1922; "The Gas Buggy," *Emporia Gazette*, 2 February 1925. Paula S. Fass, *The Damned and the Beautiful: American Youth in the 1920s* (Oxford: Oxford University Press, 1977) remains a strong resource; for the automobile see James J. Flink, *The Car Culture*, (Cambridge: MIT Press, 1975). One of the great issues intricately tied to changing manners and mores for White was Prohibition. Many editorials appeared in the *Gazette* throughout the twenties advocating stricter enforcement of the law. The issue for White was not morality but the social and economic welfare of the nation. See for example, "Chickens," *Emporia Gazette*, 18 January 1926: "the prohibition question is not a question of morals or trying to make people good, but is a question of social conservation, trying to make a complex world safe." On the intricacies of Prohibition see Joseph R. Gusfield, *Symbolic Crusade: Status, Politics, and the American Temperance Movement*, 2nd ed. (Urbana, University of Illinois Press, 1986); Norman H. Clark, *Deliver Us from Evil: An Interpretation of American Prohibition* (New York: W. W. Norton, 1976); and W. J. Rorabaugh, *The Alcoholic Republic: An American Tradition* (Oxford: Oxford University Press, 1979).

20. "Nearer and Nearer," *Emporia Gazette*, 23 August 1923. For the development and influence of radio upon American culture see Susan J. Douglas, *Inventing American Broadcasting, 1899–1922* (Baltimore: John Hopkins University Press, 1987), and Eric Barnouw, *A Tower in Babel: A History of Broadcasting in the United* States, vol.1—to 1933 (New York: Oxford University Press, 1966).

21. White plays upon railroad "robber baron" Commodore Cornelius Vanderbilt's famous declaration in "Old Stuff," *Emporia Gazette*, 18 August 1919.

22. "Townley and the Farmers" and "'One Big Union,'" *Emporia Gazette*, 14 July 1919.

23. "What Labor Really Wants," *Emporia Gazette*, 13 November 1919.

24. "Wages for Workers," *Emporia Gazette*, 15 January 1926.

25. "Nix on the Socialists," *Emporia Gazette*, 21 December 1920; "Middle Class," *Emporia Gazette*, 4 November 1920; "Cheap, Cheap, Cheap," *Emporia Gazette*, 11 August 1925.

26. "Distribution of Wealth," *Emporia Gazette*, 3 December 1926.

27. "Labor and Wait," *Emporia Gazette*, 9 June 1921. Sharing space on the editorial page was a partial reprint of an excessively laudatory *Saturday Evening Post* piece praising Kansas as a middle-class paradise.

28. Kansas, Lyon County, and Emporia demographic analysis drawn from Carroll D. Clark and Roy L. Roberts, *People of Kansas: A Demographic and Sociological Study* (Topeka: Kansas State Planning Board, 1936); Kansas, Office

of the State Board of Agriculture, *Report of the Kansas State Board of Agriculture for the Quarter Ending December, 1925: Containing the State's Dicennial Census of 1925, Tabulated, Classified and Arranged as Contemplated by the Law* (Topeka: n. p., 1926); Department of Commerce, Bureau of the Census, *Fifteenth Census of the United States, 1930: Population*, vol. 3.

29. "The Passing Decade," *Emporia Gazette*, 24 December 1920.

30. Ibid.

31. "The New Well," *Emporia Gazette*, 26 May 1921; "An Editor and His Town," *Emporia Gazette*, 4 December 1924.

32. Amongst helpful works on the second incarnation of the Ku Klux Klan, see Robert Moats Miller, "The Ku Klux Klan," in *Change and Continuity in Twentieth-Century America: The 1920s*, ed. John Braeman, Robert H. Bremner, and David Brody (Columbus: Ohio State University Press, 1968), 215–55; Kenneth T. Jackson, *The Ku Klux Klan in the City 1915–1930* (New York: Oxford University Press, 1970; Chicago: I. R. Dee, 1992); Nancy MacLean, *Behind the Mask of Chivalry: The Making of the Second Ku Klux Klan* (New York: Oxford University Press, 1994); Leonard Moore, "Historical Interpretations of the 1920s Klan: The Traditional View and the Populist Revision," *Journal of Social History* 24 (winter 1990): 341–57; and Shawn Lay, "Hooded Populism: New Assessments of the Ku Klux Klan of the 1920s," *Reviews in American History* 22 (December 1994): 668–73, for a synopsis and good bibliographical directives.

33. "Nix on Ku Klux," *Emporia Gazette*, 28 July 1921.

34. "Seeing Red," *Emporia Gazette*, 27 December 1919; "The Ku Klux Klan Again," *Emporia Gazette*, 25 May 1922. For a Klan tarring of White, see "The Truth at Last," *Emporia Gazette*, 2 August 1923, which is a reprint of an Enid, Oklahoma, Klan newspaper attack depicting the editor as a "little self styled cheese smelling demagogue" too often expressing "his brainless block on the klan." For a sampling of White's racial, religious, regional, and class prejudices, see "Why the Dark Horse Wins," *Emporia Gazette*, 2 July 1924, which is a reprint of one of his syndicated articles covering the strife-torn cultural landscape at the 1924 Democratic convention.

35. The cartoon ran in the *Emporia Gazette*, 13 October 1924. For a general analysis of the campaign, see Jack Wayne Traylor, "William Allen White's 1924 Gubernatorial Campaign," *Kansas Historical Quarterly* 42 (summer 1976): 180–91. For an in-depth assessment of the legal battle to oust the Klan from Kansas, see Charles William Sloan Jr., "Kansas Battles the Invisible Empire: The Legal Ouster of the KKK from Kansas, 1922–1927," *Kansas Historical Quarterly* 40 (autumn 1974): 393–409.

36. Quoted in Everett Rich, *William Allen White: The Man from Emporia*, (New York: Farrar and Rinehart, 1941), 255; "A Holy American Day," *Emporia Gazette*, 17 September 1924.

37. "White Announces," *Emporia Gazette*, 20 September 1924.

38. "Forward or Backward," *Emporia Gazette*, 27 September 1924.

39. "Wiped Out," *Emporia Gazette*, 5 August 1926. White remained ever alert to reaction, keeping tabs on "bigotry, fantiscism [*sic*], communism—the devil's

own brew of the ill-bred and misconceived." For an insightful commentary see "Power and Ignorance," *Emporia Gazette*, 6 June 1925: "The world is going through a queer phase in which ignorance armed in democracy and conscious of the strength of mere numbers, is arousing, organizing and becoming emotionalized. The third and fourth-raters are getting a taste of power. Leadership in the world is leveling down as the standards of living of the masses are leveling up. The vast masses of the half-baked, the unintelligent but literate, the unthinking but plausible are crowding into high places by the sheer power of numbers, and with stupid or unscrupulous leaders are messing up the world."

40. "Virtue's Own Reward," *Emporia Gazette*, 12 October 1921; "Our Daily Jolt," *Emporia Gazette*, 8 September 1923; "Greater Wichita," *Emporia Gazette*, 21 April 1924; "The Millennium," *Emporia Gazette*, 30 December 1921. For more on the demographic and cultural divide, see Don S. Kirchner, *City and Country: Rural Responses to Urbanization in the 1920s* (Westport: Greenwood Publishing, 1970).

41. "Hickville on the Hudson," *Emporia Gazette*, 9 October 1922; "'Impressions of America,'" *Emporia Gazette*, 11 December 1924.

42. "Mirrors of Emporia," *Emporia Gazette*, 10 May 1923.

43. Ellison Hoover, "An Impression of Emporia, Kansas, By One Who Has Never Been There," *Life*, 20 August 1925, 23; "Emporia and New York," *Emporia Gazette*, 21 August 1925.

44. Sinclair Lewis, *Main Street* (1920; reprint, New York: New American Library, 1961). For an attack on Gotham, see the front page story, "Gotham Naughty, Also Essential," *Emporia Gazette*, 15 October 1925. For an ideal community, see the editorial "Service Above Self," *Emporia Gazette*, 27 March 1926. For the review of "The Home Town Mind," see "Book Stuff," *Emporia Gazette*, 5 April 1926. For Fitzgerald's criticism, see the editorial "Where the People Live," *Emporia Gazette*, 15 November 1921. For the friendly reviews, see "Victor Murdock's Book," *Emporia Gazette*, 9 March 1921; "The Brimming Cup," *Emporia Gazette*, 24 August 1921; "A New Kansas Book," *Emporia Gazette*, 16 August 1924; and "Grayson's New Book," *Emporia Gazette*, 15 October 1925. For a critique of the realists, see "Back to Tok," *Emporia Gazette*, 26 April 1922. For a survey of authors see, "Our Women Novelists," *Emporia Gazette*, 12 September 1922. For praise of Howe and Garland, see "Ed Howe Rebels," *Emporia Gazette*, 6 April 1926, and "The Revival of Old Stuff," *Emporia Gazette*, 4 September 1922.

45. "A Great American Novel," *Emporia Gazette*, 23 November 1920. On the same day he ran the editorial, White wrote Lewis. He kept to himself the reservations which he expressed to others regarding the author's neglect of the kindlier side of Main Street. Something more important had been achieved—as he wrote fellow-Kansan, newspaper owner, and novelist Victor Murdock, "It is the sort of thing that puts discontent into the hearts of folks." He asked Lewis to inscribe and autograph copies of the novel he and Sally intended to distribute as Christmas gifts: "If I were a millionaire, I should buy a thousand of those books and send them to my friends, and then I would go and bribe the legislature of Kansas to make "Main Street" compulsory reading in the public schools. No

American has done a greater service for his country in any sort of literature, than you have done." Quoted in Walter Johnson, ed., *Selected Letters of William Allen White, 1899–1943* (New York: Henry Holt and Company, 1947), 211–12.

46. Mark Schorer, *Sinclair Lewis: An American Life* (New York: McGraw-Hill Book Company, 1961), 231. Lewis was one of the most popular authors of the era; Hollywood in the twenties capitalized on his draw, filming his works— clearly, again, the "middling message" carried weight with millions. Based upon my own study of Lewis's twenties work, I agree with Schorer's analysis of Lewis's affinity for the heartland; see in particular the last novel of the decade, *Dodsworth* (1929; reprint, New York: New American Library, 1980) for a decade's resolution of Lewis's search for an inhabitable, middle-ground enclave.

47. Sinclair Lewis, *Babbitt* (1922; reprint, New York: New American Library, 1961); "Babbitt," *Emporia Gazette*, 2 October 1922. In "Arrowsmith," *Emporia Gazette*, 21 April 1925, White would bestow high praise upon the novel and its author, "a man of power and distinction in our letters." In "A Healthy Spirit," *Emporia Gazette*, 10 February 1926, White applauded one of Lewis's "fellow protestors": "A lively discussion is going on in the Kansas press about the merits of Sinclair Lewis and Mencken. It is a healthy discussion, which could not have appeared five years ago. For no one would have defended the two recalcitrant and intransigent authors. Now they are well-supported—and that in Kansas. The world does need its satirists and lampoonists. Human nature is such that it needs the rod; we are all children who will be spoiled if the rod is spared. So here's to the strong right arms of our two leading literary mentors. Long may they wave!"

48. "What Is a Good Town?" *Emporia Gazette*, 23 November 1920.

49. Lynd and Lynd, *Middletown*, 3. Not incidentally, Mencken's own biases, including that towards Baltimore, could be dubbed characteristic of a "village mentality"—many took him to account for "small-mindedness."

50. Fgc [artist], "Main Street," *Life*, 9 July 1925; "Babbitt," *Emporia Gazette*, 2 October 1922; "The New Masses," *Emporia Gazette*, 20 April 1926. Add to this mix of sophisticated outlooks on main street Walter Lippmann's exacerbated assessment of his friend as they parted company over New Yorker Al Smith's 1928 presidential candidacy: "White surely is about the best thing that the Middle West and the small town in the Buick–radio age has produced. . . ." See Ronald Steel, *Walter Lippmann*, 248.

Chapter Five
Raising Middle American Barricades: Smith, Depression, and War

1. For an excellent assessment of the decade's trauma and its particularly disturbing political, social, economic, and cultural milestones, see Robert S.

McElvaine, *The Great Depression: America, 1929–1941,* rev. ed. (New York: Times Books, 1993).

2. William Allen White, "The Leaven of the Pharisees," *Saturday Evening Post,* 29 May 1920, 20–21 and 77, quoted 20; "Why I Am a Progressive," *Saturday Evening Post,* 23 April 1921, 3–4, 52, and 54; the *Nation* remark was made in introducing "These United States," a series designed to offer divergent views of the evolving American commonwealth. White led off with "Kansas: A Puritan Survival," *Nation,* 19 April 1922, 460–62. H. L. Mencken followed up with "Maryland: Apex of Normalcy," *Nation,* 3 May 1922, 517–19, a depressed counterpoint to White's paean to Middle America. For an excellent assessment of the emotion-laden and tense political and social environment, see David Burner, 1919: "Prelude to Normalcy" in *Change and Continuity in Twentieth-Century America: The 1920's,* eds. John Braeman, Robert H. Bremner, and David Brody (Columbus: Ohio State University Press, 1968). Many pieces in this volume still offer strong insights into the decade.

3. William Allen White, "Blood of the Conquerors," *Collier's,* 10 March 1923, 5–6, 30, and back page for editorial comment; "The Dawn of a Great Tomorrow: We Are Making America Over to Give an Equal Chance to Every Man," *Collier's,* 17 March 1923, 11–12 and 27. For an earlier 1920s example of White's attempt to identify Emporia as a generic Middle American locale see his defensive correspondence, W. A. White, "'Ever Been in Emporia?'" *New Republic,* 12 May 1920, 348–49.

4. William Allen White, "What's the Matter with America," *Collier's,* 1 July 1922, 3–4 and 18.

5. Ibid., 3 and 18; Heywood Broun, "What's the Matter with White," *Collier's,* 1 July 1922, 18.

6. For the more typically restrained but still dismal analysis of regional differences over Prohibition, see William Allen White, "A Dry West Warns the Thirsty East," *Collier's,* 2 September 1922, 3–4 and 18–19. In William Allen White, "The Solid West—Free and Proud of It: Bumping Together the Heads of the Solid South and the Solid East," *Collier's,* 30 December 1922, 5 and 24, White suggested the possibility of reconciliation. In this piece he clearly identifies his constituency as progressive, middle class, and Middle Western. Beyond Prohibition, disappointment with the Harding administration and progressive setbacks in Congress possibly weighed in to trigger White's vitriolic attack in "What's the Matter with America." Important, too, nativist sentiment for anti-immigration legislation was peaking at the same time.

7. William Allen White, "Cheer Up, America!" *Harper's Magazine,* March 1927, 405–11, editors quoted 533.

8. William Allen White, "Al Smith, city feller," *Collier's,* 21 August 1926, 8–9 and 42–43. For a succinct biography of Smith, see Oscar Handlin, *Al Smith and His America* (Boston: Little, Brown and Company, 1958); see also Paula Eldot, *Governor Alfred E. Smith: The Politician as Reformer* (New York, Garland, 1983). For more in particular on the 1928 campaign see Lawrence W. Levine's excellent analysis in *The Unpredictable Past: Explorations in American Cultural History*

(New York: Oxford University Press, 1993), chapter ten, "Progress and Nostalgia: The Self Image of the Nineteen Twenties," 189–205. Allan J. Lichtman offers lengthier insights in *Prejudice and the Old Politics: The Presidential Election of 1928* (Chapel Hill: University of North Carolina Press, 1979).

9. For White's 1920 efforts for Hoover see his pre-convention article, William Allen White, "The Leaven of the Pharisees," *Saturday Evening Post,* 29 May 1920, 20–21 and 77. For a succinct biography of Hoover see Joan Hoff Wilson, *Herbert Hoover: Forgotten Progressive* (Boston: Little, Brown and Company, 1975); see also David Burner, *Herbert Hoover: A Public Life* (New York: Knopf, 1979).

10. White's statement appeared in the *Christian Science Monitor,* 16 July 1928, and is quoted in Walter Johnson, *William Allen White's America* (New York: Henry Holt and Company, 1947), 408. Broun, writing on 18 July 1928, is quoted in ibid.

11. William Allen White, "Battle Hum of the Republic," *Collier's,* 18 August 1928, 8–9, 32, and 34, quoted 34.

12. Quoted in Johnson, *William Allen White's America,* 411.

13. William Allen White, "We Have Ceased to Mark Time: New Blood and Leadership Enter with Hoover," *Public Affairs Magazine,* May 1929, 23.

14. White led off the untitled commentary in "Where Are the Pre-War Radicals?" *Survey [Graphic Number],* 1 February 1926, 556–66, quoted 556.

15. Quoted in Johnson, *William Allen White's America,* 425 and 430. For a prescient analysis of Hoover as a capable public servant but a poor politician with little understanding of public sentiment, see White's pre-convention piece, William Allen White, "The Education of Herbert Hoover," *Collier's,* 9 June 1928, 8–9, 42, and 44. The political and ideological death-throes of the Hoover administration were complex. Hoover, while buttressing the economic establishment, similar to Theodore Roosevelt decades earlier, would lash out at the narrow-mindedness of the capitalists. McElvaine, *Great Depression* offers a fine analysis.

16. William Allen White, "If I Were Dictator," *Nation,* 2 December 1931, 596–98.

17. William Allen White, "Herbert Hoover—The Last of the Old Presidents or the First of the New?" *Saturday Evening Post,* 4 March 1933, 6–7 and 53–56.

18. Amongst many valuable works on the politics of the Depression see McElvaine, *Great Depression;* William E. Leuchtenberg, *Franklin D. Roosevelt and the New Deal, 1932–1940* (New York: Harper and Row, 1963); Paul K. Conkin, *The New Deal,* 2d ed. (Arlington Heights: AHM Publishing, 1975).

19. William Allen White, "The Farmer Takes His Holiday," *Saturday Evening Post,* 26 November 1932, 6–7, 64, 66, and 68–70.

20. William Allen White, "The Republic Totters," *Capper's Magazine,* February 1931, 35; quoted in Johnson, *William Allen White's America,* 432; William Allen White, "On Our Way—But Where Are We Going?" *Saturday Review of Literature,* 14 April 1934, 625 and 632.

21. William Allen White, "Here Was a Man," *Saturday Review of Literature,* 7 November 1931, 257 and 260.

22. William Allen White, "Good Newspapers and Bad," *Atlantic Monthly,* May 1934, 581–86, quoted 586.

23. Quoted in Walter Johnson ed., *Selected Letters of William Allen White*

1899–1943 (New York: Henry Holt and Company, 1947), 366. William Allen White, "Landon: I Knew Him When," *Saturday Evening Post,* 18 July 1936, 5–7, 68, 70, and 72–73. White combined this article with an August 9 *New York Times* piece and some additional material into his book *What It's All About; Being a Reporter's Story of the Early Campaign of 1936* (New York: Macmillan Company, 1936). Alan Brinkley's *Voices of Protest: Huey Long, Father Coughlin, and the Great Depression* (New York: Knopf, 1982) superbly assesses the fissuring of class and politics during this period.

24. William Allen White, "The Challenge to the Middle Class," *Atlantic Monthly,* August 1937, 196–201, quoted 196. Interestingly enough, in researching and writing *Middletown in Transition: A Study in Cultural Conflicts* (New York: Harcourt Brace, 1937), Robert Lynd, according to Richard Wightman Fox [see Fox's "Epitaph for Middletown: Robert S. Lynd and the Analysis of Consumer Culture," in *The Culture of Consumption: Critical Essays in American History, 1880–1980,* ed. Richard Wightman Fox and T. J. Jackson Lears (New York: Pantheon Books, 1983), 101–41], had lost faith in the ability of a materially corrupted middle class to save itself; elite, Marxist leadership was now necessary. White seems to have missed or overlooked this aspect of the study, although in his article he does note the positive contribution of Marxism toward helping raise the lot of the proletariat; middle-class America, however, had the distribution and production capacity to offer ever more. Richard H. Pells, *Radical Visions and American Dreams: Culture and Social Thought in the Depression Years* (New York: Harper Torchbooks, 1973), offers the most comprehensive analysis of intellectual thought during this period.

25. William Allen White, "A Yip from the Doghouse," *New Republic,* 15 December 1937, 160–62. In three articles criticizing the increasing conservatism of the press, White condemned the conservatism of the middle class as bolstering the attitude and exacerbating the problems of class struggle. See White's "How Free Is Our Press," *Nation,* 18 June 1938, 693–95; "How Free Is the Press?" *Collier's,* 8 April 1939, 16 and 88–89; and "Don't Indulge in Name-Calling with Press Critics—W. A. White," *Editor and Publisher,* 22 April 1939, 14 and 68. For the Depression Era difficulties of the aging progressives, see Otis L. Graham Jr., *An Encore for Reform: The Old Progressives and the New Deal* (New York: Oxford University Press, 1967). Graham addresses at length White's tentative thirties positioning along with that of a good many other bewildered old-liners. For a compelling literary take on the middle class dangers running amuck in democratic society see White's class compatriot Sinclair Lewis, *It Can't Happen Here* (1935; reprint, New York: New American Library, 1970).

26. William Allen White, "Speaking for the Consumer: We Must All Give a Little," *Vital Speeches,* 1 November 1938, 41–49. The speech was delivered before the Seventh International Management Congress in Washington, D.C., September 20. White at different times came to make the dictator charge; for an example see his article written in opposition to Roosevelt's court-packing scheme, William Allen White, "Supreme Court—Or 'Rule by Impulses,'" *New York Times* [magazine], 25 April 1937, 3, 23, and 25.

27. William Allen White, "The Challenge to Democracy: It Is a Glib

Shibboleth," *Vital Speeches,* 1 June 1938, 494–96. The speech was delivered before the Economic Club in New York on May 3. White's confusion and quest for resolution were indicative of the thought of a wide array of social commentators—not to mention politicians—during the decade. Many argue that the multi-angled New Deal—or New Deals—most pointedly exemplifies the tangled state of affairs.

28. W. A. White, "The Eternal Bounce in Man," *Vital Speeches,* 15 July 1937, 606–08. The address was delivered June 12.

29. William Allen White, "Moscow and Emporia," New Republic, 21 September 1938, 177–80.

30. Upton Sinclair, "An Open Letter to William Allen White," *New Republic,* 7 December 1938, 131–32.

31. William Allen White, untitled response to Upton Sinclair, "An Open Letter to William Allen White," *New Republic,* 7 December 1938, 132. The editors' note of the additional correspondence also appears on 132.

32. William Allen White, "We Are Coming, Father Abraham!" *Abraham Lincoln Quarterly,* June 1940, 71–81, quoted 79 and 81. White was a hearty supporter of Republican Wendell Willkie, and he worked closely with Franklin Roosevelt in support of internationalism—clearly, both candidates in 1940 fit his Lincolnesque leadership bill.

Chapter Six
Forging a Middle American Ethos

1. Benjamin DeMott, *The Imperial Middle: Why Americans Can't Think Straight About Class* (New York: William Morrow and Co., 1990; New Haven: Yale University Press, 1992). In his provocative if weakly argued study, De Mott observes the enduring phenomenon of a middle-class idyll. He is scathing as he argues it is one thing to acknowledge a "culture-wide consensual evasion" and another "altogether to blink away the essential truth: America as a classless society is, finally, a deceit, and today, as yesterday, the deceit causes fearful moral and social damage"; see p. 12.

2. William Allen White, *The Changing West: An Economic Theory About Our Golden Age* (New York: Macmillan Company, 1939), vi–vii. A good number of academics and non-academics in his day surely would have disagreed with White's interpretation. The West's history still remains contenious ground. See chapter one.

3. Ibid., 5–7.

4. Ibid., 3, 26, 47, 42, and 51. Further into the analysis the upper range of such a country town expands to 150,000; see p. 82. White went on to offer up a more detailed description of archetypal "semi-urban" Emporia; see pp. 83–89.

5. Ibid., 57.

6. Ibid., 39, 41, 137, and 108.

7. Quoted in Walter Johnson ed., *Selected Letters of William Allen White* (New York: Henry Holt and Company, 1947), 402.

8. Quoted in Walter Johnson, *William Allen White's America* (New York: Henry Holt and Company, 1947), 529; and Johnson, *Selected Letters,* p. 48.

9. Quoted in Johnson, *William Allen White's America,* 516.

10. *Emporia Gazette,* 6 November 1939, quoted in ibid., 519–20.

11. Quoted in ibid., 527–28. Johnson offers a good synopsis of White's committee activity. For additional information see his more detailed analysis: Walter Johnson, *The Battle Against Isolation* (Chicago: University of Chicago Press, 1944). See also Richard L. McBane, "The Crisis in the White Committee," *Midcontinent American Studies Journal* 4 (fall 1963): 28–38; and William M. Tuttle Jr., "Aid-to-the-Allies Short-of-War versus American Intervention, 1940: A Reappraisal of William Allen White's Leadership," *Journal of American History* 56 (March 1970): 840–58.

12. Quoted in Johnson, *William Allen White's America,* 549.

13. William Allen White, "Unity and American Leadership," *Yale Review* 32 (September 1942): 1–17, quoted 17. For White's views on the need to "compromise," see William Allen White, "Be of Good Cheer, Little Guy!" *Rotarian,* July 1943, 10–13 and 58. White strongly supported Roosevelt's war leadership. Still, he had campaigned for Wendell Willkie in 1940; an enthusiastic Willkie backer, White favored his second run for the 1944 Republican nomination.

14. White, "Unity and American Leadership," 10–11.

15. William Allen White, "Emporia in Wartime," *New Republic,* 13 April 1942, 490–92.

16. Richard W. Resh, "A Vision in Emporia: William Allen White's Search for Community," *Midcontinent American Studies Journal* 10 (fall 1969): 19–35, quoted 26.

17. White, *Changing West,* 10.

18. William Allen White, "It's Been a Great Show," *Collier's,* 12 February 1938, 16 and 63–65.

19. For a thirty-year sampling of White's political sketches see William Allen White, *Masks in a Pageant* (New York: Macmillan Company, 1928).

20. Johnson, *Selected Letters,* 414–15; *William Allen White's America,* 574.

21. White, "It's Been a Great Show," 65.

22. *Newsweek* (Election Extra), November/December 1984, 38 and 89–90.

23. *Newsweek* (Anniversary Issue), spring 1983, cover and 3.

24. David E. Shi, *The Simple Life: Plain Living and High Thinking in American Culture* (New York: Oxford University Press, 1985), 280.

25. Gannett recalled the day in his New York *Herald Tribune* remembrance of White two days after the journalist's death; quoted in Johnson, *William Allen White's America,* 79.

Bibliography

Work by William Allen White: Books

The Autobiography of William Allen White. New York: Macmillan Company, 1946.

The Autobiography of William Allen White. 2nd. ed., rev. and abr. Edited by Sally Foreman Griffith. Lawrence: University Press of Kansas, 1990.

Calvin Coolidge: The Man Who Is President. New York: Macmillan Company, 1925.

A Certain Rich Man. 1909. Reprint, Lexington: University Press of Kentucky, 1970.

The Changing West: An Economic Theory about Our Golden Age. New York: Macmillan Company, 1939.

The Court of Boyville. New York: Doubleday & McClure Company, 1899.

God's Puppets. New York: Macmillan Company, 1916.

In Our Town. 1906. Reprint, New York: Doubleday, Page & Company, 1909.

In the Heart of a Fool. New York: Macmillan Company, 1918.

The Martial Adventures of Henry and Me. New York: Macmillan Company, 1918.

Masks in a Pageant. New York: Macmillan Company, 1928.

The Old Order Changeth: A View of American Democracy. New York: Macmillan Company, 1910.

Politics: The Citizen's Business. New York: Macmillan Company, 1924.

A Puritan in Babylon: The Story of Calvin Coolidge. New York: Macmillan Company, 1938.

The Real Issue: A Book of Kansas Stories. 1896. Reprint. New York: Doubleday and McClure Company, 1899.

Rhymes by Two Friends. In collaboration with Albert Bigelow Paine. Fort Scott, Kans.: M. L. Izor & Sons, 1893.

Stratagems and Spoils: Stories of Love and Politics. New York: Charles Scribner's Sons, 1901.

What It's All About: Being a Reporter's Story of the Early Campaign of 1936. New York: Macmillan Company, 1936.

Woodrow Wilson: The Man, His Times, and His Task. Boston: Houghton Mifflin Company, 1924.

Work by William Allen White: Articles

"Kansas: Its Present and Its Future." *Forum,* March 1897.

"The Business of a Wheat Farm." *Scribner's Magazine,* November 1897.

"An Appreciation of the West: Apropos of the Omaha Exposition." *McClure's Magazine,* October 1898.

"Bryan." *McClure's Magazine,* July 1900.

"Hanna." *McClure's Magazine,* November 1900.

"Croker." *McClure's Magazine,* February 1901.

"Carrie Nation and Kansas." *Saturday Evening Post,* 6 April 1901.

"Lawton—The Metropolis of the Wilderness." *Saturday Evening Post,* 7 September 1901.

"Theodore Roosevelt." *McClure's Magazine,* November 1901.

"Platt." *McClure's Magazine,* December 1901.

"The New Congress." *Saturday Evening Post,* 28 December 1901.

"Cleveland." *McClure's Magazine,* February 1902.

"Harrison." *Cosmopolitan,* March 1902.

"Ready-Made Homes Out West." *Saturday Evening Post,* 26 April 1902.

"Uncommercial Traveling." *Saturday Evening Post,* 3 May 1902.

"The Building Up of the Prairie West." *Collier's,* 10 May 1902.

"One Year of Roosevelt." *Saturday Evening Post,* 4 October 1902.

"A Tenderfoot on Thunder Mountain: I—The Trail." *Saturday Evening Post,* 8 November 1902.

"II—The Foot of the Rainbow." *Saturday Evening Post,* 15 November 1902.

"[The Foot of the Rainbow]: Continued." *Saturday Evening Post,* 22 November 1902.

"The Pot of Gold." *Saturday Evening Post,* 29 November 1902.

"The Politicians: Our 'Hired Men' at Washington." *Saturday Evening Post,* 14 March 1903.

"The Brain Trust: The Oligarchy That Rules the Country." *Saturday Evening Post,* 21 March 1903.

"The Balance-Sheet of the Session: A Survey of Things Done and Left Undone by the Most Important Peace Congress the Country Has Yet Known." *Saturday Evening Post,* 28 March 1903.

"The President: The Friends and the Enemies He Has Made—The Curious Spectacle of a Smiling Support Ready with the Knife in the Hand behind the Back." *Saturday Evening Post,* 4 April 1903.

"Swinging Round the Circle with Roosevelt." *Saturday Evening Post,* 27 June 1903.

"McKinley and Hanna: A Study of Hanna the Man, and the Ruling Passion of His Life." *Saturday Evening Post,* 12 March 1904.

"Grafting and Things." *Saturday Evening Post,* 7 May 1904.

"The Boom in the Northwest: Opening Up a Country That Must Be Developed by Capital." *Saturday Evening Post,* 21 May 1904.

"The Boom in the Northwest: With Pick and Shovel in the Mining Camps of Montana, Wyoming and Idaho." *Saturday Evening Post,* 28 May 1904.

"William Allen White on Mr. Steffens's Book, 'The Shame of the Cities.'" *McClure's Magazine,* June 1904.

"The Dollar in Politics: Some Modern Methods in Popular Misgovernment." *Saturday Evening Post,* 2 July 1904.

"Seconding the Motion: How a Great National Convention Became a Manikin." *Saturday Evening Post,* 23 July 1904.

"The Natural History of a Gentleman: Being the Autobiography of Mr. Herbert Spencer." *Saturday Evening Post,* 30 July 1904.

"The Democratic Revival: A Near View of the Building of a Safe and Sane Platform at St. Louis." *Saturday Evening Post,* 13 August 1904.

"The Reorganization of the Republican Party: The Great Problems before the Nation." *Saturday Evening Post,* 3 December 1904.

"Why the Nation Will Endure." *Saturday Evening Post,* 4 March 1905.

"Political Signs of Promise." *Outlook,* 15 July 1905.

"The Golden Rule." *Atlantic Monthly,* October 1905.

"The Kansas Conscience: Its Revolt against the Iniquities of an Unrestrained Competitive System—The Deeper Meaning of the Oil Fight and the Wider Significance of the Struggle for Industrial Independence." *Reader Magazine,* October 1905.

"Folk: The Story of a Little Leaven in a Great Commonwealth." *McClure's Magazine,* December 1905.

"The Partnership of Society." *American Magazine,* October 1906.

"What's the Matter with America: I The County." *Collier's,* 20 October 1906.

"What's the Matter with America: The State." *Collier's,* 10 November 1906.

"What's the Matter with America: III The Nation." *Collier's,* 1 December 1906.

"Emporia and New York." *American Magazine,* January 1907.

"Roosevelt: A Force for Righteousness." *McClure's Magazine,* February 1907.

"A National Responsibility." *City Club Bulletin,* 20 March 1908.

"Taft, A Hewer of Wood." *American Magazine,* May 1908.

"A Brief for the Defendant: Being a View of the Chicago Republican Convention through Friendly Eyes." *Collier's,* 4 July 1908.

"Twelve Years of Mr. Bryan: 1896–1908, A Period of Political Progress in Which New Doctrines Have Become Familiar and Radicalism Has Stepped Faster Than Its Prophet." *Collier's,* 17 October 1908.

"Certain Voices in the Wilderness." *Kansas Magazine,* January 1909.

"'The Old Order Changeth.'" *American Magazine,* January 1909.

"The Old Order Changeth: II—The Beginnings of the Change." *American Magazine,* February 1909.

"The Old Order Changeth: III Certain Definite Tendencies." *American Magazine,* March 1909.

"The Old Order Changeth: IV—Progress in American Cities." *American Magazine*, April 1909.

"The Old Order Changeth: V. The Leaven in the National Lump." *American Magazine*, May 1909.

"'The Old Order Changeth': VI The Schools—The Main Spring of Democracy." *American Magazine*, August 1909.

"'The Old Order Changeth': What About Our Courts?" *American Magazine*, February 1910.

"A Theory of Spiritual Progress." *Columbia University Quarterly*, 12 (September 1910): 408–20.

"The Insurgence of Insurgency: What the Radical Wing of the Republican Party Stands For, and What It Has Accomplished." *American Magazine*, December 1910.

"The Progressive Hen and the Insurgent Ducklings." *American Magazine*, January 1911.

"The Old Problem of the Dog and the Engine." *American Magazine*, February 1911.

"'When the World Busts Through.'" *American Magazine*, April 1911.

"Storming the Citadel: Capture of the Outworks of the Senate by the Insurgents Significant of Greater Changes." *American Magazine*, September 1911.

"A Democratic View of Education." *Craftsman*, November 1911.

"Three Years of Progress: The Ground Covered during Three Years of Political Skirmishing." *Saturday Evening Post*, 24 February 1912.

"Should Old Acquaintance Be Forgot? A Statement of the Relations between President Taft and His Friend Colonel Roosevelt." *American Magazine*, May 1912.

"The Ebb Tide: Can the Progressives Come Back?" *Saturday Evening Post*, 19 December 1914.

"The Republican Party." *Metropolitan*, July 1915.

"The Glory of the States: Kansas." *American Magazine*, January 1916.

"Government of the People, by the People, for the People." *Independent*, 7 February 1916.

"Who Killed Cock Robin? A Post-Mortem Inquiry into Recent Republican Calamities." *Collier's*, 16 December 1916.

"The Odds against the U-Boat." *Collier's*, 8 December 1917.

"The Y.M.C.A. Huts: 'Safety Valves' for Our Boys in France." *Touchstone*, January 1918.

"In Germany with William Allen White." *Literary Digest*, 26 April 1919.

"William Allen White to F. H." *New Republic*, 17 May 1919.

"The Doughboy on Top of the World." *Red Cross Magazine*, June 1919.

"The Highbrow Doughboy." *Red Cross Magazine*, August 1919.

"'Ever Been in Emporia?'" *New Republic*, 12 May 1920.

"The Leaven of the Pharisees." *Saturday Evening Post*, 29 May 1920.

"Why I Am a Progressive." *Saturday Evening Post*, 23 April 1921.

"Kansas: A Puritan Survival." *Nation,* 19 April 1922.

"What's the Matter with America." *Collier's,* 1 July 1922.

"A Dry West Warns the Thirsty East." *Collier's,* 2 September 1922.

"The Solid West—Free and Proud of It: Bumping Together the Heads of the Solid South and the Solid East." *Collier's,* 30 December 1922.

"Blood of the Conquerors." *Collier's,* 10 March 1923.

"The Dawn of a Great To-morrow: We Are Making America Over to Give an Equal Chance to Every Man." *Collier's,* 17 March 1923.

"Where Are the Pre-War Radicals?" (untitled commentary) *Survey* [Graphic Number], 1 February 1926.

"Al Smith, city feller." *Collier's,* 21 August 1926.

"Cheer Up, America!" *Harper's Magazine,* March 1927.

"The Education of Herbert Hoover." *Collier's,* 9 June 1928.

"Battle Hum of the Republic." *Collier's,* 18 August 1928.

"We Have Ceased to Mark Time: New Blood and Leadership Enter with Hoover." *Public Affairs Magazine,* May 1929.

"The Republic Totters." *Capper's Magazine,* February 1931.

"Here Was a Man." *Saturday Review of Literature,* 7 November 1931.

"If I Were Dictator." *Nation,* 2 December 1931.

"The Farmer Takes His Holiday." *Saturday Evening Post,* 26 November 1932.

"Herbert Hoover—The Last of the Old Presidents or the First of the New?" *Saturday Evening Post,* 4 March 1933.

"On Our Way—But Where Are We Going?" *Saturday Review of Literature,* 14 April 1934.

"Good Newspapers and Bad." *Atlantic Monthly,* May 1934.

"Landon: I Knew Him When." *Saturday Evening Post,* 18 July 1936.

"Supreme Court—Or 'Rule by Impulses,'" *New York Times* [magazine], 25 April 1937, sec. 8, pp. 3, 23, and 25.

"The Eternal Bounce in Man." *Vital Speeches,* 15 July 1937.

"The Challenge to the Middle Class." *Atlantic Monthly,* August 1937.

"Imperial City." *Digest,* 16 October 1937.

"A Yip from the Doghouse." *New Republic,* 15 December 1937.

"It's Been a Great Show." *Collier's,* 12 February 1938.

"The Challenge to Democracy: It Is a Glib Shibboleth." *Vital Speeches,* 1 June 1938.

"How Free Is Our Press?" *Nation,* 18 June 1938.

"Moscow and Emporia." *New Republic,* 21 September 1938.

"Speaking for the Consumer: We Must All Give a Little." *Vital Speeches,* 1 November 1938.

[Untitled response to Upton Sinclair's "An Open Letter to William Allen White."] *New Republic,* 7 December 1938.

"How Free Is the Press?" *Collier's,* 8 April 1939.

"Don't Indulge in Name-Calling with Press Critics—W. A. White." *Editor and Publisher,* 22 April 1939.

"We Are Coming, Father Abraham!" *Abraham Lincoln Quarterly,* 1 (June 1940): 71–81.

"Emporia in Wartime." *New Republic,* 13 April 1942.

"Unity and American Leadership." *Yale Review,* 32 (September 1942): 1–17.

"Be of Good Cheer, Little Guy!" *Rotarian,* July 1943.

Additional White Resources

Emporia Gazette, 1 October 1918–2 January 1927.

Fitzgibbon, Russell H. comp. *Forty Years on Main Street.* New York: Farrar and Rinehart, 1937.

Johnson, Walter, ed. *Selected Letters of William Allen White 1899–1943.* New York: Henry Holt and Company, 1947.

Johnson, Walter, and Alberta Pantle. "A Bibliography of the Published Works of William Allen White." *Kansas Historical Quarterly* 15 (February 1947): 22–41.

Mahin, Helen Ogden, comp. *The Editor and His People: Editorials by William Allen White.* New York: Macmillan Company, 1924.

Pady, Donald S. "GLR Bibliography: William Allen White." *Great Lakes Review* 5 (summer 1978): 49–66.

Primary Sources

Anderson, Sherwood. *Winesburg, Ohio.* 1919. Reprint, New York: Viking Compass, 1958.

Becker, Carl L. "Kansas." In *Everyman His Own Historian: Essays on History and Politics,* edited by Carl L. Becker. 1935. Reprint, Chicago: Quadrangle Books, 1966.

Book of the Month Club. *William Allen White: In Memoriam.* n.p., n.d.

Bourne, Randolph. "Morals and Art from the West." *Dial,* 65 (14 December 1918): 556–57.

Broun, Heywood. "What's the Matter with White." *Collier's,* 1 July 1922.

Croly, Herbert David. *The Promise of American Life.* Edited by Arthur M. Schlesinger Jr. 1909. Reprint, Cambridge: Harvard University Press: Belnap Press, 1965.

Drew, Elizabeth. "Letter from Washington." *New Yorker,* 4 July 1988.

Fgc. [artist] "Main Street." *Life,* 9 July 1925.

F. H. [Francis Hackett]. "In the Heart of a Fool," review of *In the Heart of a Fool,* by William Allen White. *New Republic,* 15 February 1919.

———. "The Lilies of the Field." *New Republic,* 17 May 1919.

———. "The Voice of Kansas," review of *The Martial Adventures of Henry and Me,* by William Allen White. *New Republic,* 17 August 1918.

Garland, Hamlin. *Back-Trailers from the Middle Border.* New York: Macmillan Company, 1928.

Glenn, John. "Remarks of Senator John Glenn. Declaration of Candidacy for the Office of President of the United States." New Concord, Ohio, Thursday, April 21, 1983.

Hoover, Ellison. "An Impression of Emporia, Kansas, By One Who Has Never Been There." *Life,* 20 August 1925.

Howe, E. W. *The Story of a Country Town.* 1882. Reprint, New York City: Blue Ribbon Books, n.d.

Kansas, Office of the State Board of Agriculture. *Report of the Kansas State Board of Agriculture for the Quarter Ending December, 1925: Containing the State's Dicennial Census of 1925, Tabulated, Classified and Arranged as Contemplated by the Law.* Topeka: n.p., 1926.

Leonard, Olen and C. P. Loomis. *Culture of a Contemporary Rural Community: El Cerrito, New Mexico.* Washington, D.C.: U.S. Department of Agriculture, 1941.

Lewis, Sinclair. 1922. *Babbitt.* Reprint, New York: New American Library, 1961.

———. 1929. *Dodsworth.* Reprint, New York: New American Library, 1980.

———. *It Can't Happen Here.* 1935. Reprint, New York: New American Library, 1970.

———. *Main Street.* 1920. Reprint, New York: New American Library, Inc., 1961.

Lynd, Robert S., and Helen Merrell Lynd. *Middletown: A Study in American Culture.* New York: Harcourt Brace Jovanovich, 1956.

———. *Middletown in Transition: A Study in Cultural Conflicts.* New York: Harcourt Brace, 1937.

Mencken, H. L., "Maryland: Apex of Normalcy." *Nation,* 3 May 1922.

Nation, 89 (19 August 1909): 163.

New York Times, 10 November 1918, sec. 3, p. 4.

New York Times Review of Books, 7 April 1918, sec. 6, p. 145.

Newsweek, (Anniversary Issue) Spring 1983.

Newsweek (Election Extra), November/December 1984.

Norris, Frank. *McTeague: A Story of San Francisco.* 1899. Reprint, New York: Rinehart and Company, 1950.

Outlook, 71 (21 August 1909): 921–23.

Outlook, 120 (18 December 1918): 640.

Publishers' Weekly 94 (28 December 1918): 2033.

"Saturday Review of Books." *New York Times,* 31 July 1909, 462.

Seely, John R., R. Alexander Sim, and Elizabeth W. Looseley. *Crestwood Heights: A Study of the Culture of Suburban Life.* New York: Basic Books, 1956.

Sinclair, Upton. "An Open Letter to William Allen White." *New Republic,* 7 December 1938.

Steffens, Lincoln. *The Autobiography of Lincoln Steffens.* New York: Grosset & Dunlap Publishers, 1931.

————. *The Shame of the Cities.* 1902. Reprint, New York: Hill and Wang, 1957.

Tarbell, Ida M. *All in the Day's Work: An Autobiography.* 1939. Reprint, Boston: G. K. Hall, 1985.

Turner, Frederick Jackson. "The Significance of the Frontier in American History." In *The Frontier in American History,* edited by Frederick Jackson Turner. New York: Henry Holt and Company, 1921.

U.S. Department of Commerce. Bureau of the Census. *Fifteenth Census of the United States 1930: Population,* Vol. 3.

Vidal, Gore. *Palimpsest: A Memoir.* New York: Random House, 1995.

Vidich, Arthur J. and Joseph Bensman. *Small Town in Mass Society: Class, Power and Religion in a Rural Community.* Princeton: Princeton University Press, 1958.

von Hoffman, Nicholas. "Contra Reaganum." *Harper's,* May 1982.

Secondary Sources

Allen, Frederick Lewis. *Only Yesterday: An Informal History of the Nineteen Twenties.* New York: Harper and Row, 1964.

Ayers, Edward L., Patricia Nelson Limerick, Stephen Nissenbaum, and Peter S. Onuf. *All over the Map: Rethinking American Regions.* Baltimore: Johns Hopkins University Press, 1996.

Bader, Robert Smith. *Hayseeds, Moralizers, and Methodists: The Twentieth-Century Image of Kansas.* Lawrence: University Press of Kansas, 1988.

Barnouw, Erik. *A Tower in Babel: A History of Broadcasting in the United States.* (Vol. 1—to 1933). New York: Oxford University Press, 1966.

Bender, Thomas. *Community and Social Change in America.* Baltimore: Johns Hopkins University Press, 1982.

Bergman, Andrew. *We're in the Money: Depression America and Its Films.* New York: New York University Press, 1971; Chicago: Ivan R. Dee, 1992.

Blight, David W. "'For Something beyond the Battlefield': Fredrick Douglass and the Memory of the Civil War." *Journal of American History* 75 (March 1989): 1156–78.

Blotner, Joseph. *The Modern American Political Novel, 1900–1960.* Austin: University of Texas Press, 1966.

Bodnar, John. "Power and Memory in Oral History: Workers and Managers at Studebaker." *Journal of American History* 75 (March 1989): 1201–21.

Boyer, Paul, ed. *Reagan as President: Contemporary Views of the Man, His Politics, and His Policies.* Chicago: Ivan R. Dee, 1990.

Braeman, John, Robert W. Bremner, and David Brody, eds. *Change and Continuity in Twentieth-Century America: The 1920's.* Columbus: Ohio State University Press, 1968.

Brinkley, Alan. *Voices of Protest: Huey Long, Father Coughlin, and the Great Depression.* New York: Knopf, 1982.

Brooks, Patrick Alan. "William Allen White: A Study of Values." Ph.D. diss., University of Minnesota, 1969.

Burner, David. *Herbert Hoover: A Public Life.* New York: Knopf, 1979.

———. "1919: Prelude to Normalcy." In Change and Continuity in Twentieth-Century America. Edited by John Braeman, Robert W. Bremner, and David Brody. Columbus: Ohio State University Press, 1968.

Carter, Paul A. *Another Part of the Twenties.* New York: Columbia University Press, 1977.

———. "Country Bumpkin vs. City Slicker in the Halls of Congress: or How're You Gonna Keep 'Em Down on the Farm after They've Seen Paree?" *Reviews in American History* 19 (June 1991): 232–37.

———. *The Twenties in America.* 2nd. ed. Arlington Heights: Harlan Davidson, 1975.

Chambers, John Whiteclay II. *The Tyranny of Change: America in the Progressive Era, 1890–1920.* 2nd. ed. New York: St. Martin's Press, 1992.

Clark, Carroll D. and Roy L. Roberts. *People of Kansas: A Demographic and Sociological Study.* Topeka: Kansas State Planning Board, 1936.

Clark, Norman H. *Deliver Us from Evil: An Interpretation of American Prohibition.* New York: W. W. Norton, 1976.

Clough, Frank C. *William Allen White of Emporia.* 1941. Reprint, Westport, Conn.: Greenwood Press, Publishers, 1970.

Conkin, Paul K. *The New Deal.* 2nd. ed. Arlington Heights: AHM Publishing, 1975.

Cooper, John Milton, Jr. *The Warrior and the Priest: Woodrow Wilson and Theodore Roosevelt.* Cambridge: Harvard University Press, Belknap Press, 1983.

Cornish, Dudley T. "Carl Becker's Kansas: The Power of Endurance." *Kansas Historical Quarterly* 41 (spring 1975): 1–13.

Crunden, Robert M. *Ministers of Reform: The Progressives' Achievements in American Civilization, 1889–1920.* New York: Basic Books, 1982; Urbana: University of Illinois Press, 1984.

———. "Thick Description in the Progressive Era." *Reviews in American History* 19 (December 1991): 463–67.

Davis, Natalie Zemon. "Toward Mixtures and Margins." *American Historical Review* 97 (December 1992): 1409–16.

DeMott, Benjamin. *The Imperial Middle: Why Americans Can't Think Straight about Class.* New York: William Morrow, 1990; New Haven, Conn.: Yale University Press, 1992.

Dorman, Robert L. *Revolt of the Provinces: The Regionalist Movement in America, 1920–1945.* Chapel Hill: University of North Carolina Press, 1993.

Douglas, George H. *H. L. Mencken: Critic of American Life.* Hamden: Archon, 1978.

Douglas, Susan J. *Inventing American Broadcasting, 1899–1922.* Baltimore, MD: Johns Hopkins University Press, 1987.

Dubbert, Joe L. "William Allen White's American Adam." *Western American Literature* 7 (winter 1973): 271–78.

Dubbert, Joseph Lynn. "The Puritan in Babylon: William Allen White." Ph.D. diss, University of Minnesota, 1967.

Dumenil, Lynn. *The Modern Temper: American Culture and Society in the 1920s.* New York: Hill and Wang, 1995.

Eldot, Paula. *Governor Alfred E. Smith: The Politician as Reformer.* New York: Garland, 1983.

Fabian, Ann. "Back to *Virgin Land.*" *Reviews in American History* 24 (September 1996): 542–53.

Fass, Paula S. *The Damned and the Beautiful: American Youth in the 1920s.* Oxford: Oxford University Press, 1977.

Fischer, Dorothy Canfield. *Country Editor . . . and Cosmopolite.* In *William Allen White: In Memoriam.* N.p.: Book of the Month Club, n.d.

Flanagan, John T. "The Middle Western Historical Novel." *Journal of the Illinois State Historical Society* 37 (March 1944): 7–47.

Flink, James J. *The Car Culture.* Cambridge: MIT Press, 1975.

Fox, Richard Wightman. "Epitaph for Middletown: Robert S. Lynd and the Analysis of Consumer Culture." In *The Culture of Consumption: Critical Essays in American History, 1880–1980.* Edited by Richard Wightman Fox and T.J. Jackson Lears. New York: Pantheon Books, 1983.

Fox, Richard Wightman, and T. J. Jackson Lears. eds. *The Culture of Consumption: Critical Essays in American History, 1880–1980.* New York: Pantheon Books, 1983.

———. *The Power of Culture: Critical Essays in American History.* Chicago: University of Chicago Press, 1993.

Frisch, Michael. "American History and the Structures of Collective Memory: A Modest Exercise in Empirical Iconography." *Journal of American History* 75 (March 1989): 1130–55.

Gilkeson, John S., Jr. *Middle-Class Providence, 1820–1940.* Princeton: Princeton University Press, 1986.

Glassberg, David. *American Historical Pageantry: The Uses of Tradition in the Early Twentieth Century.* Chapel Hill: University of North Carolina Press, 1990.

Goodwyn, Lawrence. *The Populist Moment: A Short History of the Agrarian Revolt in America.* Oxford: Oxford University Press, 1978.

Graham, Otis L., Jr. *An Encore for Reform: The Old Progressives and the New Deal.* New York: Oxford University Press, 1967.

Griffith, Sally F. "Mass Media Come to the Small Town: The 'Emporia Gazette' in the 1920s." In *Mass Media Between the Wars: Perceptions of Cultural Tension, 1918–1941,* edited by Catherine L. Covert and John D. Stevens. Syracuse: Syracuse University Press, 1984.

Griffith, Sally Foreman. *Home Town News: William Allen White and the "Emporia Gazette."* New York: Oxford University Press, 1989.

Groman, George L. "W. A. White's Political Fiction: A Study in Emerging Progressivism." *Midwest Quarterly* 8 (October 1966): 79–93.

Gusfield, Joseph R. *Symbolic Crusade: Status Politics and the American Temperance Movement.* 2nd ed. Urbana: University of Illinois Press, 1986.

Handlin, Oscar. *Al Smith and His America.* Boston: Little, Brown and Company, 1958.

Hawley, Ellis W. *The Great War and the Search for a Modern Order: A History of the American People and Their Institutions, 1917–1933.* 2nd. ed. New York: St. Martin's Press, 1992.

Hays, Samuel P. *The Response to Industrialism: 1885–1914.* Chicago: University of Chicago Press, 1957.

Haywood, C. Robert. *Tough Daisies: Kansas Humor from "The Lane County Bachelor" to Bob Dole.* Lawrence: University Press of Kansas, 1995.

Herron, Ima Honaker. *The Small Town in American Literature.* 1939. Reprint, New York: Pageant Books, 1959.

Herzstein, Robert E. *Henry R. Luce: A Political Portrait of the Man Who Created the American Century.* New York: Charles Scribner's Sons, 1994.

Hilfer, Anthony Channell. *The Revolt from the Village 1915–1930.* Chapel Hill: University of North Carolina Press, 1969.

Hinshaw, David. *A Man from Kansas: The Story of William Allen White.* New York: G. P. Putnam's Sons, 1945.

Hoffman, Frederick J. *The Twenties: American Writing in the Postwar Decade.* New York: Viking Press, 1955.

Jackson, Kenneth T. *Crabgrass Frontier: The Suburbanization of the United States.* New York: Oxford University Press, 1985.

———. *The Ku Klux Klan in the City 1915–1930.* New York: Oxford University Press, 1970; Chicago: I. R. Dee, 1992.

Jernigan, E. Jay. *William Allen White.* Boston: Twayne Publishers, 1983.

———. *William Lindsay White: In the Shadow of His Father.* Norman: University of Oklahoma Press, 1997.

Johnson, Walter. *The Battle against Isolation.* Chicago: University of Chicago Press, 1944.

———. *William Allen White's America.* New York: Henry Holt and Company, 1947.

Kaplan, Amy. *The Social Construction of American Realism.* Chicago: University of Chicago Press, 1992.

Kelley, Robin D. G. "Notes on Deconstructing 'The Folk.'" *American Historical Review* 97 (December 1992): 1400–08.

Kennedy, Jean Lange. "William Allen White: A Study of the Interrelationship of Press, Power and Party Politics." Ph.D. diss., University of Kansas, 1981.

Kirschner, Don S. *City and Country: Rural Responses to Urbanization in the 1920s.* Westport, Conn.: Greenwood Publishing, 1970.

Kraus, Joe W. "The Publication of William Allen White's 'The Real Issue.'" *Kansas Historical Quarterly* 43 (summer 1977): 193–202.

Kurth, Peter. *American Cassandra: The Life of Dorothy Thompson.* Boston: Little Brown and Company, 1990.

La Forte, Robert Sherman. *Leaders of Reform: Progressive Republicans in Kansas, 1900–1916.* Lawrence: University Press of Kansas, 1974.

Lay, Shawn. "Hooded Populism: New Assessments of the Ku Klux Klan of the 1920s." *Reviews in American History* 22 (December 1994): 668–73.

Lears, T. J. Jackson. "The Concept of Cultural Hegemony: Problems and Possibilities." *American Historical Review* 90 (June 1985): 567–93.

———. "Making Fun of Popular Culture." *American Historical Review* 97 (December 1992): 1417–26.

———. *No Place of Grace: Antimodernism and the Transformation of American Culture, 1880–1920.* New York: Pantheon Books, 1981; Chicago: University of Chicago Press, 1983.

Leisy, Ernest E. *The American Historical Novel.* Norman: University of Oklahoma Press, 1950.

Leuchtenberg, William E. *Franklin D. Roosevelt and the New Deal, 1932–1940.* New York: Harper & Row, 1963.

———. *The Perils of Prosperity, 1914–1932.* 2nd. ed. Chicago: University of Chicago Press, 1993.

Levine, Lawrence W. "The Folklore of Industrial Society: Popular Culture and Its Audiences." *American Historical Review* 97 (December 1992): 1369–99.

———. "Levine Responds." *American Historical Review* 97 (December 1992): 1427–30.

———. *The Unpredictable Past: Explorations in American Cultural History.* New York: Oxford University Press, 1993.

Levy, Emanuel. *Small-Town America in Film: The Decline and Fall of Community.* New York: Continuum Publishing Company, 1991.

Lichtman, Allan J. *Prejudice and the Old Politics: The Presidential Election of 1928.* Chapel Hill: University of North Carolina Press, 1979.

Limerick, Patricia Nelson. "Turnerians All: The Dream of a Helpful History in an Intelligible World." *American Historical Review* 100 (June 1995): 697–716.

Link, Arthur S., and Richard L. McCormick. *Progressivism.* Arlington Heights: Harlan Davidson, 1983.

Livingston, James. "Why is There Still Socialism in the United States?" *Reviews in American History* 22 (December 1994): 577–83.

MacLean, Nancy. *Behind the Mask of Chivalry: The Making of the Second Ku Klux Klan.* New York: Oxford University Press, 1994.

Marchand, Roland. *Advertising the American Dream: Making Way for Modernity, 1920–1940.* Berkeley: University of California Press, 1985.

Martin, Jay. *Harvests of Change: American Literature, 1865–1914.* Englewood Cliffs, N.J.: Prentice-Hall, 1967.

May, Henry F. *The End of American Innocence: A Study of the First Years of Our Own Time, 1912–1917.* 1959. Reprint, Oxford: Oxford University Press, 1979.

May, Lary. *Screening Out the Past: The Birth of Mass Culture and the Motion Picture Industry.* New York: Oxford University Press, 1980; Chicago: University of Chicago Press, 1983.

McBane, Richard L. "The Crisis in the White Committee." *Midcontinent American Studies Journal* 4 (fall 1963): 28–38.

McElvaine, Robert S. *The Great Depression: America, 1929–1941.* Rev. ed. New York: Times Books, 1993.

McGlone, Robert E. "Rescripting a Troubled Past: John Brown's Family and the Harpers Ferry Conspiracy." *Journal of American History* 75 (March 1989): 1179–1200.

McKee, John DeWitt. *William Allen White: Maverick on Main Street.* Westport: Greenwood Press, 1975.

Meinig, D. W. "Symbolic Landscapes: Some Idealizations of American Communities." In *The Interpretation of Ordinary Landscapes,* edited by D. W. Meinig. New York: Oxford University Press, 1979.

Miller, Robert Moats. "The Ku Klux Klan." In *Change and Continuity in Twentieth-Century America: The 1920s,* Edited by John Braeman, Robert H. Bremner, and David Brody. Columbus: Ohio State University Press, 1968.

Moore, Leonard. "Historical Interpretations of the 1920s Klan: The Traditional View and the Populist Revision." *Journal of Social History* 24 (winter 1990): 341–57.

Mott, Frank Luther. *A History of American Magazines, 1885–1905.* Cambridge: Harvard University Press, Belknap Press, 1957.

Mowry, George E. *The Urban Nation, 1920–1960.* New York: Hill and Wang, 1965.

Nash, Roderick. *The Nervous Generation: American Thought, 1917–1930.* Chicago: Rand McNally, 1970; Chicago: Ivan R. Dee Publisher, 1990.

Nye, Russel B. *Midwestern Progressive Politics: A Historical Study of Its Origins and Development, 1870–1958.* East Lansing: Michigan State University Press, 1959.

Painter, Nell Irvin. *Standing at Armageddon: The United States, 1877–1919.* New York: W. W. Norton & Company, 1987.

Pells, Richard H. *Radical Visions and American Dreams: Culture and Social Thought in the Depression Years.* New York: Harper Torchbooks, 1973.

Peterson, Thomas. *Magazines in the Twentieth Century.* Urbana: University of Illinois Press, 1956.

Quandt, Jean B. *From the Small Town to the Great Community: The Social Thought of Progressive Intellectuals.* New Brunswick: Rutgers University Press, 1970.

Resh, Richard W. "A Vision in Emporia: William Allen White's Search for Community." *Midcontinent American Studies Journal* 10 (fall 1969): 19–35.

Rich, Everett. *William Allen White: The Man from Emporia.* New York: Farrar and Rinehart, 1941.

Richmond, Robert W. *Kansas: A Land of Contrasts.* 3rd ed. Arlington Heights: Forum Press, 1989.

Riley, Donn Charles. "William Allen White: The Critical Years: An Analysis of the Changing Political Philosophy of William Allen White during the Progressive Period, 1896–1908." Ph.D. diss., Saint Louis University, 1960.

Robertson, James Oliver. *American Myth, American Reality.* New York: Hill & Wang, 1980.

Rodgers, Daniel T. *Contested Truths: Keywords in American Politics Since Independence.* New York: Basic Books, 1987.

—————. "In Search of Progressivism." *Reviews in American History* 10 (December 1982): 113–32.

—————. *The Work Ethic in Industrial America, 1850–1920.* Chicago: University of Chicago Press, 1979.

Rorabaugh, W. J. *The Alcoholic Republic: An American Tradition.* Oxford: Oxford University Press, 1979.

Rubin, Joan Shelley. "In Retrospect: Henry F. May's 'The End of American Innocence.'" *Reviews in American History* 18 (March 1990): 142–49.

—————. *The Making of Middlebrow Culture.* Chapel Hill: University of North Carolina Press, 1992.

Schneirov, Matthew. *The Dream of a New Social Order: Popular Magazines in America, 1893–1914.* New York: Columbia University Press, 1994.

Schorer, Mark. *Sinclair Lewis: An American Life.* New York: McGraw-Hill, 1961.

Seymour, Thaddeus, Jr. "A Progressive Partnership: Theodore Roosevelt and the Reform Press—Riis, Steffens, Baker, and White." Ph.D. diss., University of Wisconsin-Madison, 1985.

Shi, David E. *Facing Facts: Realism in American Thought and Culture, 1850–1920.* New York: Oxford University Press, 1995.

—————. *The Simple Life: Plain Living and High Thinking in American Culture.* New York: Oxford University Press, 1985.

Shortridge, James R. *The Middle West: Its Meaning in American Culture.* Lawrence: University Press of Kansas, 1989.

Simon, Bryant. "One Side of Main Street." *Reviews in American History* 22 (September 1994): 461–67.

Sklar, Robert. *Movie-Made America: A Cultural History of American Movies.* New York: Random House, 1975.

Sloan, Charles William, Jr. "Kansas Battles the Invisible Empire: The Legal Ouster of the KKK from Kansas, 1922–1927." *Kansas Historical Quarterly* 40 (autumn 1974): 393–409.

Slotkin, Richard. *The Fatal Environment: The Myth of the Frontier in the Age of Industrialism, 1800–1890.* New York: Macmillan, 1985; New York: Harper Perennial, 1994.

Smith, Henry Nash. *Virgin Land: The American West as Symbol and Myth.* Cambridge: Harvard University Press, 1970.

Socolofsky, Homer E., and Virgil W. Dean, comp. *Kansas History: An Annotated Bibliography.* New York: Greenwood Press, 1992.

Steel, Ronald. *Walter Lippmann and the American Century.* Boston: Little, Brown and Company, 1980.

Sussman, Warren I. *Culture as History: The Transformation of American Society in the Twentieth Century.* New York: Pantheon Books, 1984.

Thelen, David. "Memory and American History." *Journal of American History* 75 (March 1989): 1117–29.

Thelen, David P. *Robert M. La Follette and the Insurgent Spirit.* Boston: Little, Brown and Company, 1976; Madison: University of Wisconsin Press, 1985.

Trachtenberg, Alan. *The Incorporation of America: Culture and Society in the Gilded Age.* New York: Hill and Wang, 1982.

Traylor, Jack Wayne. "William Allen White and His Democracy, 1919–1944." Ph.D. diss., University of Oklahoma, 1978.

———. "William Allen White's 1924 Gubernatorial Campaign." *Kansas Historical Quarterly* 42 (summer 1976): 180–91.

Tuttle, William M., Jr. "Aid-to-the-Allies Short-of-War versus American Intervention, 1940: A Reappraisal of William Allen White's Leadership." *Journal of American History* 56 (March 1970): 840–58.

Vidal, Gore. "Ronnie and Nancy: A Life in Pictures." In *At Home: Essays, 1982–1988,* edited by Gore Vidal. New York: Random House, 1988.

Wallace, Mike. *Mickey Mouse History and Other Essays in American Memory.* Philadelphia: Temple University Press, 1996.

Warren, Roland L. *The Community in America.* 2nd ed. Chicago: Rand McNally, 1972.

White, Morton, and Lucia White. *The Intellectual versus the City: From Thomas Jefferson to Frank Lloyd Wright.* Cambridge: Harvard University Press and MIT Press, 1962.

Wicker, Tom. *One of Us: Richard Nixon and the American Dream.* New York: Random House, 1991.

Wiebe, Robert H. *The Search for Order, 1877–1920.* New York: Hill and Wang, 1967.

Wilholt, Robert Lee. "The Rhetoric of the Folk Hero: William Allen White." Ph.D. diss., University of Illinois, 1962.

Wilson, Joan Hoff. *Herbert Hoover: Forgotten Progressive.* Boston: Little, Brown and Company, 1975.

Worley, Lynda F. "William Allen White: Kansan Extraordinary." *Social Science* 41 (April 1966): 91–98.

Wrobel, David M. *The End of American Exceptionalism: Frontier Anxiety from the Old West to the New Deal.* Lawrence: University Press of Kansas, 1993.

Zornow, William Frank. *Kansas: A History of the Jayhawk State.* Norman: University of Oklahoma Press, 1957.

Index

Abilene, Kansas, 28
Abraham Lincoln Association, 157
Addams, Jane, 3, 13, 25
Aiken, Duncan, 123
Allen, Henry, 62
America First Committee, 167
American Magazine, 51; White's writings published in, 77, 79, 81
Anderson, Sherwood, 57, 91, 123
Arbuckle, Fatty: trial covered in *Emporia Gazette*, 96
Armstead, Andy, 97
Ashfield: New England rural village, 23, 24
Aspen, Colorado, 27
Associated Press, 96
Atlantic Monthly, 4; White's writings published in, 76, 147, 149
Austin, Mary, 19

Baker, Ray Stannard, 123
Barrymore, Ethel, 111
Barthes, Roland, 6
Barton, Bruce, 17
Beaume, France, 85–86, 173
Becker, Carl, 21–22
Bender, Thomas, 36, 39–42
Beverly Hills, California, 29
Boise, Idaho, 120
Book of the Month Club, 18, 20, 89
Borsodi, Ralph, 22, 27
Botkin, B. A., 19
Boulder, Colorado, 27
Bourne, Randolph, 63
Brandeis, Louis, 140
Broun, Heywood, 135–36, 139
Bryan, William Jennings, 11, 15, 30, 50, 71, 74, 173
Bull Moose platform, 2, 81, 82, 83, 84, 86, 129, 131, 138, 141, 148–53, 168
Bush, George, 29, 176
Butler, Nicholas Murray, 173

Canton, Ohio, 28, 30
Capper's Magazine: White's writings published in, 144
Capra, Frank, 15
Carnegie, Dale, 17
Cather, Willa, 17, 123
Chambers, John, 15, 26
Chicago, Illinois, 44, 50, 81, 93, 162
Chicago News, 63
Christian Science Monitor, 147
Cleveland, Grover, 142, 173
Cleveland, Ohio, 100, 162
Clinton, William Jefferson (Bill), 28, 29, 30, 176; and Hope, Arkansas, 28, 29, 30, 176
Cobb, Frank, 25
College of Emporia, 111, 112, 137
Collier's, 4, 51, 121; White's writings published in, 85, 129, 133, 135, 136, 172
Columbia University, 25, 173
Committee for Unemployment Relief, 141
Committee to Defend America by Aiding the Allies, 164, 166, 167
Congress of Industrial Organizations, 150
Cooley, Charles Horton, 13, 26
Coolidge, Calvin, 89, 91, 96, 100, 107, 129, 131, 137, 138, 140, 173
Cooper, James Fenimore, 3
Cooper, John Milton, 74
Craftsman, 60
Croly, Herbert, 70

Danville, Kentucky, 27
Daughters of the American Revolution, 130
Davis, Nancy, 4. *See also* Nancy Reagan
Dell, Floyd, 123
Democratic Party, 114, 130
Denver Post, 147
Depression Era. See Great Depression
Dewey, John, 13, 25, 63–64
Dixon, Illinois, 28, 29, 31
Doe, John, 15
Dole, Bob (Robert), 30

Dorman, Robert L., 18, 19, 20
Duluth, Minnesota, 120
Dust Bowl, 22

Eisenhower, Dwight D., 4, 175; and Abilene,
    28
El Dorado, Kansas, 48, 53
El Dorado *Republican*, 49
Emporia, Kansas, 21, 28, 31, 32, 35, 36, 41,
    42, 50, 51, 62, 77, 86, 88, 89, 92, 96, 97,
    100, 109, 111, 112, 119, 120, 121, 124,
    125, 128, 163, 164, 166, 168, 169–71,
    172–73, 174, 177; during the Depression,
    141, 154–55; hometown of William
    Allen White, 21, 33, 90–91, 131, 134;
    and the KKK, 114; as White's rhetorical
    model, 21, 31–36, 42, 45, 95, 109–13,
    121–28
Emporia Gazette, 47, 49, 50, 65, 89, 95, 96,
    97, 98, 100, 109, 110, 111, 112, 114, 132,
    154, 166, 172; and the KKK, 116, 118;
    White's editorials published in, 65, 89,
    95–98, 100–128, 166

Ferber, Edna, 90, 123
Finley, John, 35
First Hundred Days, 143–44
First World War. See World War I
Fisher, Dorothy Canfield, 91, 123
Fitzgerald, F. Scott, 123
Follett, Mary Parker, 13
Ford, Henry, 17
Forum: White's writings published in, 66–67
Four Freedoms, 4, 132
Fox Movietone News, 172
Frankfurter, Felix, 25
Frenau, Philip, 10, 11
frontier myth, 5, 9

Gale, Zona, 91, 123
Gannett, Lewis, 178
Garland, Hamlin, 54, 55, 123
Garvey, Marcus, 15
Gazette. See Emporia Gazette
Gemeinschaft, 40, 41, 42, 45, 55, 56, 93, 174;
    in Emporia, 90–91, 92, 95, 110; in
    Muncie, 92–95
Gesellschaft, 40, 41, 42, 45, 56, 93, 174; in
    Emporia, 90–91, 92, 95, 110; in Muncie,
    92–95
Giddings, Franklin, 13
Gilpin, William, 10, 11
Glassberg, David, 18
Gompers, Samuel, 97

Graphic, 60
Grayson, David, 123
Great Depression, 2, 17, 23, 131, 132,
    140–57

Hackett, Francis, 62–63
Hagedorn, Hermann, 33
Hanna, Marcus (Mark), 30, 50, 74
Harding, Warren, 28, 91, 100, 129, 131, 133,
    138; and Marion, 28
Harper's Magazine: White's writings pub-
    lished in, 136
Harvard University, 10, 12, 23, 159, 163
Hearst, William Randolph, 131–32
Hearst's, 121
Herron, Ima, 55
Hilfer, Anthony Channell, 55
Hitler, Adolph, 42, 166
Hoover, Herbert, 91, 129, 130, 131, 138,
    139, 140–44, 146
Hope, Arkansas, 28, 30, 176
Howe, Ed, 54, 55, 123
Howe, Frederick, 13
Howells, William Dean, 11, 59

Ickes, Harold, 149
Independence, Missouri, 28
Indiana, Pennsylvania, 29

Jackson, Bruce, 16
James, William, 11
Johnson, Lyndon, 4

Kansas, 2, 21, 34, 35, 49, 56, 65–67, 76, 77,
    91, 110, 111, 138, 149, 168; Dust Bowl,
    22; and the KKK, 34, 114–19, 130;
    Populism in, 2, 56, 65–67, 135;
    Republican Party in, 49–51, 175
Kansas Charter Board, 116–17
Kansas City, Missouri, 96, 119, 120
Kansas City *Journal*, 49
Kansas City *Star*, 49
Kansas Magazine: White's writings pub-
    lished in, 129
Kansas State Teachers College, 111, 112
King, Martin Luther, Jr., 3
Kirby, Rollin, 116
Kirkland, Joseph, 55
Ku Klux Klan, 34, 42, 96, 113, 114–19, 130

Ladies' Home Journal, 121
La Follette, Robert "Fighting Bob," 11, 87, 96
Landon, Alfred M., 149
Laski, Harold, 174

Lauder, Harry, 111
Lawrence, Kansas, 49
League of Nations, 52, 98, 99, 130
Lears, T. J. Jackson, 18, 19–20, 25, 30
Levine, Lawrence, 15–17, 24
Lewis, John, 150
Lewis, Sinclair, 91, 122–24, 125, 126, 128, 132
Life, 4, 172
Life, (humor magazine), 121, 122, 127
Limerick, Patricia Nelson, 9
Lippmann, Walter, 2, 4, 12, 25, 35, 64
Lodge, Henry Cabot, 97, 130
Look, 4, 172
Los Angeles, California, 28, 44
Luce, Henry, 2, 3, 132
Lynd, Helen Merrell, 32, 41, 92, 126, 149
Lynd, Robert S., 32, 41, 92–95, 126, 149

MacLeish, Archibald, 17
Madeira, Ohio, 27
Madison, Wisconsin, 27
Madison Avenue, 19, 26
Manifest Destiny, 10
Marchand, Roland, 18, 19
Marion, Ohio, 28
Mason, Walt, 121
May, Henry, 11
McClure's Magazine, 51; White's writings published in, 71, 79
McKinley, William, 28, 30, 34, 50, 66, 76, 148, 173
Meinig, D. W., 21
Mencken, H. L., 2, 91, 126, 128
Minneapolis symphony, 111
Mumford, Lewis, 19, 22, 23, 24
Muncie, Indiana, 32, 41, 92, 94, 95, 126
Munsey, Frank, 97
Murdock, Victor, 123
Mussolini, [Benito], 166

Nation, 60, 129, 133, 142
National Enquirer, 3
Nearing, Helen Knothe, 22, 27
Nearing, Scott, 22, 27
Nelson, William Rockhill, 49
New Deal, 143–46, 149–53, 155
New Era, 18, 47, 86, 88, 89, 100, 106, 133
New Masses, 127
New Republic, 120, 129, 155; White's writings published in, 150, 154, 155–56, 169
Newsweek, 175, 177
New York City, 42, 44, 50, 77, 90, 96, 120, 121, 122, 135, 166

New York State, 130, 137, 143
New York *Telegram*, 139
New York Times, 3, 35, 60, 167
New York Times Magazine, 129
New York *World*, 25, 116
Niebuhr, Rheinhold, 17
Nixon, Richard, 4; and Whittier, California, 28
Non-Partisan Committee for Peace through Revision of the Neutrality Law, 165, 166
Non-Partisan League, 106
Norris, Frank, 57
Northwestern University, 153
Norton, Charles Eliot, 23, 24, 97
Nye, Russell B., 87

Odum, Howard, 19
Olathe, Kansas, 138
Outlook, 60; White's writings published in, 76

Palmer, A. Mitchell, 130
Palm Springs, California, 29
Paris, 52, 63, 86, 90, 96, 98, 121
Parker, Alton, 74
Park, Robert, 13, 93
Paulen, Ben S., 116, 118
Pavlova, Anna, 111
Platt, Thomas, 173
Populism, 49, 50, 51, 56, 65; in Kansas, 2, 56, 58, 65–69, 135
Post. See Saturday Evening Post
Pringle, Henry, 147
Prinkipo Conference, 52
Progressive Era, 12–15, 24–30, 36, 37, 39, 41, 45, 48, 53, 60, 65, 69, 82–88, 89, 97, 102, 130, 133–37, 156, 173
Progressive Party, 38, 39, 52, 81–85, 135
progressivism, 14, 15–18, 24, 26, 36–37, 45, 82–83, 87, 134, 169, 172
Prohibition, 14, 136, 139–40
Public Affairs Magazine, 140, 144
Pulitzer Prize: awarded to White, 89

Quandt, Jean B., 12, 13, 14, 25, 26

Reagan, Nancy, 29
Reagan, Ronald, 4, 22–23, 28, 29, 30, 31, 175, 176, 177; and hometown of Dixon, Illinois, 28, 29, 31
Red Cross, 35, 52, 85
Red River Valley, 67
Red Scare, 52, 114, 130
Reno, Milo, 131

Republican Party, 47, 49, 50, 70, 81, 84, 99, 100, 114, 115, 116, 131, 140, 175
Riley, James Whitcomb, 55
Robertson, James Oliver, 36, 43–44
Rockwell, Norman, 4, 172
Rodgers, Daniel T., 26, 27, 36, 37, 39
Rogers, Will, 29
Roosevelt, Eleanor, 3
Roosevelt, Franklin Delano, 4, 34, 131, 132, 142, 149, 151–52, 163, 164–65, 166; author of *On Our Way*, 145; and the Four Freedoms, 4, 132; and the New Deal, 4, 143–46, 149–52, 155
Roosevelt, Theodore, 11, 12, 14, 34, 37, 38, 50, 51, 52, 60, 63, 69–76, 79, 81, 82, 87, 97, 99, 100, 142, 145, 147, 173, 174; memorialized by White, 103; and the Progressive Movement, 97; and the Republican Party, 70; Roosevelt Memorial Association, 33, 165; and the Square Deal, 63; and William Allen White, 50–51, 52, 60, 69–75
Ross, Edward, D., 12
Rotarian, 129
Royce, Josiah, 13, 25
Rubin, Joan Shelley, 18
Russia, 156. *See also* Soviet Union
Ruth, Babe, 17

Sacco, [Nicola], 130
St. Louis symphony, 111
San Francisco, California, 12
Santa Barbara, California, 29
Santa Fe Magazine, 129
Santa Fe Railroad, 111, 112
Saturday Evening Post, 4, 51, 63, 67, 68, 72, 73, 75, 83, 129, 133, 142, 144, 149, 172; White's writings published in, 67, 68, 72, 73, 75, 83, 133, 142, 144, 149
Saturday Review of Literature, 4, 129, 173
Scherman, Robert, 18
Schlessinger, Arthur, Jr., 4
Schorer, Mark, 124
Schrag, Peter, 44
Schumacher, E. F., 22
Scribner's: White's writings published in, 67
Seldes, Gilbert, 149
Shakespeare, William, 15
Sharpless, John, 27
Sheldon, Charles M., 123
Shi, David E., 21, 22, 23, 24, 25, 30, 178
Shortridge, James R., 21
Sinclair, Upton, 131, 155, 156, 159, 162, 174

Slotkin, Richard: approach to cultural myth, 4–8, 9, 30
Smith, Alfred E., 15, 34, 42, 91, 130, 137; Democratic nominee for president, 91, 130, 137–40; governor of New York, 130, 137
Smith, Henry Nash, 9, 10, 11
Smith, Jefferson, 15, 29
Soviet Union, 154. *See also* Russia
Springfield, Ohio, 177
Standard Oil Company, 76
Steffens, Lincoln, 2
Stein, Gertrude, 2
Stewart, Jimmy, 29, 30
Studio City, California, 28
Survey, 141
Sussman, Warren, 17–18

Taft, William Howard, 38, 79, 81
Tammany, 138, 140
Tarbell, Ida, 2
Teapot Dome scandal, 96
Theodore Roosevelt Medal, 165
Thompson, Dorothy, 2
Thunder Mountain, Idaho, 67, 173
Time, 4
Tönnies, Ferdinand, 40
Topeka, Kansas, 51
Truman, Harry, 28
Turner, Frederick Jackson, 9, 17, 22, 25, 54
Twain, Mark, 55

United Nations, 169
University of Kansas, 49, 51, 145, 166
USA Today, 3
U.S. Constitution, 116

Valentino, Rudolph, 97
Vanzetti, [Bartolomeo], 130
Versailles, (Peace Confeence and Treaty), 52, 62, 63, 85, 86, 98, 99, 168, 173
Vidal, Gore, 2
Vital Speeches of the Day, 129, 151

Walker, Charles Rumford, 149
Wallace, Anthony F. C., 16
Wallace, Henry, 132
Walpole, Hugh, 111
Washington, D.C., 30, 90, 98, 143, 168
Washington Post, 33
Webster, Noah, 3
West, Rebecca, 120
Wharton, Edith, 123

White, Allen: father of William Allen White, 49

White, Bill: son of William Allen White, 115

White, Mary Ann Hatton: mother of William Allen White, 49

White, Sally Lindsay: wife of William Allen White, 49, 90, 115, 164

White, William Allen: abandons fiction, 47, 53, 63–64; and the biography of Calvin Coolidge, 89, 173; and the biography of Woodrow Wilson, 89, 173; and Book of the Month Club, 20, 89; childhood in El Dorado, Kansas, 48–49, 53; civil rights advocate, 14, 51; on the death of his daughter, 89; and the Democratic Party, 84, 130; and the Depression, 2, 131–33, 140–46, 148–57; editor of *Emporia Gazette*, 47, 89, 95–128, 131, 132–33, 137, 166, 168; fiction writer, 14, 31, 47, 48, 51, 53–64, 172; and the New Era, 47–48; owner of *Emporia Gazette*, 47, 49, 95; political and social commentator, 31, 32, 41, 45, 47–48, 53, 65–88, 94–128, 129–57; and Populism, 2, 49, 50, 51, 56, 65–67, 72; and the Progressive Movement, 2, 4, 13, 20, 26–27, 37, 45, 47, 52, 69, 81–85, 87–88, 89, 130, 133–40; Progressive Party advocate, 38, 52, 81–84; prohibitionist, 14, 51, 136; recipient of Roosevelt Memorial Association Award, 33; recipient of the Theodore Roosevelt Medal, 165; Red Cross observer, 35, 52, 85; and the Republican Party, 14, 34, 47–53, 84, 131–33, 140, 165; and rhetoric of America's changing mainstream, 1–4, 6, 8–15, 20–21, 25–28, 38–39, 41–42, 163, 171–73; views on the KKK, 42, 130; articles and editorials: "Al Smith—city feller," 137; "Battle Hum of the Republic," 139; "Blood of the Conquerers," 134; "But Where Are We Going?" 145; "The Challenge to Democracy: It Is a Glib Shibboleth," 152; "The Challenge to the Middle Class," 149; "Cheer Up, America!" 136; "The Cock-Eyed World," 102; "The Conduct of Great Businesses," 67; "The Dawn of a Great Tomorrow: We Are Making America Over to Give an Equal Chance to Every Man," 134; "The Doughboy on Top of the World," 85;

"The Ebb Tide: Can the Progressives Come Back?" 83, 136; "An Editor and His Town," 113; "Moscow and Emporia," 154, 162, 163; "Emporia and New York," 77; "Emporia and New York" (editorial), 121, 122; "Emporia in Wartime," 169, 170; "The Farmer Takes His Holiday," 144; "The Gas Buggy," 104; "Good Newspapers and Bad," 147; "Herbert Hoover: The Last of the Old Presidents or the First of the New?" 142; "The Highbrow Doughboy," 85; "If I Were a Dictator," 142; "The Kansas Conscience," 76; "The Ku Klux Klan Again," 115; "Mary White," 89; "The New Well," 112; "One Year of Roosevelt," 73; "The Partnership of Society," 77, 78; "The Passing Decade," 111; "The President's Message," 103; "Ready-Made Homes Out West," 68; "The Republic Totters," 144; "Roosevelt: A Force for Righteousness," 79; "The Second Coming of Wilson," 98; "Should Old Acquaintance Be Forgot," 81; "Swinging Round the Circle with Roosevelt," 73; "'Them As Has Gits,'" 103; "To an Anxious Friend," 89; "Uncommercial Traveling," 68; "We Have Ceased to Mark Time: New Blood and Leadership Enter with Hoover," 140; "What Is a Good Town?" 125; "What Labor Really Wants," 107; "What's the Matter with America?" 135, 136, 171; "What's the Matter with Kansas?" 50, 56, 65, 136, 171; "When the World Busts Through," 81; "Why I Am a Progressive," 133; "A Yip from the Doghouse," 150

literary works: *A Certain Rich Man*, 54, 59–61; *The Changing West: An Economic Theory about Our Golden Age*, 10, 159–63, 171; *The Court of Boyville*, 58; *In the Heart of a Fool*, 59, 61–63; *The Martial Adventures of Henry and Me*, 35, 62, 171; *In Our Town*, 55, 58–59; *The Real Issue: A Book of Kansas Stories*, 56–58, 59; *Strategems and Spoils*, 59

White Committee, 167

Whitehead, Alfred North, 24

Whiteman, Paul, 111

Wichita, Kansas, 62, 119

Wicker, Tom, 4

Willkie, Wendell, 132

Wilmington, Ohio, 27

Wilson, Woodrow, 48, 52, 62, 82, 85, 89, 97, 98, 99, 142, 173
Winchell, Walter, 35
Winrod, Gerald, 155
World War I, 12, 47, 48, 52, 130, 153, 168, 171, 173; effects on community, 95–96, 98, 129; postwar, 26, 38–39, 47–48, 52–53, 89, 90, 95–96, 129–37, 168–69
World War II, 9, 17, 39, 168, 173

Yale Review, 129; White's writings published in, 168, 169
YMCA, 111, 112
YWCA, 111, 112